Early Identification and Intervention of Suicide Risk in Chinese Young Adults

Elsie Ong

Early Identification and Intervention of Suicide Risk in Chinese Young Adults

Springer

Elsie Ong
Faculty of Health, Education and Society
University of Northampton
Northampton, UK

Division of Information and Technology
Studies, Faculty of Education
The University of Hong Kong
Hong Kong, China

ISBN 978-981-16-7640-6 ISBN 978-981-16-7641-3 (eBook)
https://doi.org/10.1007/978-981-16-7641-3

This Springer imprint is published by the registered company Springer Nature Singapore Pte Ltd.
The registered company address is: 152 Beach Road, #21-01/04 Gateway East, Singapore 189721, Singapore

Preface

The central theme of the various parts of this book will be to explore cognitive and neurological factors that could serve as valid indicators for characterizing suicide risk in a non-clinical sample. Chapter 1 describes suicidal behaviour and enlists some of the most common risk factors and means of a suicide attempt. The following Chap. 2 aptly combines theories and models discussing the emergence and progression of suicidal behaviours. Well-established suicide models are recommended, such as the escape theory, cry of pain theory, and the more recent one: the schematic model of suicidal behaviour. A section on the existing suicide risk assessment and suicide prevention programmes in Hong Kong follows Chap. 3. The discussion reflects the critical view which enumerates the current issues in suicide assessment and interventions, for instance issues regarding the specificity and reliability of instruments used for assessment, divergent terms of suicidal thoughts and behaviours, long waiting times for interventions, etc. The traditional methods in suicide assessment and prevention programmes are challenged, both for not applying specific psychological theories and for not evaluating theoretical research findings separately and granting them more attention. The largest section of the volume is devoted to Chap. 4, which aptly combines suicide risk assessment and intervention eloquently illustrating the connection between the two. The author's recommendations for future suicide interventions are explained and argued in the respective themed chapters. While the existing approach in assessing and prevention suicidality has been critiqued by the authors, Chap. 5 opens up with potential research opportunities as to how recent development of advanced technologies such as mobile apps and cognitive games may play an important role in suicide intervention. Importantly, Chap. 5 is the concluding chapter where the author summarizes the book with a list of recommendations for future research, all of which are sound and substantiated by analysis of literature. This part is largely a collection of recommendations elaborated in the previous parts of the book.

Northampton, UK/Hong Kong, China — Elsie Ong

Preface

Acknowledgments

Writing a book about how advanced digital interventions in mental health was something I have always dreamt about. The substantial knowledge gained through the research process and the people I met through these years are valuable because this book would not have been possible without the help and assistance from many different people. First, I wish to thank my editor at Springers Nature, Shalini Monica, for her prompt response whenever I approached her for guidance and information with the proposal. I am deeply indebted to Dr. Sam Chu who has set a role model for me in being a successor of publishing more than one hundred journal articles and books. I thank him for encouraging me constantly to keep trying and never give up. I also acknowledge many graduates and postgraduates who have worked for my research over the last several years. Although I do not list them individually by name, their efforts have contributed immensely to helping me study suicidal behaviours in young adults. Thanks go to my research team at the University of Hong Kong and the University of Salford for giving me a large amount of professional advice in running my EEG experiments. Finally, my deepest thanks go to my mum and dad, my children, and my grandparents, for all of the unconditional love and support they have given. Their encouragement in all manner of issues and the confidence they have instilled have helped to turn me from a lecturer to a writer. Grandpa, your faith in me has helped me believe in myself, I miss you all the time and wish you could read my book.

Acknowledgements

Contents

About the Author

Dr. Elsie Ong has a Master of Science in Applied Cognitive Neuroscience and completed a Ph.D. in Health Sciences. She has worked as a lecturer in cognitive psychology for over ten years and is currently working as a lecturer in biological psychology in England. Initially, she considered helping students to achieve their learning outcomes as her primary goal in her teaching career; this perspective has changed since the acquaintance of few suicide cases she came across with the students who appeared to be psychologically and physically fit. Since then, she has dedicated years of work that focused exclusively on the young adults going through university transition. Her expertise in cognitive neuroscience and psychology has also initiated further exploration on the mental health issues of young adults going through university transition and later sparkle potentials for suicide prevention and interventions. She has published her research through internationally renowned conferences and reputed journals such as Frontiers in Psychiatry. These experiences have helped to keep her most up to date on the latest development in mental disorder prevention and interventions. Regarding her research interests, she has dedicated work exclusively to young adults going through university transition. In 2018, she obtained her Ph.D. in Cognitive Psychology with the thesis titled: The cognitive and neural basis of suicide: investigating factors that help to identify individuals at risk. In the write-up of my thesis, she became deeply inspired by the research on how Attentional Bias Modification (ABM) can be implemented to reduce suicidal behaviour, and this has motivated the examination of specific attentional bias in university students with suicidal ideation. Alongside many investigations, she became aware of the challenges in assessing and diagnosing individuals with suicide risk.

About the Author

Chapter 1
Introduction

Suicide is defined as death caused by self-directed injurious behaviour with intent to die as a result of the behaviour (Who.int, 2017). Each suicide is a personal tragedy that prematurely takes an individual's life and has a continuing ripple effect, dramatically affecting the lives of families, friends, and communities ("Preventing suicide," 2014). Suicide is a socially taboo topic that is rarely discussed with others, yet approximately 800,000 people die due to suicide every year, which is one person every 40 s. According to the statistics by World Health Organization (WHO) 2017, approximately 800,000 people die each year from suicide, which is equivalent to one person every 40 s. Many more attempt suicide, yet, there are indications that for each adult who died of suicide there may have been more than 20 others attempting suicide. Suicide is a universal phenomenon, with 78% of suicides in low- and middle-income countries in 2015. What's more, Suicide occupied 1.4% of all deaths around the globe, giving rise to its rank as the 17th leading cause of death in 2015 (Who.int, 2017). In that regard, it is high time to put effective and evidence-based interventions in practice at different levels, namely population, sub-population, and individual levels, in a bid to refrain from suicide and suicide attempts.[1] Suicide occurs throughout the lifespan. In contrast to suicide being the tenth leading cause of death for all ages (see Centers for Disease Control and Prevention (CDCP), 2017), suicide is the second leading cause of death for young people aged 15–24 years old and the fourth leading cause of death among individuals between the ages of 35 and 54. This draws specific attention to improving preventive measures among this age group in this book.

International recognition of suicide as a major public health problem culminated in the creation of World Suicide Prevention Day on 10 September 2003. This day has spurred campaigns both nationally and locally and has contributed to raising awareness and reducing stigma worldwide. The organization of different activities for this special day encourages more people to be engaged with each other and

[1] A suicide attempt is a non-fatal, self-directed, potentially injurious behaviour with intent to die as a result of the behaviour. A suicide attempt might not result in injury.

E. Ong, *Early Identification and Intervention of Suicide Risk in Chinese Young Adults*,
https://doi.org/10.1007/978-981-16-7641-3_1

Fig. 1.1 World suicide prevention day 2020

Fig. 1.2 Example activities organized by IASP in support of World Suicide Prevention Day, Adapted with permission from ("World Suicide Prevention Day 2018 Brochure—WSPD Brochure," n.d.) and from Centre for Suicide Research and Prevention (hku.hk)

spread awareness of suicide prevention. This observance—held on the same date every year—is organized by the International Association for Suicide Prevention (IASP) and has been cosponsored by WHO. The theme varies every year. 'Suicide Prevention: One World Connected', was an example theme in 2014, illustrating the vitalness of connections at different levels in curbing suicide (World suicide, 2014). One of the big group events IASP organizes annually is the "Cycle Around the Globe" in which valiant participants collectively cycle the globe. Participants can take part in groups, individually, at home, in the gym, or anywhere they prefer ("World Suicide Prevention Day 2018 Brochure—WSPD Brochure," n.d.). On the 10th of September 2018 at 8 pm, individuals were invited to take part in the "Light a Candle" by lighting a candle near a window as a symbol of support for suicide prevention. For many people, especially those bereaved by the suicide of their close ones, it is a means of remembering a loved one (Fig. 1.1).

In the most recent suicide prevention day in 2020, the theme was 'working together to prevent suicide', and in connection to this, The Hong Kong Jockey Club Centre for Suicide Research and Prevention (CSRP) of the University of Hong Kong (HKU) held a press conference on that day with the theme "Connect the Disconnected" (see Fig. 1.2c). This is a significant theme given that most people in 2020 have been living under the pandemic and were distressingly disconnected from others. Face-to-face interaction was replaced by online learning, online meetings, etc., and those who struggled with mental health issues struggled even more. Research has indicated that since 2019, the pandemic had taken a heavy toll on their mental health. Zhao et al. (2020) have investigated HK general population stress level, the prevalence of anxiety, and the depression symptoms by analyzing repeated cross-sectional data in 2016 (N = 4036), 2017 (N = 4051) and the COVID-19 Health Information Survey (CoVHInS) on April 9–23, 2020 (N = 1501). Using population-based random samples of general adults from the Hong Kong Family and Health Information Trend Survey (FHInTS), they found that participants' stress level has increased by 28.3%, the prevalence of anxiety increased by 42.3%, and the depression symptoms and unhappiness score have both drastically increased during the COVID-19 outbreak. The findings have added pressure to the current mental health service in HK which is already overloaded.

1.1 Suicide Problems in Young Population in Hong Kong

In China, suicide is one of the major causes of death among adults aged 15–34, taking up 19% of deaths within this age group, which occupies a higher percentage of death caused by accidents (Phillips et al., 2002). Be that as it may, these statistics are deemed to not reflect the whole picture of the situation because of the ample unidentified and under-reported samples (Nock et al., 2010). Similar to China, there is a surge in attention to students' suicide in Hong Kong. As can be seen from social media, quite a number of topics related to suicidality in students appear in newspaper headlines, ranging from "15-year-old hangs himself in ninth student suicide since September" (Hong Kong Free Press, 2016), "More Hong Kong children conduct suicide than die in accidents, study reveals" (Hong Kong Free Press, 2016), to "Third student suicide in three weeks raises alarm bells over stress levels" (Hong Kong Free Press, 2015). These headlines (see Fig. 1.3a for one example) reveal the fact that student suicide is an alarming issue. It pushes schools and educators to contemplate why students are making these attempts and identify "at stake" students as early as possible.

There are more stories about how students suffer from the pressurized educational system. On the 5th March 2016, a third-year medical student aged 22 from a Chinese University conducted suicide by jumping off the roof of the apartment she lived (Cheung & Chiu, 2017). She was taken to North District Hospital in HK and was pronounced dead shortly after. According to the police officers, no suicide note was found at the site of the accident during the initial stage of the investigation but reported that the student had been in distress because of academic issues in university. In fact, such a tragedy related to youth suicide is not rare in HK, with this one as the sixteenth report about student suicide within three months. (Cheung & Chiu, 2017). Strikingly, just four days after this incident, another Hong Kong university student aged 20 jumped to his death from his residential block (Chung, 2016). He was pronounced dead at the scene. The police officers found several suicide notes from his resident block, written to the media and others, written to his family. As revealed from those letters later, he was under immense pressure regarding academic issues but

Fig. 1.3 **a** A sharp rise of 50% in the suicide rate of Hong Kong teenagers, Image from (Chen, 2018) [photo]. Retrieved from 青少年自殺亡人數按年急增五成 逾八成人「從高處墮下

had never sought any counseling supports. This was the seventh suicide case in just nine days within the small city of HK. The two cases mentioned above (Chung, 2016; Cheung & Chiu, 2017) share a significant similarity concerning that both students complained about their unhappiness in academic-related issues. These cases foreground the importance of investigating the potential suicidal progress students might have undergone by understanding what students might have encountered during their university years.

While university life can be the first time for students to leave home, it could be thorny particularly for Chinese students (Zhang et al., 2012). Mooney (2005) shared a similar view on this, contended that Chinese students are often the only 'child' at home, making family functioning particularly essential for them. During the critical period in entering university, students start to learn different ways to cope with the real world independently, which in turn means that coping[2] may serve as a crucial factor. On top of this social and environmental challenge, university students are experiencing the transition from adolescence to adulthood. At this stage, it is of paramount importance for students to equip themselves with cognitive abilities to find flexible and adequate means in dealing with a variety of demands for work, relationships, and academic life. If one experiences aversive life events when they still do not have their psychological development in shape, this may obstruct adaptive behaviour in this situation and manifest in suicidality. In this regard, examining the student population's cognitive, coping, and emotional factors would help perceive how these risk factors interact with suicidal behaviours in different ways.

[2] coping refers to the "conscious volitional efforts to regulate emotion, cognition, behaviour, physiology, and the environment in response to stressful events or circumstances" (p. 89).

Range of suicidal behaviour:

- Suicidal ideation—Thoughts of killing oneself
- Suicide planners—A degree higher than suicidal ideation; a person plans their suicide before actually carrying it out
- Suicidal attempt—Failed or poorly executed act of killing oneself resulting in non-fatal outcomes
- Suicide completion—Death due to suicide.

The terms suicidality and suicidal behaviour are used interchangeably throughout this book; both terms collectively cover suicidal ideation, suicide plans, and suicide attempts.

Although the rate of completed suicide is lower among university students than their non-student peers (Schwartz, 1990), the prevalence of suicidal behaviour[3] in university populations is still alarmingly high. Since the start of the academic year in September 2015, 22 students in HK conducted suicide within six months, 10 of them were university students (South China Morning Post, 2016). This number of suicide cases is substantial compared to the previous statistics of only two to three cases of university students' suicides per year (figures from the University of Hong Kong's Centre for Suicide Research and Prevention 2010 to 2014). The increase put forward the urging need in probing the causes of suicidal behaviour in the student population.

Yip (2016), Director of the CSRP, drew an initial conclusion that today's students may not be ready and well prepared for university life. The stressful education in university has posed a considerable strain on more students, with too much emphasis on score-oriented assessments. (South China Morning Post, 2016). Yip (2016) added that universities should increase awareness about this situation while counseling support should also be enhanced. Yet, it is argued by other university academics that the youth suicide problem is intricate, and the exact causes of the surging numbers in suicidality are left unidentified and ambiguous (South China Morning Post, 2016) (Fig. 1.4).

Upon the commencement of the university term, it is often reported that students will undergo changes and adversities that may influence their physical and psychological health (Arslan et al., 2009; Pedersen & Paves, 2014). These are times when students feel emotionally distressed, more pressured, and more doubtful of themselves because of different matters in the university. Regarding Ohayon et al. (2014), young adults experienced tremendous stress on fostering their own identities, establishing life goals, and developing friendships with peers during their university life. The transition between late adolescence and young adulthood is subject to high stress levels regarding adapting to a new social environment and increasing academic demands (Pedersen & Paves, 2014). When a drastic change occurs in students' social

[3] Suicidal behaviour includes suicidal ideation (frequent thoughts of ending one's life), suicide attempts (the actual event of trying to kill one's self), and completed suicide (death occurs). Suicidal behaviour is most often accompanied by intense feelings of hopelessness, depression, or self-destructive behaviours (parasuicidal behaviours).

777 SHARES

More Hong Kong children commit suicide than die in accidents, study reveals

More Hong Kong children commit suicide than die in accidents, study reveals

PUBLISHED : Friday, 10 July, 2015, 3:53pm
UPDATED : Saturday, 11 July, 2015, 3:45am

COMMENTS: 5

Almost half of 87 youngsters aged under 18 who died of unnatural causes in 2010 and 2011 committed suicide, with the youngest just 10 years old, a shocking study revealed.

Shirley Zhao

SCMP TODAY: HK EDITION

Fig. 1.4 More headline on student suicide in Hong Kong, Adapted with permission from Hong Kong Free Press (2016)

networking during their university years, it may aggravate levels of depression and anxiety, giving rise to a higher chance of suicide (Eisenberg et al., 2007; Potter et al., 2004). Although part of the students' social support network may still consist of parents and other family members, it is stressful for students to experience physical separation from them, which may be the first time in their lives. While leaving home may initially be a fantastic experience for some students, it may become overwhelming soon when they have to deal with finance, relationships, and independence. This is in line with Yip's study (2007), highlighting that the debt issue was the major risk factor contributing to trigger pressurized individuals in conducting suicide in HK.

In light of the drastic transition to university life, stressors related to academic issues, ranging from assignments, exams, to meeting deadlines for students, also lay a tremendous burden on students' life (Potter et al., 2004). A stressor is any activity, event, or stimulus that causes stress (The Cambridge Dictionary, 2016). It involves both cognitive and behavioural efforts aimed at reducing or controlling a stressor. On top of what students are normally experiencing, students in Hong Kong have been

Fig. 1.5 Samaritan reporting that the number of young people killed by suicide has increased by 50% year-on-year, with eight of these cases related to academic pressure, Adapted with permission from Hong Kong Free Press (2016)

going through an even harder time than ever given the significant impact of the social unrest[4] in 2018 and the pandemic in 2020 until now (Fig. 1.5).

The Hong Kong Jockey Club Suicide Prevention Research Center (HKJC) has recorded suicide rates in the past 36 years, of which the suicide rate among young people aged 15–24 has fluctuated from a minimum of 4.4 in 1982 to a maximum of 12.7 in 2002, which is lower than the overall suicide rate. However, regardless of the youth or the overall suicide rate, the distribution between 1981 and 2006 increased upwards until the past ten years which has then narrowed, and slightly adjusted downward (Figs. 1.6 and 1.7).

---

[4] In 2019, an unprecedented period of social unrest in Hong Kong (HK) was initiated by the Extradition Bill which was intended to regulate transfers of criminal fugitives who are wanted in different parts of China. This Bill constitutes a drastic change because existing laws enacted before the handover in July 1997 prohibit extradition to Mainland China. Ng (2020) reported that the proposed Bill has triggered a very strong reaction in HK, including numerous demonstrations, violence of the protesters. Social unrest has a significant impact on citizens as well as the young adults in the society, but for university students, little attention has been placed on how they thrived through this period with disconnection to social support.

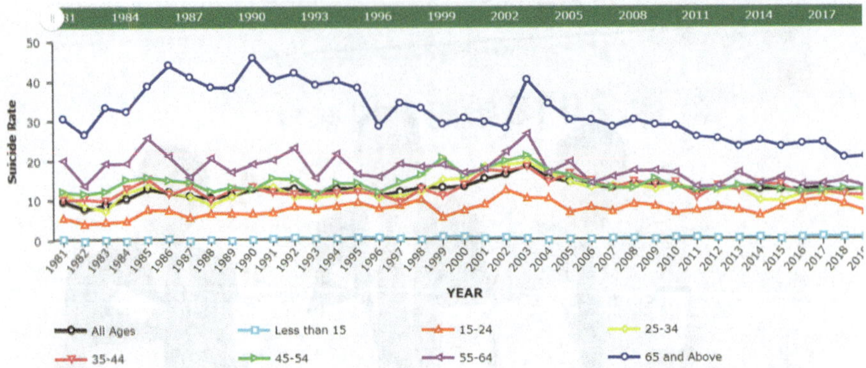

Fig. 1.6 Suicide rates by age group in HK [obtained from Suicide Rate—Centre for Suicide Research and Prevention (hku.hk)]

Fig. 1.7 On average, every 9.3 days, a young people's suicide data deconstructed why they are on the road of no return, Adapted with permission from Lui & Leung (2017)

1.1.1 *What Is Reviewed in Suicide Notes?*

Suicide notes are rarely studied and are hard to find in public or social media, but even when they are available, psychologists are still puzzled to use these fragmented messages to understand the reasons behind these attempts (Harris, 2020). there are only short or unimportant messages in the last letter, not even the last letter. At this time, we glimpse the "unspeakable pain" of life in the puzzle. Harris, a psychologist studying suicide notes left by the attempters in Taiwan commented "*The last words are often written in a sudden or hasty manner the moment before the action. They may be in a state of confusion, picking up paper, a corner of a notebook, or today's mobile messaging and web platform posts*".

One of the news reported by the South Morning China post states that nowadays, the agonizing suicide notes written by teens in Hong Kong show how they are crumbling under the burden of expectations (Abraham, 2018). The news of a "*teenage boy's suicide on the mainland*" reported that the boy had completed suicide by drowning himself in a reservoir after leaving a suicide note (Li, 2016). In the note, the boy expressed that he did not want to add any more burden on his mum and dad since he could not make it to the high school. He also perceived himself to be worthless. Similarly, analysis of suicide notes written by local students also showed a pattern whereby 'being a burden to others was a constant theme for suicide. Followed from this, a recent study was conducted by Li et al. (2020) which involved a large-scale analysis of suicide notes in China (2004–2016). Based on the 2407 cases, some common features were identified. Similar to what was reported by Li in 2016, they found that only 19% (N = 458) of them have left a suicide note, of which 27.4% of the suicide note written by adolescents mentioned having a negative interpersonal relationship with someone.

Although the geological distance between HK and China is relatively small compared to other Asian countries, there are some differences from a cultural perspective. For example, Li et al. (2020) compared suicide notes left by the individuals in Hong Kong with those in Shanghai. They discovered that note leavers from Shanghai expressed more feelings of regret in their notes. The percentage of note leavers who "asked for forgiveness" in Shanghai (58.8%) was significantly higher than those in Hong Kong (44.8%). It was reasoned that concern for the families could be a protective factor against suicide, thus contributing to the lower suicide rates in Shanghai when compared with Hong Kong. Despite all the expressions of apologies, regrets, and gratitude towards others (parents, siblings and friends most of the time, and teachers sometimes) for being so kind as to support or care for the person, it is still unclear from the suicide notes as to what made these individuals feel so hopeless that they simply decided to take on their lives at such tender age (Fig. 1.8).

In other countries such as the United States (U.S.) suicide note also reflects the tremendous pressure expressed by students. According to Jaschik (2018), the death of a 16-year-old at a competitive high school in California leaves many asking whether too much is being asked of students. Despite being apparently happy and successful, this student from Newport Harbor High School in California ended his life. He left several suicide notes to say that he didn't want his parents or other family members to blame themselves. The notes also reviewed how much he loved his coaches and his struggles with the school due to the overwhelming pressure where going to a good college is the norm and where parents and teachers expect top performance.

According to the statement of Sean Boulton, principal from the California student's high school, teachers, administration, school counselors, and now parents/students are all feeling the pressure (Jaschik, 2018). He reflected from the past where

By primary and secondary school students By post-secondary school students

Fig. 1.8 The size of the word is proportional to the average rate of each word's appearance in each suicide note. *Source* World Health Organization (WHO). Suicide rates and absolute numbers of suicide by country (2001). Available at http://www.who.int/mental health/Topic Suicide/suicide1.html. Final report by Committee on Prevention of Student Suicides (2016)

nobody would ask about performance in the G.P.A. but now things have changed and the competitive culture has significantly impacted our young adults. Boulton the Principal added that it is essential to broaden the concepts of success. For example, some categories of jobs, including military career, plumbing, or welding, are just as important if not more and shall not be devalued. Those students who choose to enter the armed forces or want to work with their hands shall not be weighed down with the burden of being perfect in high school and shall indeed be proud of themselves. The Principal also reiterated the importance that if children don't live a perfect young adult experience, it is not the end of the world. He advised the parents that this can simply be an opportunity to head in another direction for their children rather than the end of the world.

1.1.2 Under-Reporting of Suicide Rates

Although established associations such as the World Health Organization (WHO) and the CSRP have reported national and worldwide figures for the prevalence of suicides, unlike the recording of deaths, there are no internationally accepted methods for standardizing the collection of information about suicide attempts ("Preventing suicide," 2014). This is due to several methodological deviations when comparing rates across different fields or countries. Currently, the estimates of the rates based on medically treated suicide attempts from the hospital reports may be inaccurate if the selected hospitals are not representative of all hospitals in the community. This is especially problematic when local clinics rather than hospitals treat a substantial number of suicide attempts. Moreover, it should be noted that only some suicide attempts result in injuries that receive medical treatment, so case-fatality estimates based on medically treated suicide attempts (hospitals) are significantly higher than what was reported. Therefore, standardizing the recording processes of suicide rates within and between countries is essential for better understanding and preventing suicides. Currently, the reported rates of medically treated suicide attempts are based on the recording processes in hospital settings which may be unreliable because they may not:

- distinguish individuals from treatment episodes which means patients with multiple suicide attempts in a year are duplicated;
- exclude those who die in the hospital during treatment for the suicidal behaviour or are discharged so they can die at home (and thus are not suicide attempts);
- distinguish between patients with non-suicidal self-injury and suicidal self-injury;
- include individuals treated in hospital emergency departments who are subsequently discharged before formal inpatient hospital admission;
- include individuals directly admitted to hospital wards without going through the emergency department;
- record the method of the suicide attempt which makes it difficult to assess method-specific case-fatality rates;
- correctly report cases as suicide attempts but instead record them as "accidents" due to stigma, lack of insurance coverage for suicidal behaviour, or concern about potential legal complications.

1.1.3 Divergent Definitions of Suicide

A major issue that has challenged the study of suicide and reporting of suicide rates is the divergent definitions use for different degrees of suicidality. Klonsky et al. (2016) echoed this notion. While most researchers have raised concern on the different suicidality terms and definitions, it has been a struggle to reach a consensus on a set of agreed terms due to the variations in the use of terminology between different subfields. For example, terms used by psychologists, mental health professionals, researchers, school systems, and coroners. The diversity becomes a stumbling block to mingle disparate knowledge suicide studies and confine the likelihood in comparing different factors attributed to suicidality (Posner et al., 2014). The segregation also obstructs the integration of findings across different published studies. In this regard, Klonsky et al. (2016) also raised concern over the current approach in examining suicidality because of the suicidality measures, particularly the divergent aims and various methods adopted in previous studies to measure suicidal behaviour, ranging from the simplest to the more complex assessment forms on suicidal behaviour. The simplest screening form comprises solely one or two items such as "Did you ever seriously consider suicide?" or, "Have you ever attempted suicide?" Both questions would be followed by a yes or no answer (CDC, 2015). Alternatively, more comprehensive forms of assessments may include a series of multiple-choice and open-ended questions. The inventories cover many aspects of suicidal behaviour such as frequency, severity, planning, communication, and intent of suicide at present as well as in the future (Nock et al., 2007). Slightly different definitions may have been adopted even for assessing lifetime suicidal ideation. For instance, May and Klonsky (2015) highlighted some assessments that would define suicidal ideation as "thoughts of serving as the agent of one's death,". In contrast, others may be "seriously thinking about conducting suicide". This foregrounds the disparity in assessment within different instruments ranging from structured, semi-structured, and non-structured clinical interviews, review of medical charts, to self-report questionnaires used in the current protocol.

Examples illustrating the divergent decisions made by coroners as to whether a death is adjudged as a suicide from Tait et al. (2018)

> I don't think you require an intent to kill yourself for suicide. All you have to intend is a dangerous act against yourself and the consequence is death. What your intent or what your motivation was is beside the point.
>
> There has to be evidence that the person intended to die, or they intended to take their life.
>
> If you're having a psychotic episode and you think you're superman, and you're going to stop the train . . . that's not suicide.
>
> So a psychotic episode, I'm jumping off a building, I think I'm a bird. Am I conducting suicide?

Because of these differences in the assessment of suicidality, the sample populations vary across various studies regarding the degree of suicide severity, stage of suicide, the measures used in assessing suicidality, and the comorbidity of other affective disorders. While versatile approaches in measurement render flexibility in assessing different settings and time frames, it also gives rise to problems in literature reviews (Klonsky et al., 2016). For instance, suicidal ideation is sometimes operationalized as fleeting thoughts about suicide but at other times requires heightened intensity, duration, or frequency. Such disparity in the suicidality assessment has imposed problems on comparing empirical findings and integration of knowledge across the literature. Given the diversity of suicide measures and the combined definitions of suicidality (Burton et al., 2011; Nangle et al., 2006), the existing knowledge about the underlying causes of suicidality remains ambiguous and indefinite.

1.2 Means of Suicide

To understand more about suicidal thoughts and behaviour, it is essential to consider the different means of suicide and how they vary from country and gender. For example, the firearm is considered the most common method in the U.S., Argentina, and Uruguay but is not apparent in any other countries possibly due to restriction by law (Ajdacic-Gross, 2008). In contrast, hanging is the most common means of suicide in most countries with the highest proportions (around 90% in men and 80% in women) found in Eastern Europe (i.e., Estonia, Latvia, Lithuania, Poland, and Romania). Gould et al. (2003) stated that Hanging varies from Europe to the U.S as it is considered the second most prevalent method of suicide in the U.S. regardless of age or ethnicity. Still, this method is only used by 10- to 14-year-olds or by African American youths. It is generally assumed that hanging is one of the most traditional suicide methods, yet many people consider it a violent method that requires some preparation. Therefore it needs some degree of courage and determination to generate particular obstacles to this act (Ajdacic-Gross et al., 2008). Typically, the greater the obstacles, the lower the acceptability of the method. In this perspective, the selection of suicide methods one takes is governed by their acceptability,[5] obstacles, and sociocultural norms.[6]

International or intercultural comparisons of suicide methods help increase understanding of the interplay between these two factors and provide a basis for preventive strategies. In relation to this, WHO (2014) claimed that restriction of access to lethal means would be one of the most straightforward strategies for suicide prevention, efforts should therefore be made to study the common means of suicide in HK, so that targeted measures could be implemented. Restricting access to the means of suicide is one of the most direct efforts in suicide prevention. However, means restriction policies in HK such as limiting access to pesticides or putting barriers in MTR[7] platforms require an understanding of the method preferences of different groups in society. It also depends on cooperation and collaboration between multiple sectors ("Preventing suicide," 2014). Therefore, although restricting access to the means of suicide can be an important component of suicide prevention but it is crucial to gain knowledge of the national, regional, and local suicide patterns, as well as having a better understanding of underlying mechanisms on suicidal behaviours (local examples of restriction of means will be discussed in more details in Chap. 3). In short, the suicide patterns across gender, culture, and societal patterns reflect that the availability and acceptability of suicide methods play an important role in the choice people make (Ajdacic-Gross et al., 2008).

Based on the statistics for the most common means of suicide in HK for all ages across 2007–2016, it is evident that jumping from height is the most common method one chooses to attempt suicide (see Graph 1.1; CSRP, 2015). Jumping from a height plays an important role in small, predominantly urban societies such as HK, Luxembourg, and Malta. In contrast, in rural Latin American countries (e.g., El Salvador, Nicaragua, and Peru), Asian countries (e.g., the Republic of Korea and Thailand), and also in Portugal (Ajdacic-Gross et al., 2008). Following jumping from heights, other common means are hanging, charcoal burning,[8] poisoning (see Graph

[5] acceptability is the beliefs about whether or not to commit suicide and which method to use.

[6] sociocultural norms relates to how one may proceed suicide such as how to deal with obstacles to suicide.

[7] MTR is a abbreviation for Mass Transit Railway, it is a major public transport network serving Hong Kong.

[8] Burning barbecue charcoal in a confined space leading to carbon monoxide poisoning.

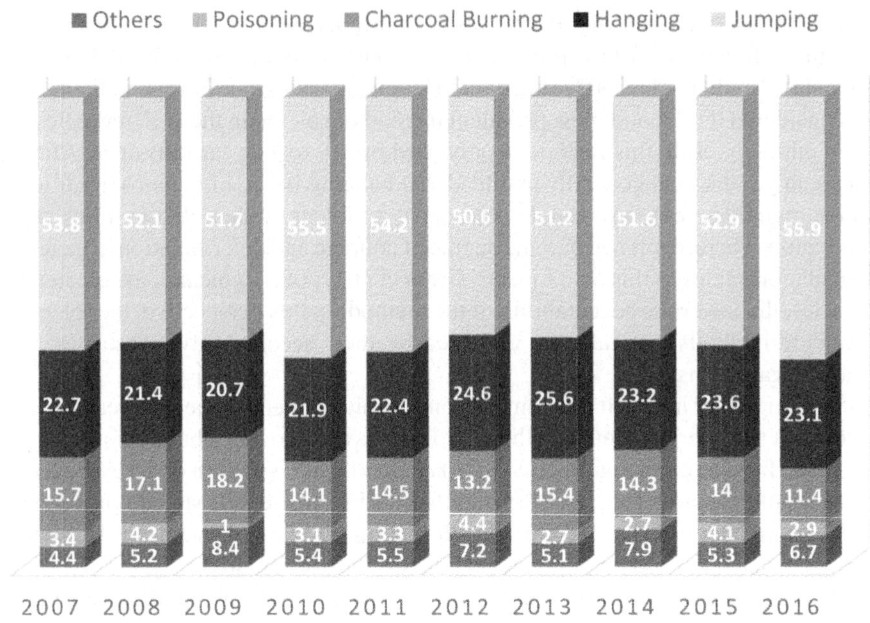

Graph 1.1 Showing means of suicide in HK from 2007 to 2016 (Hong Kong Jockey Club for suicide research and prevention, 2018)

1.1; CSRP, 2015). In particular, poisoning with pesticides or drugs was a major problem, notably among women, and this is very common in women from Canada, the Nordic countries, and the United Kingdom (UK). It also played an important role in male suicide in other countries. In comparison, the role of pesticide suicide in Asian countries was only apparent in the 1990s but soon came to the emergence of a new method, charcoal-burning suicide, in HK, China, and urban Taiwan, China has been a surprise but serves as a warning that research and prevention efforts should be reinforced.

Alongside the cultural difference in means of suicide, it also differs in terms of gender too. For instance, the second most common suicide method for females is poisoning by ingestion, occupying 30% of all female suicides, with only 6.7% of male suicides using this method. The difference is even more apparent in the age group of 15–19, in which poisoning by ingestion takes up 15.7% of female suicides but only 2% of male suicides (Hogan & Kennedy, 2011). Likewise, a similar situation is reflected in the age group of 20–24, with 18.9% female suicides adopted ingestion, comparing to male suicides by ingestion with only 3.2%. Violent and highly lethal methods such as firearm suicide and hanging are more frequent among men. In contrast, women often choose poisoning by ingestion or drowning, which are less violent and less lethal (Ajdacic-Gross et al., 2008).

1.3 Suicidal Thought to Behaviour

Suicide isn't very often regarded as an isolated event. Instead. It is conceptualized as a continuum of processes (see Fig. 1.9), beginning with suicidal ideation, moving to a suicide plan and preparation, a suicide attempt, and finally suicide completion (Potter et al., 2004). Noteworthily, the term suicidality is interchangeable with the term suicidal behaviour in this book, with both terms referring to any actions, thoughts (also known as suicidal ideation), intentions, motivations, plans, and attempts of suicide (Silverman, 2006). In the prevention of suicidality at an earlier stage, it is utmost to pay attention to the initial step of the whole suicide path, which is suicidal ideation. Suicidal ideation refers to the experience of thoughts, ruminations (repetitive action of focusing on the same feelings and thoughts) or fantasies about conducting suicide, and/or verbalizing threats to conduct suicide (Reynolds, 1988). It is contended to be the most crucial stage of the suicide process since it comes before a suicide attempt (Gould & Kramer, 2001; Lee et al., 2009). Perceiving the progression from thoughts of suicide to taking action is favorable to early detection as well as possible prevention of suicidality (Palmer, 2004; Klonsky & May, 2015).

Figure 1.9. depicting the path of suicide reveals progression as a series of suicidal behaviours that are hierarchical and ongoing (Potter et al., 2004; Thompson et al., 2012). Reynolds (1988) suggested that along the suicide continuum, a milder form of suicidal behavior is reflected by suicidal ideation, further progressing into more severe suicidal behaviours such as suicide planning and attempts. Researchers Glenn and Nock (2014) and Prinstein et al. (2008) supported such proposed progression, concluding that more severe suicidal acts can be strongly predicted by suicidal ideation. The intensity of self-harm is directly proportionate to the intensity of suicidal ideation experienced. Nevertheless, May and Klonsky (2016) argued that it is not a must to assume suicidal ideation as the beginning point of suicidal acts that will be progressed into more life-threatening behaviours. The ideation-to action framework is developed by Klonsky and May (2015) to progress suicide research regarding risk assessment, theory, treatment, and prevention. It is stated clearly by the ideation-to action framework that suicidal ideation development and progression from ideation to suicide attempts should be perceived as individual processes with distinct predictors and explanations. In addition to this framework, Baca-Garcia et al. (2011) stated that only one-third of individuals with experiences in attempting suicide reported suicidal ideation. Likewise, there were some suicide reports in absence of any early stages' signs. Based on these incidents, the first suicide attempts have

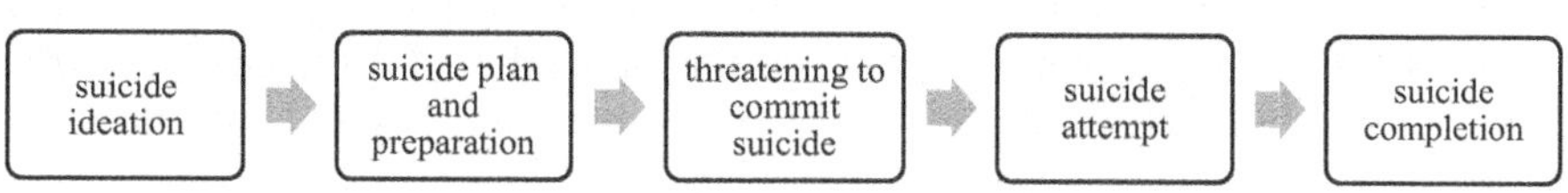

Fig. 1.9 The suicide continuum, from the escalation of suicidal ideation to the complete act of suicide (Potter et al., 2004)

become lethal suicide and do not follow the suicide continuum as stated in Fig. 1.9 (Schlebusch, 2005).

Some researchers have conceptualized suicidal ideation as having two distinct categories; active and passive suicide forms of ideation. Active suicidal ideation comprises active thoughts regarding self-harm or comprehensive planning on conducting suicide (Schulberg et al., 2005). Contrarily, passive suicidal ideation occurs when one feels unworthy of their own life or thinks that going dead is better than staying alive. These thoughts may include but are not limited to ideas of being fed up with life and a wish to not get up from sleep. Compared with active suicidal ideation, passive thoughts consist of fewer particular intentions or plans for self-killing (Schulberg et al., 2005). Szanto et al. (1996) measured the clinical correlates of active versus passive suicidal ideation in patients with recurrent depression. The data confronted the need to differentiate active and passive suicidal ideation because the features of both sides overlapped highly. They also stated that the suicidal ideation could transfer from passive to active during an episode of a suicide crisis, leading to difficulty in defining distinctive features (Schulberg et al., 2005). Despite that it is not the emphasis of this book, it should be noted that suicidal ideation can be active or passive; both are significant and substitutable.

Notwithstanding a variety of current suicide prevention programmes given, there has not been a significant decline in the suicide rates in proportion to the number of resources spent (Centers for Disease Control and Prevention, 2014). It is put forward that even with substantial work in prevention and prediction, suicide rates still pose a considerable strain on healthcare (Mathers & Loncar, 2006) and are foreseen to surge around the globe through 2030 (WHO, 2013). Not only does suicide make families and friends devastated, but it also imposes a tremendous financial burden on society (Shepard et al., 2015). In this regard, it is vital to identify people who display warning signs of suicide risks as early as possible.

1.4 Risk and Protective Factors Associated with Suicide

The decision as to whether someone proceeds from one stage of suicide to the next can be influenced by individual risk factors (also known as *vulnerability*) or protective factors (also known as *resilience*). Resilience generally refers to factors associated with reduced rates of affective disorders[9] or other negative outcomes. In terms of suicide resilience, it has a protective effect on suicide risk and can buffer against setbacks in life (Bonanno et al., 2007). Some protective factors counter specific risk factors, while others protect individuals against a number of different suicide risk factors. While risk factors can add to the risk of one's likelihood of taking their life,

[9] Affective disorders refer to a set of psychiatric diseases related to disturbance in mood that ranges from mild to severe. The main types of affective disorders include depression, bipolar disorder, and anxiety disorder. An affective disorder is also termed as a mood disorder by the Diagnostic and Statistical Manual of Mental Disorders, Fifth Edition (DSM-5).

for those high in suicide resilience, the association between the risk of suicide and suicidal behaviour can be less significant.

The listed risk factors may contribute directly or indirectly (e.g., increasing susceptibility to mental disorders) to suicidal behaviours. Moreover, each risk factor interrelates with others, and the areas are not mutually exclusive; nonetheless, all of these factors are generally viewed as moving from systemic through to individual category. It is important to note that those risk factors listed are far from exhaustive; thus the way they are classified/categorized varies greatly depending on the context ("Preventing suicide," 2014). Specific risk factors could sit within more than one of the areas simultaneously. One example will be that loss of a job or financial support could influence a person individually and lead to the deterioration of close relationships. Still, it could also be linked to an economic recession at a systemic level.

From the research perspective, there has been a substantial investigation of suicidality through exploring risk factors. In other words, it reveals the intention of researchers on explicating psychological vulnerabilities and maladaptive cognitive processes related to suicidal behaviour (Nierenberg et al., 2012). With references to Baumeister (1990), the intention to conduct suicide germinates when one adversely regards themselves as inadequate, incompetent, and guilty, which develops an urge to escape undesirable thoughts by resorting to suicide attempt. Given that suicidal behaviour has been highly ascribed to a couple of psychological factors, researchers and clinicians have adopted these variables in availing early identification of individuals at stake (Homaifar et al., 2012). This is also regarded as a risk-based approach since research very often sheds light on the linkage between risk factors and the suicide act.

As mentioned, for every suicide there are many more people who attempt suicide every year. Significantly, a prior suicide attempt is the most critical risk factor for suicide in the general population. Even one year after a suicide attempt, suicide risk and premature death from other causes remain high. Based on the current literature, several other common factors associated with suicidality and act cumulatively increase a person's vulnerability to suicidal behaviour. These include the presence of recurrent suicidal ideation, feelings of hopelessness, a history of past suicide attempt(s), cognitive deficits (e.g. poor problem solving), and comorbidity with affective disorders (Baumeister, 1990; Rudd et al., 2015; WHO, 2014; see list for detail).

For this reason, these factors are studied by a wide variety of disciplines such as socio-cultural, environmental, biological, and cognitive perspectives (e.g. Hawton & van Heeringen, 2009; Nierenberg et al., 2012). Among these factors, the established link between a past suicide attempt, recurrent suicidal ideation, hopelessness, and depression are regarded as the most important risk factors for predicting future suicidal behaviour. For example, Hopelessness refers to negative self-referential processing (i.e. thinking) relating to a person's feelings about the future, loss of motivation, and expectations. It encompasses negative expectations about the future, accomplishing goals, and the likelihood of achieving success. It is generally conceptualized as a cognitive aspect of psychological functioning, often used as an indirect indicator of suicidal risk when coupled with mental disorders or prior suicide attempts

("Preventing suicide," 2014). Hopelessness is often accompanied by depression; measures of hopelessness are better correlated with suicidal behaviour than scores of depression rating scales in prospective cohort studies (Wagner et al., 2015).

Hopelessness includes the presence of thoughts such as:

- "This world will be better off without me."
- "things will never get better"
- "I can't find a reason to live."
- "I do not see things improving"
- "I can't handle it anymore. Suicide is the only way out."

1.4.1 Social-Ecological Framework for Understanding Suicidal Behaviours

The social-ecological framework (Cramer & Kapusta, 2017) is adopted to illustrate how different factors can impact individuals. The framework consists of individual factors (e.g. mental health, personal experiences, and personality), interpersonal relationships (e.g. families, peers), community (e.g. discrimination, living environment), the larger society (e.g. media, the stigma of help-seeking), and the health system. For example, individual risk factors are related to the likelihood of a person developing suicidal behaviours. These personal, interpersonal, and sociocultural factors interact with each other to mediate not only suicide risk but sometimes induce protection against suicide risk. Based on the examples listed, The WHO (2014) has identified a number of protective factors and risk factors among different levels of this Social-Ecological framework. One common personal risk factor is substance abuse. Substance use disorders are found in 25 – 50% of all suicides, and suicide risk is further increased if someone is engaged in alcohol or substance use or has psychiatric disorders. Of all deaths from suicide, 22% can be attributed to alcohol use, which means that every fifth suicide would not occur if alcohol were not consumed in the population. Dependence on other substances, including cannabis, heroin, or nicotine, is also often comorbid with the impulsive act of suicide (Education Bureau, 2018) (Fig. 1.10).

Some of the most common risk factors identified from an exhaustive list and the key ones are illustrated in Table 1.1. The factors have been grouped into five categories: systemic, societal, community, relationship (social connectedness to immediate family and friends), and individual risk factors. The groups are reflective from the Social-Ecological framework and this categorization helps to identify relevant interventions more easily (Fig. 1.11).

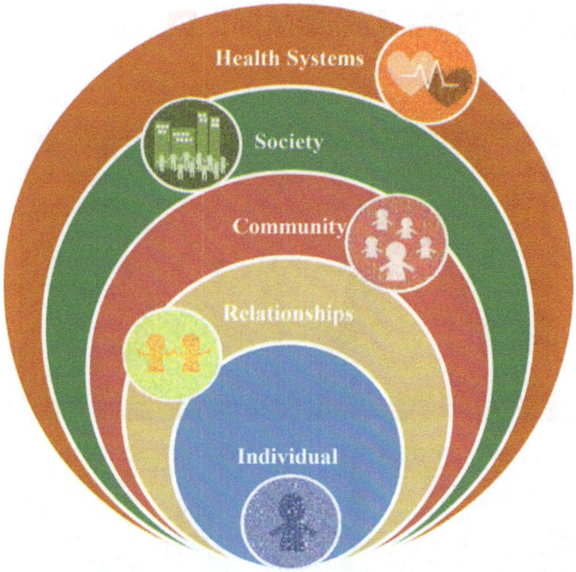

Fig. 1.10 Showing the different layers of the social-ecological framework from [resource handbook for school, 2017, p. 8 in (Education Bureau, 2018)]

Table 1.1 Risk factors identified by WHO (2018): Suicide WHO. (2018, August 24). Retrieved (Education Bureau, 2018, p. 24)

	Some examples for each layer of the social-ecological framework
Individual	• Personal e.g. previous suicide attempt, impulsivity, affective disorders (e.g. clinical depression) • Sense of hopelessness, substance abuse, chronic pain, exposure to overwhelming or chronic stress
	• Cognitive—poor problem-solving skills, the rigidity of thoughts • Extreme perfectionism • Poor emotional control
	• Biological—Genetic or neurological factors • E.g. Biological disposition of affective disorders, schizophrenia, and personality disorders • Family history of suicide, puberty, hormonal change
Relationships	• Sense of isolation and lack of social support, interpersonal/family relationship conflict, discord or loss, history of abuse
Society	• Access to means of suicide • Inappropriate media reporting • The stigma associated with help-seeking behaviour
Community	• Natural disaster, economic recession, job loss • Acculturation and dislocation, discrimination
Health systems	• Barriers to accessing health care • Long waiting times

Fig. 1.11 News reporting a girl with relationship conflict with her girl friend at school (Headline Daily, 2020), Relationship conflict is one of the common risk factors attributed to youth suicide. A recent news reported a secondary school student who jumped down from her school on the 12th November 2020. She has expressed emotional distress and having relationship conflict.

1.4.2 Cognitive and Neurological Risk Factors

As evident from Table 1.1 (as above), individuals factors such as cognitive and neurological malfunctioning are important risks factors associated with suicide. Invariably, the suicide continuum outlined in Fig. 1.9 (Potter et al., 2004) depicts that starting from the first stage of suicidal ideation to the final stage of conducting suicide, complex cognitive processes are required in the path of suicide progression. These may include but are not limited to solving problems to refrain from the accumulation of emotional pain, attending to sensitive stimuli relevant to one's emotional state, inhibition of intrusive thoughts, planning and organizing ways to conduct suicide, and decision making about the final attempt (Burton et al., 2011). These cognitive

1. Abstract ideas
2. Judgment
3. Emotion regulation
4. Impulse control
5. Reasoning
6. Planning and Organization
7. Personality
8. Social skills
9. Cognitive flexibility
10. Working memory
11. Attentional control
12. Inhibition

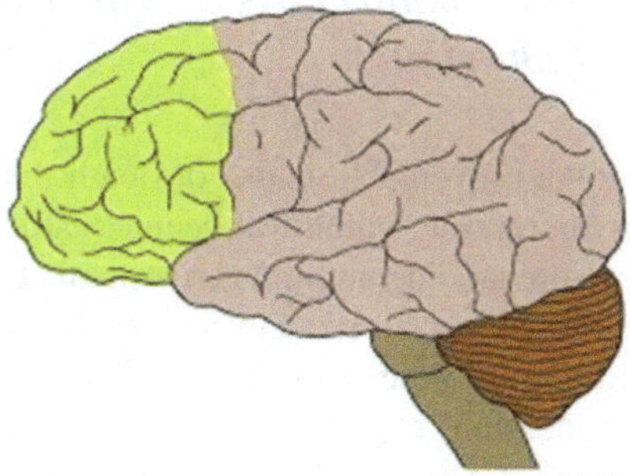

Fig. 1.12 Functions of the prefrontal cortex

processes generally fall under the umbrella term of *executive functions*,[10] responsible for controlling, organizing, and directing cognitive activity, emotional responses, and behaviour (Banich, 2009). It is put forward that there is the interaction between emotion and cognitive processing, which serves as an utmost determinant concerning whether one may proceed from one point of the suicide continuum to another (Cha et al., 2010; Van Heeringen & Marusic, 2003).

Many components in executive functions enable ones to plan and enact goal-directed behaviours, overcome unanticipated challenges, regulate emotions, exert self-control, work with information held in the mind, shift focus between multiple tasks, and modify behaviour flexibly according to a situation (Burton et al., 2011; Damasio, 1995; Diamond, 2013; Doty, 2012). It has been set forth that executive functions comprise three major processes, cognitive flexibility, inhibitory control, and working memory, and these are the building blocks for daily life (Diamond, 2013). This higher level of processing is predominant in the frontal part of the brain called the prefrontal lobe (PFC). Many brain regions will interact closely with other brain regions (e.g., the anterior cingulate and the amygdala; Anderson, 2008; Diamond, 2013) (Fig. 1.12).

[10] Since the 1980s, the term executive function, executive control, cognitive control, and frontal lobe functioning have been used interchangeably through years of different publications. All of these terms are proposed to be a psychometric construct on the activity occurring within the frontal lobes (Anderson et al., 2011).

1.4.3 *The Comorbidity of Affective Disorders and Suicidal Behaviour*

Suicide is a preventable cause of death that often coexists with affective disorders such as depression which has been considered as one of the most powerful predictors of future suicide attempts (Arsenault-Lapierre et al., 2004; Sokero et al., 2005). Depression is characterized by a range of cognitive and physical symptoms including lack of interest and energy, difficulties concentrating, feelings of guilt and sadness, suicidal ideation, change in weight and psychomotor abilities, fatigue, and sleep disturbance (CDC, 2013; Depressive Disorders, 2013). In high-income countries such as U.S and UK, the comorbidity of affective disorders and suicidal behaviour are present in up to 90% of individuals. Among the 10% without clear diagnoses, psychiatric symptoms resemble those of people who die by suicide. In comparison, affective disorders are less prevalent among suicide attempters in some Asian countries, as shown in studies from China and India (around 60%). Suicide risk varies with the type of disorder, and the most common disorders associated with suicidal behaviour are depression and alcohol use disorders ("Preventing suicide," 2014). The lifetime risk of suicide is estimated to be 4% in affective disorders, 7% with alcohol dependence, and 8% with bipolar disorder. Importantly, the risk of suicidal behaviour increases with comorbidity between these disorders.

DSM-5™ Diagnostic Criteria Major Depressive Disorder

According to the Diagnostic and Statistical Manual of Mental Disorders, Fifth Edition (DSM-5), four criteria (A, B, C, and D) have been postulated with the recommendation that an individual has to display at least five of the symptoms listed in Criterion A for a minimum duration of 2-week to be diagnosed as having clinical depression. Also at least one of the symptoms should be having a depressed mood or loss of interest or pleasure.

A. **Five (or more) of the following symptoms with the same 2-week period**

Note: Do not include symptoms that are attributable to another medical condition.

1. Depressed mood most of the day, nearly every day, as indicated by either subjective report (e.g., feels sad, empty, and hopeless) or observation made by others (e.g., appears tearful).
2. Markedly diminished interest or pleasure in all, or almost all, activities most of the day, nearly every day (as indicated by either subjective account or observation.)
3. Significant weight loss when not dieting or weight gain (e.g., a change of more than 5% of body weight in a month) decreases or increases appetite nearly every day.
4. Insomnia or hypersomnia nearly every day.
5. Psychomotor agitation or retardation nearly daily (observable by others, not merely subjective feelings of restlessness or being slowed down).
6. Fatigue or loss of energy nearly every day.

7. Feelings of worthlessness or excessive or inappropriate guilt (which may be delusional) nearly every day (not merely self-reproach or guilt about being sick).
8. Diminished ability to think or concentrate, or indecisiveness, nearly every day (either by subjective account or as observed by others).
9. Recurrent thoughts of death (not just fear of dying), recurrent suicidal ideation without a specific plan, or a suicide attempt or a specific plan for conducting suicide.

B. **The symptoms cause clinically significant distress or impairment in social, occupational, or other important areas of functioning.**
C. **The episode is not attributable to the physiological effects of a substance or another medical condition.**

Note: Criteria A-C represent a major depressive episode.

Note: Responses to a significant loss (e.g., bereavement, financial ruin, losses from a natural disaster, a serious medical illness or disability) may include the feelings of intense sadness, rumination about the loss, insomnia, poor appetite, and weight loss noted in Criterion A, which may resemble a depressive episode.

Although such symptoms may be understandable or considered appropriate to the loss, the presence of a major depressive episode in addition to the normal response to a significant loss should also be carefully considered. This decision inevitably requires the exercise of clinical judgment based on the individual's history and the cultural norms for the expression of distress in the context of loss.

D. **The occurrence of the major depressive episode is not better explained by schizoaffective disorder, schizophrenia, schizophreniform disorder, delusional disorder, or other specified and unspecified schizophrenia spectrum and other psychotic disorders.**

Sources obtained from the Diagnostic and Statistical Manual of Mental Disorders 5

Below is a note from a 28-year-old male suicide completer who revealed the dilemma of suicide he had undergone regarding the co-existing feelings of depression and suicidal thoughts. This statement fully expresses the urge to get out of the current state which is considered to be ambiguous, lonely, and not worth living for.

> There is a silent line between relief and depression, one that I have yet to master… where is the line? When do I know I have crossed it? I will tell you when… it is when everything is perfect, everything is filled, yet something is empty and I am ready. (Lester et al., 2004)

It is indicated by Bostwick and Pankratz (2000) that individuals with affective disorders are subject to suicide risk 17 times higher in comparison with those without. Statistics with steady results also denoted a significant intensity of the comorbidity between depression and suicide. More than 90% of all suicide completers were diagnosed with at least one form of affective disorder (Arsenault-Lapierre et al., 2004; Mann, 2003). This echoes the view that depression contributes to the progression of suicide to a great extent. The higher the levels of depression, the greater the suicide risk will be (Pompeo, 2014; Potter et al., 2004; Sokero et al., 2005). In that regard, a couple of programmes related to suicide prevention always attempt to identify the suicide risk of individuals through screening for early signs of depression (Wang et al., 2017). The high comorbidity between suicide and affective disorders gives rise to committee research and programmes for prevention intending to investigate these concepts together instead of regarding them as separated elements (Preuss et al., 2002; Yen et al., 2003).

Around 6.7% of 18–65 year-old-adults in the U.S. (Adaa.org, 2017) and 8.4% of adults in HK (Lee et al., 2007) are influenced by depression. Notably, depression is alarmingly dominant within the student population, with couple numbers of reports from students experiencing emotional disturbances in their studies (Mackenzie et al., 2011). This is depicted by approximately 12–18% of students being diagnosed with at least one form of affective disorder during their time at university (Mowbray et al., 2006). Depression dominance was also found within Chinese university students (N = 5245). Based on the Beck Depression Inventory (BDI; Beck et al., 1996), it was discovered that respondents with clinical levels of depressive symptoms occupied 11.7% (Chen et al., 2013). A web-based survey in a public university in the U.S. was directed by Eisenberg et al. (2007) to compare the disparities between graduate and undergraduate students. Among 2843 responses, undergraduates with depression or anxiety disorder accounted for 15.6% of 1181, whereas graduate students occupied 13% of 1662. The findings unveil that university life could be a critical period of the manifestation of affective disorders within students. Compared with around 6.7% for depression and 3.1% for generalized anxiety disorder in the national prevalence, it is apparent that the dominance of affective disorders among these students' samples is substantially high. In Eisenberg et al.'s study (2007), when putting the affective disorder dominance in graduates to undergraduates into comparison. It was stated by Pereira-Lima and Loureiro (2015) that university graduates who have finished their degrees and have integrated into the workforce are generally more capable of maintaining satisfying and longer-lasting relationships. They also possess better productivity and are mentally and physically healthier, which might be why graduates are revealed to be of lower levels of depression and anxiety levels than undergraduates. This again foregrounds university life as the critical stage that students are undergoing and the importance of selecting the right sample for studying the suicide process in research (Fig. 1.13).

Following from the studies of Arsenault-Lapierre et al. (2004) and Mann (2003), rather than reviewing the high percentage of suicide completers who had been depressed, Angst et al. (2005) explored the percentage of depressed individuals who had made at least one suicide attempt. They found that 10–15% of depressed patients have attempted suicide during the course of their disorder. This means that only a small percentage of depressed individuals proceed to suicide whilst over 85% remained in the depressed state without striving for change. Despite the high association between suicide and depression, this has raised questions as to why only a small proportion of depressed individuals proceed to a suicide act whilst others do not. It is reasoned that other factors may significantly impact whether someone decides to commit a suicide act or not. Aside from individual risk factors, some risk factors

Roche

V 0477

Beck Depression Inventory

CRTN: _____ CRF number: _____

Baseline

Page 15 patient inits: _______

11. Agitation

0 I am no more restless or wound up than usual.
1 I feel more restless or wound up than usual.
2 I am so restless or agitated that it's hard to stay still.
3 I am so restless or agitated that I have to keep moving or doing something.

12. Loss of Interest

0 I have not lost interest in other people or activities.
1 I am less interested in other people or things than before.
2 I have lost most of my interest in other people or things.
3 It's hard to get interested in anything.

13. Indecisiveness

0 I make decisions about as well as ever.
1 I find it more difficult to make decisions than usual.
2 I have much greater difficulty in making decisions than I used to.
3 I have trouble making any decisions.

14. Worthlessness

0 I do not feel I am worthless.
1 I don't consider myself as worthwhile and useful as I used to.
2 I feel more worthless as compared to other people.
3 I feel utterly worthless.

15. Loss of Energy

0 I have as much energy as ever.
1 I have less energy than I used to have.
2 I don't have enough energy to do very much.
3 I don't have enough energy to do anything.

16. Changes in Sleeping Pattern

0 I have not experienced any change in my sleeping pattern.
1a I sleep somewhat more than usual.
1b I sleep somewhat less than usual.
2a I sleep a lot more than usual.
2b I sleep a lot less than usual.
3a I sleep most of the day.
3b I wake up 1–2 hours early and can't get back to sleep.

17. Irritability

0 I am no more irritable than usual.
1 I am more irritable than usual.
2 I am much more irritable than usual.
3 I am irritable all the time.

18. Changes in Appetite

0 I have not experienced any change in my appetite.
1a My appetite is somewhat less than usual.
1b My appetite is somewhat greater than usual.
2a My appetite is much less than before.
2b My appetite is much greater than usual.
3a I have no appetite at all.
3b I crave food all the time.

19. Concentration Difficulty

0 I can concentrate as well as ever.
1 I can't concentrate as well as usual.
2 It's hard to keep my mind on anything for very long.
3 I find I can't concentrate on anything.

20. Tiredness or Fatigue

0 I am no more tired or fatigued than usual.
1 I get more tired or fatigued more easily than usual.
2 I am too tired or fatigued to do a lot of the things I used to do.
3 I am too tired or fatigued to do most of the things I used to do.

21. Loss of Interest in Sex

0 I have not noticed any recent change in my interest in sex.
1 I am less interested in sex than I used to be.
2 I am much less interested in sex now.
3 I have lost interest in sex completely.

Fig. 1.13 The Beck Depression Inventory (BDI; Beck et al., 1996). Adapted with permission from Beck Depression Inventory (BDI; Beck et al., 1996) associated with the health system and society should also be accounted for. These include

- difficulties in accessing health care and in receiving the care needed,
- easy availability of the means for suicide,
- inappropriate media reporting that sensationalizes suicide and increases the risk of imitative suicidal behaviours (also known as "**copycat**" suicides[11])
- stigma against people who seek help for suicidal behaviours, or for mental health and substance abuse problems
- ("Preventing suicide," 2014).

1.4.4 Problems with Too Many Risk Factors Identified

Past findings have tried to identify a range of risk factors associated with suicide including depression, hopelessness, impulsivity, cognitive rigidity, difficulty regulating emotions, a lack of rescue factors, and information processing bias (Cuijpers et al., 2012; O'Connor & Nock, 2014; Rajappa et al., 2011). However, the current problem is that many of these factors have not successfully predicted and prevented suicide. For instance, not all depressed patients are suicidal (i.e. only 12–18% of students report having at least one form of affective disorder were suicidal; Mowbray et al., 2006) and many individuals who are often exposed to a number of risk factors show no suicidal tendencies. A review on the psychological treatment for reducing depression and suicidal behaviour by Cuijpers et al. (2012) evaluated studies from 1966 to 2012, with 52 studies regarding psychological treatment (e.g., psychotherapy, medication, or a combination of both). Among the 616 participants included in the review that were analyzed on the effects of treatment on suicidal ideation and suicide risk and levels of hopelessness, depression was assessed by diagnostic interview or an elevated level of depressive symptoms (such as using the Beck Depression Inventory; BDI; Beck et al., 1996). It was concluded that there was insufficient evidence to establish whether suicidality in depressed patients could be reduced by reducing depressive symptoms through psychotherapy. The conclusion also reflected the limited ability to reduce suicidal behaviour by reducing depressive symptoms and hopelessness. Despite the fact that reducing depression alone may not be an effective way to prevent suicide, more researchers have turned to explore resilience factors instead. This has led to the emergence to focus on the resilient factors for suicide instead (Seligman et al., 2006; Tarrier, 2010).

Traditionally, suicide has been considered best to be addressed through clinical interventions, especially through the treatment of depression. These interventions include but are not limited to pharmaceutical and therapeutical interventions that stem from medical and clinical models involving intensive professional care. However, due

[11] A copycat suicide is defined as an emulation of another suicide that the person attempting suicide knows about either from local knowledge or due to accounts or depictions of the original suicide on television and in other media.

to a number of issues with the clinical approach such that the majority of people who completed suicide had not received psychiatric services prior to death, this approach has recently been questioned for its effectiveness in helping those who most in need of the service are. Given the issues raised, The CSRP (2015) has adopted a more holistic public health approach for suicide prevention instead. Using information and knowledge generated from research studies, they have integrated a multilayer intervention approach together with community collaboration. This means that individuals who are at a dangerous level of suicide risk will be catered for and those in the community who display signs of suicide risks. This holistic approach addresses risk factors of suicide and looks at protective factors that may help individuals build resilience to emotional concerns and suicidal behaviours.

1.4.5 What Protects People from the Risks of Suicide?

Some researchers challenged that the recognition of factors alone cannot fully explain suicidal behaviour, it is also important to explore positive psychological factors that may cultivate psychological wellbeing (Seligman et al., 2006; Tarrier, 2010) and protective factors associated with reduced suicidality (Johnson et al., 2008; Perkins & Jones, 2004). In contrast to risk factors, protective factors guard people against the risk of suicide. While many interventions are geared towards reducing risk factors in suicide prevention, it is equally important to consider how to strengthen factors that have been shown to increase resilience and connectedness and protect against suicidal behaviour ("Preventing suicide," 2014).

1.4.6 Protective Factors Highlighted by WHO (2018)

- Individual—e.g. self-worth, coping skills, religious belief, impulse control, positive well-being, healthy self-esteem and self-identity, good sense of self-efficacy
- Cognitive—e.g. effective problem-solving skills, management of stress
- Community—e.g. Support from teachers and others, willingness to seek and receive help when difficulties arise connectedness with groups and associations, stable living environment, healthy lifestyle choices such as regular exercise
- Close relationships—e.g. having strong and healthy close relationships and support from family are robust protective factors for adolescents and the elderly
- Hold religious or spiritual beliefs—socially cohesive and supportive community with a shared set of values.

1.4.7 Strong Personal Relationships

The risk of suicidal behaviour increases when people suffer from relationship conflict, loss, or discord. Conversely, the cultivation and maintenance of healthy close relationships can increase individual resilience and act as a protective factor against the risk of suicide ("Preventing suicide," 2014). Individual's interpersonal relationships with others such as their family, peers, friends, and partners can have the most influence in times of crisis. Friends and family can be a significant source of social, emotional, and financial support, and can protect against the impact of stressors. In particular, resilience gained from this support mitigates the suicide risk especially for adolescents who still have a high dependency on others. According to an interview with a girl who studies business administration and law at the University of Hong Kong (see Fig. 1.14, Ma, 2016). She expressed that suicide in the student population may not necessarily be due to academic problems, but rather is this the overly demanding expectations and perfectionism or self-pressure set by the students themselves. She believes that everyone has their psychological barrier, but she and her classmates have their own tactics to withstand stress. She claimed: "When you can't solve it yourself, you can talk to your friends, you can relieve the pressure that accumulates in your heart and laugh" (Ma, 2016).

Fig. 1.14. Showing double-degree female college students "find a friend to talk to is the best anti-pressure approach". Image by (Ma, 2016) Ma (2016, March 10). 雙學位女大學生抗壓之道: 找朋友傾訴最好

Religious or spiritual beliefs

The impact of religious beliefs may be considered as a double-edged saw ("Preventing suicide," 2014). The protective value of religion and spirituality may arise from providing access to a socially cohesive and supportive community with a shared set of values, this can at times confer protection against suicidal thoughts and behaviour. Although it provides a structured belief system that advocates for physically and mentally healthy behaviour, it may also have the opposite effect. For instance, many religious and cultural beliefs and behaviours promote stigmatism against suicide due to their moral stances, which can discourage help-seeking behaviours. A number of religious groups has forbidden suicide risk factors such as the use of alcohol. On top of that, the social practices adopted by some religions have also promoted self-destruction by fire amongst specific groups, particularly for South Asian women who are widows. As a result, the influence of religion and spiritual beliefs on suicide varies depending across various cultural and contextual practices and interpretations.

Lifestyle practice of positive coping strategies and well-being

Other protective factors to overcoming suicide are positive well-being and effective coping strategies. Personality traits help shape well-being which determines vulnerability for and resilience against stress and trauma. Emotional stability helps cultivate self-identity and offer an optimistic point of view for a range of coping strategies despite difficulties in life. To ease the influence of stressors and childhood adversities, one needs to have high self-esteem, self-efficacy[12], and effective problem-solving skills, including the ability to seek help when in need. While people normally stigmatize mental disorders, seeking help is a specifically crucial factor that depends on personal attitudes. Individuals who are less willing to seek help will have their mental health issues aggravated, leading to a surge in the suicidal risk that may have been efficaciously prevented by early intervention ("Preventing suicide," 2014). Some healthy lifestyle habits favor mental and physical well-being, ranging from regular exercise and sport, adequate sleep and diet, consideration of the impact on the health of alcohol and drugs, healthy relationships, and social contact, to effective management of stress.

The recent works on protective factors have aided cultivation in certain theoretical frameworks strengthening resilience. People who are regarded as having greater resilience to suicide may possess some personal characteristics that allow them to exert adaptation in adversities and recover from undesirable events. (Olsson et al., 2003). These are some indispensable protective factors combating suicidality development despite adversity and risk factors (Perkins & Jones, 2004). Examples include having high self-esteem, social and emotional competence (Flemming et al., 2007), and using more self-appraisal (Johnson et al., 2008).

In light of all the risk factors and protective factors mentioned, it is worth highlighting that the external factor can also have a significant impact. For example, the

[12] Self-efficacy is an individual's belief that one has competent to complete tasks, learn knowledge, or achieve goals.

COVID-19 pandemic has profound impacts on everyone (World Health Organization, 2020) and Hong Kong is no exception. Since the initial wave of COVID-19 outbreak in late January 2020, the HK government has implemented a set of emergency arrangements, including the suspensions of schools and non-emergency public services, lockdown, and stay-at-home orders (New Zealand Chamber of Commerce in Hong Kong, n.d.). This meant that some protective factors such as help-seeking, relationship building, and maintaining healthy living habits were all severely disrupted. During the difficult times of the lockdown, although people spent more time together at home with their family it did not necessarily mean they had more opportunities to build a stronger relationship with each other. In fact, the findings yield were quite the opposite and a recently published paper title reflects the situation globally. The paper titled: "The Stay at Home Order is Causing Things to Get Heated Up": Family Conflict Dynamics During COVID-19 From the Perspectives of Youth Calling a National Child Abuse Hotline' (Sinko et al., 2021). This is only a reflecting a tip of the ice-burg for the family conflict built during the pandemic. There is was disruptions of face-to-face interaction and had severe impacts on relationship building which have ruined the key protective factor on mental health in young adults which is why Chang et al. (2020) regarded the pandemic as a mental health catastrophe.

References

Adaa.org. (2017). Depression. *Anxiety and Depression Association of America, ADAA*. Available at: https://www.adaa.org/understanding-anxiety/depression.

Anderson, P. J. (2008). Towards a developmental model of executive function. In V. Anderson, R. Jacobs, & P. J. Anderson (Eds.), Neuropsychology, neurology, and cognition. Executive functions and the frontal lobes: A lifespan perspective (pp. 3–21). Philadelphia, PA, US: Taylor & Francis.

Angst, J., Angst, F., Gerber-Werder, R., & Gamma, A. (2005). Suicide in 406 mood-disorder patients with and without long-term medication: a 40 to 44 years' follow-up. *Archives of Suicide Research, 9*(3), 279-300. https://doi.org/10.1080/13811110590929488.

Arsenault-Lapierre, G., Kim, C., & Turecki, G. (2004). Psychiatric diagnoses in 3275 suicides: a meta-analysis. *BMC Psychiatry, 4*(1). https://doi.org/10.1186/1471-244x-4-37.

Baca-Garcia, E., Perez-Rodriguez, M. M., Oquendo, M. A., Keyes, K. M., Hasin, D. S., Grant, B. F., & Blanco, C. (2011). Estimating risk for suicide attempt: Are we asking the right questions? *Journal of Affective Disorders, 134*(1-3), 327-332. https://doi.org/10.1016/j.jad.2011.06.026.

Banich, M. T. (2009). Executive function. *Current Directions in Psychological Science, 18*(2), 89-94. https://doi.org/10.1111/j.1467-8721.2009.01615.x.

Beck, A., Steer, R., & Brown, G. (1996). BDI-II, Beck depression inventory. San Antonio, Tex.: Psychological Corporation.

Bostwick, J., & Pankratz, V. (2000). Affective disorders and suicide risk: A reexamination. *American Journal of Psychiatry, 157*(12), 1925-1932. https://doi.org/10.1176/appi.ajp.157.12.1925.

Cha, C., Najmi, S., Park, J., Finn, C., & Nock, M. (2010). Attentional bias toward suicide-related stimuli predicts suicidal behavior: Correction. *Journal of Abnormal Psychology, 119*(4), 874-874. https://doi.org/10.1037/a0021512.

Chen, L., Wang, L., Qiu, X. H., Yang, X. X., Qiao, Z. X., Yang, Y. J., & Liang, Y. (2013). Depression among Chinese university students: prevalence and socio-demographic correlates. *PLoS ONE, 8*(3), e58379. https://doi.org/10.1371/journal.pone.0058379.

Cheung, E., & Chiu, P. (2017, March 12). Students at breaking point: Hong Kong announces emergency measures after 22 suicides since the start of the academic year. *South China Morning Post*. Retrieved from: http://www.scmp.com/news/hong-kong/health-environment/article/1923465/students-breaking-point-hong-kong-announces.

Chung, F. (2016, March 10). HKU student latest case in grim toll. *The Standard*. Retrieved from: http://www.thestandard.com.hk/section-news.php?id=167079.

Cuijpers, P., Reynolds, C., Donker, T., Li, J., Andersson, G., & Beekman, A. (2012). Personalized treatment of adult depression: medication, psychotherapy, or both? A systematic review. *Depression and Anxiety*, *29*(10), 855-864. https://doi.org/10.1002/da.21985.

Damasio, A. (1995). Nervous function after right hemispherectomy. *Neurocase*, *1*(2), 179–181.

Eisenberg, D., Gollust, S. E., Golberstein, E., & Hefner, J. L. (2007). Prevalence and correlates of depression, anxiety, and suicidality among university students. *American Journal of Orthopsychiatry*, *77*(4), 534-542. https://doi.org/10.1037/0002-9432.77.4.534.

Glenn, C. & Nock, M. (2014). Improving the short-term prediction of suicidal behavior. *American Journal of Preventive Medicine*, *47*(3), 176-180.

Hawton, K. & van Heeringen, K. (2009). Suicide. *The Lancet*, *373*, 1372-1381.

Homaifar, B., Bahraini, N., Silverman, M., & Brenner, L. (2012). Executive functioning as a component of suicide risk assessment: clarifying its role in standard clinical applications. *Journal of Mental Health Counseling*, *34*(2), 110-120. https://doi.org/10.17744/mehc.34.2.r70331307tx03871.

Johnson, J., Gooding, P., & Tarrier, N. (2008). Suicide risk in schizophrenia: Explanatory models and clinical implications, The Schematic Appraisal Model of Suicide (SAMS). *Psychology and Psychotherapy: Theory, Research and Practice*, *81*(1), 55-77.

Lee, A., Wong, S., Tsang, K., Ho, G., Wong, C., & Cheng, F. (2009). Understanding suicidality and correlates among Chinese secondary school students in Hong Kong. *Health Promotion International*, *24*(2), 156-165. https://doi.org/10.1093/heapro/dap011.

Lee, S., Tsang, A., & Kwok, K. (2007). Twelve-month prevalence, correlates, and treatment preference of adults with DSM-IV major depressive episode in Hong Kong. *Journal of Affective Disorders*, *98*(1-2), 129-136. https://doi.org/10.1016/j.jad.2006.07.009.

Lester, D., Wood, P., Williams, C., & Haines, J. (2004). Motives for suicide: A study of Australian suicide notes. *Crisis*, *25*, 33-34.

Mackenzie, S., Wiegel, J. R., Mundt, M., Brown, D., Saewyc, E., Heiligenstein, E., & Fleming, M. (2011). Depression and suicide ideation among students accessing campus health care. American Journal of Orthopsychiatry, 81(1), 101-107. https://doi.org/10.1111/j.1939-0025.2010.01077.x.

Mann, J. J. (2003). Neurobiology of suicidal behaviour. *Nature Reviews Neuroscience*, *4*(10), 819-828. https://doi.org/10.1038/nrn1220.

Mathers, C., & Loncar, D. (2006). Projections of global mortality and burden of disease from 2002 to 2030. *PLoS Medicine*, *3*(11), 2011-2030. https://doi.org/10.1371/journal.pmed.0030442.

Mooney, P. (2005, November 25). Campus life proves difficult for China's little emperors. *The Chronicle of Higher Education*. Retrieved from http://pjmooney.com/che-studentlife.html.

Mowbray, C. T., Megivern, D., Mandiberg, J. M., Strauss, S., Stein, C. H., Collins, K., & Lett, R. (2006). Campus mental health services: Recommendations for change. *American Journal of Orthopsychiatry*, *76*, 226–237.

Nangle, J., Clarke, S., Morris, D. W., Schwaiger, S., McGhee, K., & Donohoe, G. (2006). Neurocognition and suicidal behaviour in an Irish population with major psychotic disorders. Schizophrenia Research, *85*(1-3), 196–200. https://doi.org/10.1093/epirev/mxn00210.1016/j.schres.2006.03.035.

Nock, M. K., Park, J. M., Finn, C. T., Deliberto, T. L., Dour, H. J., & Banaji, M. R. (2010). Measuring the suicidal mind: implicit cognition predicts suicidal behavior. *Psychological Science*, *21*(4), 511–517. https://doi.org/10.1177/0956797610364762.

Nock, M. K., Borges, G., Bromet, E. J., Cha, C. B., Kessler, R. C., & Lee, S. (2007). Suicide and suicidal behavior. *Epidemiological Review*. 30,133–154. https://doi.org/10.1093/epirev/mxn002.

Olsson, C. A., Bond, L., Burns, J. M., Vella-Brodrick, D. A., & Sawyer, S. (2003). Adolescent resilience: a concept analysis. **Journal of Adolescence**, *26*, 1-11.

Palmer, C. J. (2004). Suicide attempt history, self-esteem, and suicide risk in a sample of 116 depressed voluntary inpatients. *Psychological Reports*, *95*, 1092–1094.

Perkins, D. F. & Jones, K. R. (2004). Risk behaviors and resiliency within physically abused adolescents. *Child Abuse & Neglect*, 28, 547-563.

Phillips, M. R., Li, X., & Zhang, Y. (2002). Suicide rates in China, 1995–99. *The Lancet*, *359*(9309), 835–840. https://doi.org/10.1016/s0140-6736(02)07954-0.

Pompeo, A. (2014). College students' perceived and personal mental health stigma: the influence on help-seeking attitudes and intentions (Ph.D.). Montclair State University, United States - New Jersey. Retrieved from: http://search.proquest.com/psycinfo/docview/1525999386/abstract/C28 4EBEFBCCF4BBFPQ/14?accountid=13265.

Preuss, U. W., Schuckit, M. A., Smith, T. L., Danko, G. P., & Buckman, K. (2002). Comparison of 3190 alcohol-dependent individuals with and without suicide attempts. *Alcoholism: Clinical and Experimental Research*, *26*, 471–477.

Prinstein, M., Nock, M., Simon, V., Aikins, J., Cheah, C., & Spirito, A. (2008). Longitudinal trajectories and predictors of adolescent suicidal ideation and attempts following inpatient hospitalization. *Journal of Consulting and Clinical Psychology*, *76*(1), 92-103.

Reynolds, W. M. (1988). Suicidal ideation questionnaire for adolescents. *Psychological Assessment Resources*. Odessa, Florida.

Schwartz, A. J. (1990). The epidemiology of suicide among students at colleges and universities in the United States. *Journal of College Student Psychotherapy*, *4*(3-4), 25-44. https://doi.org/10.1300/j035v04n03_03.

Seligman, M. E. P., Rashid, T., & Parks, A. C. (2006). Positive psychotherapy. *American Psychologist*, *61*(8), 774-788. https://doi.org/10.1037/0003-066X.61.8.774.

Silverman, M. (2006). The language of suicidology. *Suicide and Life-Threatening Behavior*, *36*(5), 519-532. https://doi.org/10.1521/suli.2006.36.5.519.

Sokero, T. P., Melartin, T. K., Rytsälä, H. J., Leskelä, U. S., Lestelä-Mielonen, P. S., & Isometsä, E. T. (2005). Prospective study of risk factors for attempted suicide among patients with DSM–IV major depressive disorder. *British Journal of Psychiatry*, *186*(4), 314-318. https://doi.org/10.1192/bjp.186.4.314.

Sokero, T. P., Melartin, T. K., Rytsälä, H. J., Leskelä, U. S., Lestelä-Mielonen, P. S., & Isometsä, E. T. (2005). Prospective study of risk factors for attempted suicide among patients with DSM–IV major depressive disorder. *British Journal of Psychiatry*, *186*(4), 314-318. https://doi.org/10.1192/bjp.186.4.314.

Szanto, K., Reynolds, C. F., Frank, E., Stack, J., Fasiczka, A. L., Miller, M., & Kupfer, D. J. (1996). Suicide in elderly depressed patients: is active vs. passive suicidal ideation a clinically valid distinction? *The American Journal of Geriatric Psychiatry*, *4*(3), 197-207. https://doi.org/10.1097/00019442-199622430-00003.

Tarrier, N. (2010). Broad minded affective coping (BMAC): a "positive" CBT approach to facilitating positive emotions. *International Journal of Cognitive Therapy*, *3*, 64-76.

Thompson, A. H., Dewa, C. S., & Phare, S. (2012). The suicidal process: age of onset and severity of suicidal behaviour. Social Psychiatry and Psychiatric Epidemiology, 47(8), 1263-1269. https://doi.org/10.1007/s00127-011-0434-0.

Van Heeringen, C. & Marusic, A. (2003). Understanding the suicidal brain. *The British Journal of Psychiatry*, *183*(4), 282-284.

Yen, S., Shea, M. T., Pagno, M., Sanislow, C. A., & Grilo, C. M. (2003). Axis I and axis II disorders as predictors of prospective suicide attempts: findings from the collaborative longitudinal personality disorders study. *Journal of Abnormal Psychology*, *112*, 375–381.

Zhao, S. (2015, July 10) More Hong Kong children commit suicide than die in accidents, study reveals. *South China Morning Post*. Retrieved 24 March 2016, from http://www.scmp.com/news/hong-kong/health-environment/article/1835675/suicide-biggest-cause-unnatural-death-hong-kong.

A resource handbook for school. (2017). Retrieved from Education Bureau website. https://www.edb.gov.hk/attachment/en/teacher/prevention-of-student-suicides/Resource_Handbook_for_Schools_En.pdf.

Abraham, A. (2018, July 4). *Talk openly with HK youth about suicide and stress.* Retrieved from https://www.scmp.com/comment/insight-opinion/article/2075761/its-time-talk-openly-hong-kongs-youth-about-suicide-and.

Ajdacic-Gross, V. (2008). Methods of suicide: International suicide patters derived from the WHO mortality database. *Bulletin of the World Health Organization, 86*(9), 726–732. https://doi.org/10.2471/blt.07.043489.

Ajdacic-Gross, V., Weiss, M. G., Ring, M., Hepp, U., Bopp, M., Gutzwiller, F., & Rössler, W. (2008). Methods of suicide: International suicide patterns derived from the WHO mortality database. *Bulletin of the World Health Organization, 86*, 726–732. Retrieved from http://www.who.int/bulletin/volumes/86/9/07-043489/en/.

Arslan, G., Ayranci, U., Unsal, A., & Arslantas, D. (2009). Prevalence of depression, its correlates among students, and its effect on health-related quality of life in a Turkish university. *Upsala Journal of Medical Sciences, 114*(3), 170–177. https://doi.org/10.1080/03009730903174339.

Baumeister, R. (1990). Suicide as escape from self. *Psychological Review, 97*(1), 90–113. https://doi.org/10.1037//0033-295x.97.1.90.

Bonanno, G., Galea, S., Bucciarelli, A., & Vlahov, D. (2007). What predicts psychological resilience after disaster? The role of demographics, resources, and life stress. *Journal of Consulting and Clinical Psychology, 75*(5), 671–682. https://doi.org/10.1037/0022-006x.75.5.671.

Burton, C., Vella, L., Weller, J., & Twamley, E. (2011). Differential effects of executive functioning on suicide attempts. *Journal of Neuropsychiatry, 23*(2), 173–179.

Chen, S. T. (2018). 青少年自殺亡人數按年急增五成 逾八成人「從高處墮下 [photo]. Retrieved from 青少年自殺亡人數按年急增五成 逾八成人「從高處墮下.

Cramer, R. J., & Kapusta, N. D. (2017). A social-ecological framework of theory, Assessment, and prevention of suicide. *Frontiers in Psychology, 8*. https://doi.org/10.3389/fpsyg.2017.01756.

Diamond, A. (2013). Executive functions. *Annual Review of Psychology, 64*(1), 135–168.

Doty, L. (2012). Executive function and memory/cognition changes. *Florida Department of Elder Affairs Alzheimer's Disease Initiative*. Retrieved from http://alzonline.phhp.ufl.edu/en/reading/executivefxlatest.pdf.

Education Bureau. (2018, March). *A resource handbook for schools: Detecting, supporting and making referral for students with suicidal behaviours*. Retrieved from https://www.edb.gov.hk/attachment/en/student-parents/crisis-management/about-crisis-management/Resource_Handbook_for_Schools_e.pdf.

Eisenberg, D., Gollust, S. E., Golberstein, E., & Hefner, J. L. (2007). Prevalence and correlates of depression, anxiety, and suicidality among university students. *American Journal of Orthopsychiatry, 77*(4), 534–542. https://doi.org/10.1037/0002-9432.77.4.534.

Final report by Committee on Prevention of Student Suicides. (2016). Education bureau. Retrieved form https://www.edb.gov.hk/attachment/en/student-parents/crisis-management/about-crisis-management/CPSS_final_report_en.pdf.

Gould, M. S., Shaffer, D., & Greenberg, T. (2003). The epidemiology of youth suicide. In R. A. King & A. Apter (Eds.), *Suicide in children and adolescents* (pp. 1–40). Cambridge University Press.

Harris, H. (2020). 哈理斯專欄|寫在台大生自殺案後, 透過遺書, 心理學家看見了什麼?|女人迷 Womany. Retrieved 31 July 2021, from https://cn.womany.net/read/article/25726?_ga=2.166198590.109207954.1627721879-642427947.1627391720.

Hogan, M., & Kennedy, K. (2011). Suicide in Hong Kong: epidemiology, changing patterns, associated phenomena and prevention. *In Irish psychiatrist, 12* (1). Retrieved from http://www.mindmap.hk/wordpress/wp-content/uploads/2011/05/2011-Irish-Psychiatrist-Suicide-in-Hong-Kong.pdf.

Hong Kong Jockey Club for suicide research and prevention. (2018, July 31*). Proportion by method*. Retrieved from https://csrp.hku.hk/statistics/.

Jaschik. S. (2018, February 12). Suicide note calls out pressure on students. *Inside the higher Ed*. Retrieved from https://www.insidehighered.com/admissions/article/2018/02/12/suicide-note-16-year-old-renews-debate-about-pressure-top-high-schools.

Klonsky, E. D., & May, A. M. (2015). The three-step theory (3ST): A new theory of suicide rooted in the "ideation-to-action" framework. *International Journal of Cognitive Therapy, 8*(2), 114–129. https://doi.org/10.1521/ijct.2015.8.2.114.

Klonsky, E., May, A., & Saffer, B. (2016). Suicide, suicide attempts, and suicidal ideation. *Annual Review of Clinical Psychology, 12*(1), 307–330. https://doi.org/10.1146/annurev-clinpsy-021815-093204.

Li, F., Lu, X., & Yip, P. (2020). A study of the characteristics of suicide notes in China. *Crisis, 41*(1), 32–38. https://doi.org/10.1027/0227-5910/a000601.

Li, J. (2016, October 14). 'I don't want to add any more burden on you, Mum and Dad', says Chinese boy, 15, in suicide note. *South China Morning Post*. Retrieved from https://www.scmp.com/news/china/society/article/2028075/i-dont-want-add-any-more-burden-you-mum-and-dad-says-chinese-boy.

Ma, K. F. (2016, March 10). 雙學位女大學生抗壓之道: 找朋友傾訴最好. Retrieved from http://202.125.90.231/hk/bkn/cnt/news/20160310/bkn-20160310152645066-0310_00822_001.html?eventid=402882b0533bcabd01535b747d3d6cb1&eventsection=hk_news.

Nierenberg, A. A., Bentley, K. H., Farabaugh, A. H., Fava, M., & Deckersbach, T. (2012). The absence of depressive symptoms is not the presence of wellness: Validation of the Clinical Positive Affect Scale. *Australian and New Zealand Journal of Psychiatry, 46*(12), 1165–1172. https://doi.org/10.1177/0004867412459810.

Pedersen, E. R., & Paves, A. P. (2014). Comparing perceived public stigma and personal stigma of mental health treatment seeking in a young adult sample. *Psychiatry Research, 219*(1), 143–150. https://doi.org/10.1016/j.psychres.2014.05.017.

Pereira-Lima, K., & Loureiro, S. R. (2015). Burnout, anxiety, depression, and social skills in medical residents. *Psychology, Health & Medicine, 20*(3), 353–362. https://doi.org/10.1080/13548506.2014.936889.

Posner, K., Brodsky, B., Yershova, K., Buchanan, J., & Mann, J. (2014). The classification of suicidal behaviour. In M. K. Nock (Ed.), *Oxford handbook of suicide and self-injury* (pp. 7–22). Oxford University Press.

Potter, L., Silverman, M., Connorton, E., & Posner, M. (2004). *Promoting mental health and preventing suicide in college and university settings*. Presented at the Center for Mental Health Services, Substance Abuse and Mental Health Services Administration, U.S. Department of Health and Human Services: SPRC: Suicide Prevention Resource Center. Retrieved from: http://www.sprc.org/sites/sprc.org/files/library/college_sp_whitepaper.pdf.

Preventing suicide: A Global imperative. (2014). *World Health Organization*. Retrieved from http://apps.who.int/iris/bitstream/handle/10665/131056/9789241564779_eng.pdf;jsessionid=969F67939D60B3E3E0C962C06CEF30E2?sequence=1.

Rajappa, K., Gallagher, M., & Miranda, R. (2011). Emotion dysregulation and vulnerability to suicidal ideation and attempts. *Cognitive Therapy and Research, 36*(6), 833–839. https://doi.org/10.1007/s10608-011-9419-2.

Rudd, M., Bryan, C., Wertenberger, E., Peterson, A., Young-McCaughan, S., Mintz, J., et al. (2015). Brief cognitive-behavioural therapy effects on post-treatment suicide attempts in a military sample: Results of a randomized clinical trial with 2-year follow-up. *American Journal of Psychiatry, 172*(5), 441–449. https://doi.org/10.1176/appi.ajp.2014.14070843.

Schlebusch, L. (2005). *Suicidal behaviour in South Africa*. University of KwaZulu-Natal Press.

Schulberg, H. C., Lee, P. W., Bruce, M. L., Raue, P. J., Lefever, J. J., Williams, J. W., Dietrich, A. J., & Nutting, P. A. (2005). Suicidal ideation and risk levels among primary care patients with uncomplicated depression. *The Annals of Family Medicine, 3*, 523–528.

Shepard, D., Gurewich, D., Lwin, A., Reed, G., & Silverman, M. (2015). Suicide and suicidal attempts in the United States: Costs and policy implications. *Suicide and Life-Threatening Behaviour, 46*(3), 352–362. https://doi.org/10.1111/sltb.12225.

Sinko, L., He, Y., Kishton, R., Ortiz, R., Jacobs, L., & Fingerman, M. (2021). "The stay at home order is causing things to get heated up": Family conflict dynamics during COVID-19 from the perspectives of youth calling a national child abuse hotline. *Journal of Family Violence*. https://doi.org/10.1007/s10896-021-00290-5.

Tait, G., Carpenter, B., & Jowett, S. (2018). Coronial practice, indigeneity and suicide. *International Journal of Environmental Research and Public Health, 15*(4), 765. https://doi.org/10.3390/ijerph15040765.

Wagner, G., Bär, K., & Sobanski, T. (2015). Neural, cognitive, and neuroimaging markers of the suicidal brain. *Reports in Medical Imaging, 71*. https://doi.org/10.2147/rmi.s55532.

World suicide prevention day—life-saving crisis app is available to download now. (2014, September 9). *DCP strategic communication ltd*. Retrieved from http://www.dcppr.co.uk.

Zhang, X., Wang, H., Xia, Y., Liu, X., & Jung, E. (2012). Stress, coping and suicide ideation in Chinese college students. *Journal of Adolescence, 35*(3), 683–690. https://doi.org/10.1016/j.adolescence.2011.10.003.

Zhao, S., Wong, J., Luk, T., Wai, A., Lam, T., & Wang, M. (2020). Mental health crisis under COVID-19 pandemic in Hong Kong, China. *International Journal of Infectious Diseases, 100*, 431–433. https://doi.org/10.1016/j.ijid.2020.09.030.

Chapter 2
Psychological Theories and Models in Depicting Suicidal Behaviour

Why do so many young people end their lives every year? Is it due to the increasing level of stress put on our children today? What triggers their thoughts of suicide? The breakdown of relationships, academic pressure? Or is it because of depression? Are suicides the result of an impulsive act, or are they result from a prolonged period of hopelessness? There are many questions like these but no simple answers. No single factor can provide solutions to any of these questions because suicidal behaviour is a complex phenomenon influenced by several interacting factors ("Preventing suicide," 2014). These include personal, social, psychological, cultural, biological, and environmental factors. For example, psychiatric disorder, negative life events, alcohol and drug misuse, family history of suicide, physical or mental illness, exposure to the suicidal behaviour of others, and access to methods of self-harm are just some of the examples from the exhaustive list. In any individual case, multiple factors are usually involved. Whilst many suicides occur impulsively in moments of crisis and, in these circumstances, ready access to the means of suicide—such as pesticides or firearms—can determine whether a person lives or dies. Other risk factors for suicide include a breakdown in the ability to deal with acute or chronic life stresses, such as financial problems. In addition, suicide rates also vary within age groups, countries, and social classes with higher rates among those who are minorities or experience discrimination. Therefore it is imminent to understand the motivation that drives someone towards having suicidal thoughts and behaviours.

2.1 Suicide Pathway Model

Many established theories and models on suicidal behaviour have been developed in recent decades that posit the interplay between cognitive, neurological, social, environmental, and cultural factors in determining suicidal behaviours. At the same time, epidemiology has helped identify many risks and protective factors for suicide both in the general population and in vulnerable groups ("Preventing suicide," 2014).

E. Ong, *Early Identification and Intervention of Suicide Risk in Chinese Young Adults*,
https://doi.org/10.1007/978-981-16-7641-3_2

Cultural variability in suicide risk has also become apparent, with culture having roles in increasing risk and protection from suicidal behaviour (Fig. 2.1).

The roots of the recent models of suicide can be traced back to Baechler (1979). With references to the early theoretical framework, Baechler (1979) was among the first researchers to uphold suicide as a learned technique to solve problems, in which ones might attempt to conduct suicide acts with a purpose to lessen their internal agonies such as feelings of sadness, guilt, or loss. In addition, Baechler put forward that the major driving factor behind suicide is the desire to escape from intolerable conditions. With that said, suicide was regarded as a means to escape from emotional breakdowns and adversities. Later, Shneidman (1984) added that when one overpasses their threshold for tolerance in emotional or psychological pain, suicide occurs, noted that the threshold is subject to change depending on different individuals. As a corollary, in comparison with individuals with a high threshold, those with a low threshold ponder on suicide more often. While Baechler did not conduct research to validate his ideas of escape, his proposals have enlightened other researchers to continue postulating suicide as an escape attempt. (Baumeister, 1990; Williams, 1997, 2001; Williams & Pollock, 2001). On top of Baechler's ideas, Baumeister (1990) uphold the proposal that when ones possess an inferior feeling of themselves comparing to their expectations (i.e. an outcome to a situation/stressor falls below the standards the individual has set for themselves). It ignites the urge to escape from the state of emotional breakdown as well as self-awareness (Fig. 2.2).

2.1.1 *Escape Theory*

As revealed by its name, **the Escape theory** (Baumeister, 1990) emphasizes the potential to escape a distressing condition, where the greater the feeling of inability to escape, the higher the chance of attempting suicide. Six major stages are proposed to be in the progress of suicide attempts (Fig. 2.4). First of all, there will be an influential interpersonal experience that fails to live up to one's expectations stemming from an unrealistic expectation or a major downfall. Then, the individual may attribute the blame internally thinking that they were the cause of that failure or setback. Then, the individual may attribute the blame internally thinking that they were the cause of that failure or setback. For example, the suicide attempter in the news report of Fig. 2.3 (Law, 2016) reported: 我做得唔好. Next, the individual will have an increasing sense of negative self-awareness with more feelings of inadequacy, incompetence, or low self-esteem. At this point, the increased negative self-awareness may slowly lead to negative affect.

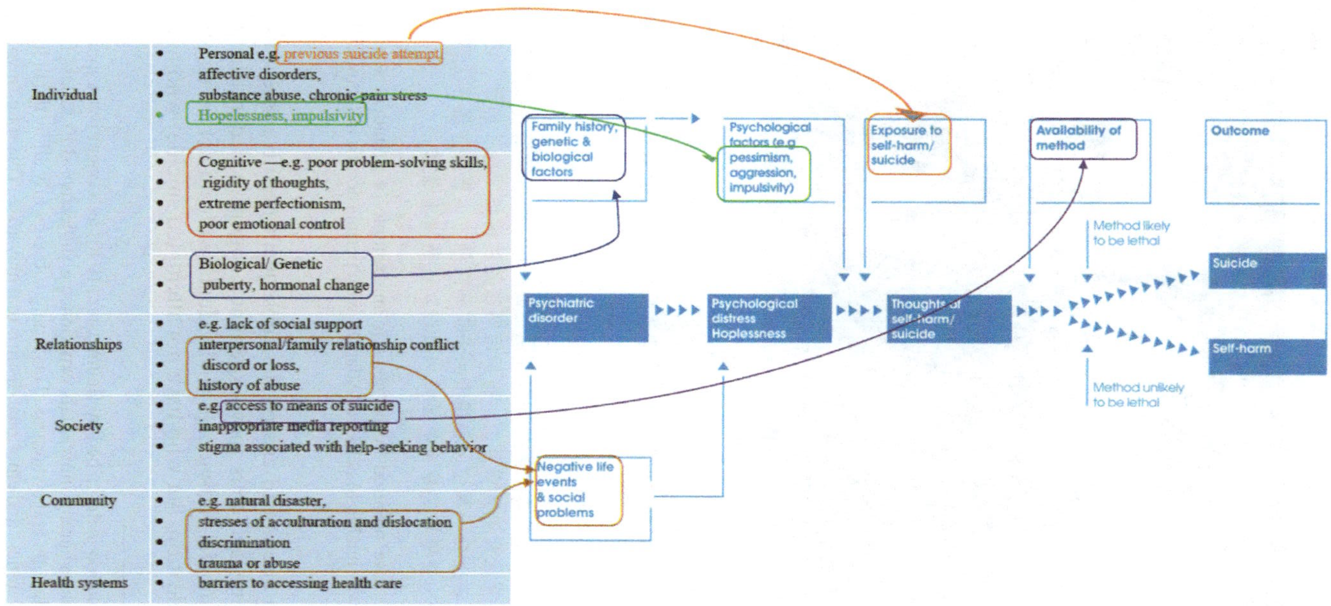

Fig. 2.1 The suicide pathway model interacts with risk factors identified by WHO (2018): Adapted with permission from ("Preventing suicide," 2014)

墮斃港大文學院男生　遺書「未能做得完美」

2016年03月10日(四) 07:08更新 00:26建立　推介 24　Tweet　G+　分享

警員在港大生墮樓現場調查。（羅貴明攝）

昨晚在黃大仙上邨跳樓斃命的20歲姓蘇港大學生，為文學院三年級學生，警方到住所調查，在睡房的枱上發現遺書，內容表示：「自己追求完美，但自己做得唔好」，他又囑咐父母好好生活。港大發言人表示，初步獲知死者是文學院學生，將會與家人保持聯絡，以便提供協助。

昨晚6時許，20歲姓蘇男生，被發現在黃大仙上邨啟善樓天台墮樓，救護員到場證實他當場死亡，警員用帳篷蓋住屍體調查。據悉，死者與父母同住上址一單位，為香港大學文學院學生，是家中獨子。蘇亦品學兼優，曾獲取獎學金，警員稍後在其住所檢獲遺書。

Fig. 2.2 The suicide case reported in the news is an example of a student setting overly high expectations that he was unable to achieve. Adapted with permission from (Law, 2016)

Ones will then attempt to escape the subsequent negative effect by neglecting meaningful thinking and thus may experience cognitive deconstruction.[1] This is apparent in pre-suicidal individuals (individuals with milder forms of suicidality such as suicidal ideation, but who have not attempted suicide) who may attempt to

[1] Cognitive deconstruction is described by Baumeister (1990) as a cognitive response to a psychologically aversive state whereby individuals experience a subjective shift to less meaningful, less integrative forms of thought and awareness. This would subsequently allow the individual to escape from aversive self-awareness and emotional distress that may arise. This state "involves focusing on physical sensations, one's surroundings, and immediate, proximal goals, thus avoiding any higher level of thoughts" (Baumeister, 1990 p. 92).

廿歲港大生墮樓亡

23:13 2016/03/09 讚好 0

事發傍晚6時，黃大仙上邨啟善樓墜下的死者蘇俊僖（20歲），就讀港大文學院，據悉是家中獨子，警方檢獲死者遺書，上寫有「我做得唔好」，疑因學業壓力尋死，事件無可疑；死者家人事後在警員陪同下認屍，跪地傷心欲絕。

Fig. 2.3 Another suicide case of a university student suffering from academic pressure. Copied from ("廿歲港大生墮樓亡—香港經濟日報—TOPick—新聞—社會", 2019)

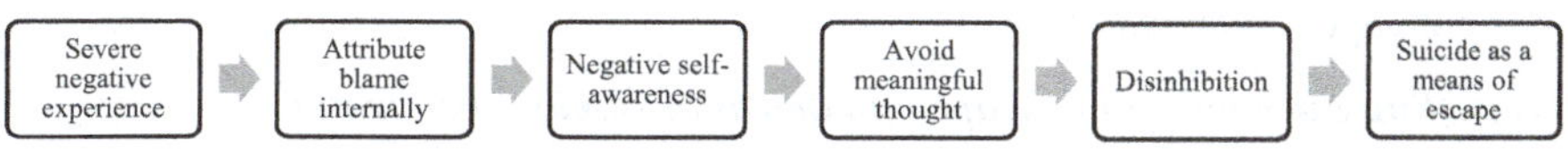

Fig. 2.4 The six main steps proposed in the progression of a suicide attempt by the Escape theory (Baumeister, 1990)

hide their emotions by suppressing them in their mind (Baumeister, 1990; Gross & John, 2003). As they are reluctant to encounter their genuine internal emotions, they are also less likely to be aware of the need to retrieve any thoughts associated with emotional disturbance. Cognitive disinhibition is the next level, which categorizes the inability in constraining or filtering out information such as suicide intentions (Baumeister, 1990). Executing inhibitory control is crucial to empower individuals to respond properly and behave appropriately in accordance with social acceptance. It also helps refrain from the generation of unwanted thoughts or distractions that are presented simultaneously with other important information (Joormann & Gotlib, 2010). It has been suggested that these characteristics result from impaired inhibition because the inability to inhibit negative thoughts may lead to accumulation in the long run.

Follows from the stage of cognitive disinhibition is a stage when individuals possess an intense urge to escape from their own negative experience by going into a comparatively numb and deconstructed state that precedes a suicide attempt right away (Baumeister, 1990; Kaplow et al., 2014). The final stage is when ones are overloaded by a critical state of negative affect that is regarded as uncontainable. If ones still cannot figure out ways to lessen their intolerable state of emotion, the urge to self-kidding manifests, which might be viewed as a way to escape (Baumeister, 1990).

While the **Escape theory** has gained widespread acceptance, empirical evidence is quite inadequate as there are insufficient studies to test the theory. Regarding an early study, Reich et al. (1996) attempted to investigate how the development of suicide progression fits with the Escape theory. This study examined older adults who were undergoing pressures because of rapid deterioration of their physical health, with the health decline related to a surge in suicidal ideation. Despite that, they discovered a substantial path from which health declines to low self-esteem, then helplessness to increased suicidal ideation, most of which echo well with the concepts upheld by Baumeister (1990). Yet, some of the concepts in the Escape theory are not utterly justifiable. For instance, the measures of confused thinking are overwhelmingly due to aging and physical illness in older adults. This assumption seems theoretically unfitting to signify the conceptof cognitive deconstruction of the model which specifies less meaningful and integrative forms of thought (which is not due to aging).

Although the model suggests that individuals have difficulty in finding alternative strategies to cope with their emotions, the findings of Reich et al. (1996) have not explained clearly why one would escape through suicide instead of choosing other options such as running away from home or drug abuse. Concerning the evidence for this model as it stands, Baumeister's (1990) view of suicide as a means of escape does not appear to be valid.

Supporting the concept of escape and defeat in suicidal behaviour

In an interview with BBC Chinese, the executive director of the Samaritan Befrienders association Tsang (2018) explained that from the status of 'not feeling happy' to 'feeling suicidal' there is a very big step to make. For someone to make such a big move they must be suffering from an overwhelming intensity of hopelessness. Indeed, 'feeling there is no way out—Chinese translated as 但最終就是他找不到出路' is a common phrase found in a suicide note and this is one example where individuals feel defeat and entrap of the situation and consequently leading to suicidal behaviour as an escape route. In the incident reported by Tsang (2018), he stated that youngsters, especially men in HK, are under tremendous pressure when there is a norm that men should be independent and capable of dealing with their problems instead of being emotional and help-seeking. He also criticized that the current suicide prevention measures are too conservative and not enough to cater to the needs of young people. Recently he promotes 「家長每天給孩子一分鐘擁抱」 in order to strengthen closeness in the family relationship thus to enhance interpersonal communication skills. This is believed to help relieve the feelings of defeat and hopelessness that may attribute to suicidal behaviour (Fig. 2.5).

Fig. 2.5 BBC interview with Tsang (2018). Image from (Lau, 2016) Lau (2016, March 16). 分析: 香港為何學生自殺事件不斷

2.1.2 The Cry of Pain Model

Occasionally, some people will threaten suicide multiple times to seek attention. In those cases suicide is considered impetuous, manipulative behaviour. However suicide may also be a reflection that someone is in extreme despair, and that s/he needs help. Therefore, every suicidal threat or intent cannot be simply overlooked. Intending to further expand on the Escape theory's psychological mechanisms, Williams and colleagues (Williams, 1997, 2001; Williams & Pollock, 2000, 2001) developed the **Cry of Pain model**. Williams and Pollock (2001) put forward that the urge to escape consists of two particular aspects; defeat and entrapment (see Fig. 2.7). Defeat is categorized by perceptions of a failed struggle associated with the loss of status or identity, while entrapment refers to the lack of motivation in moving forward because of a constrained ability to figure out solutions to cope with stress or a threat (Taylor et al., 2011). For example, stress varies depending on the form of environmental factors (e.g. exams and assignments) or negative life experiences (e.g. pressure from family). When accumulative feelings of loss and failure keep piling up alongside stress, one becomes susceptible to feelings of defeat. Failure to resolve problems (e.g. recurrent attempts at an exam without success) can manifest the feeling of powerlessness in an individual escaping from undesirable conditions (entrapment). The Cry of Pain model was examined by O'Connor (2003) who has investigated both defeat and entrapment following suicidal behaviour. This is achieved by using self-report measures assessing defeat, escape potential, and social support. The study recruited 30 adult samples with past suicide attempts (i.e. they were recruited the day after admission to a hospital due to a suicide attempt) and 30 matched hospital controls on measures. Results echoed with the Cry of Pain model and illustrated that people with past suicide acts were substantially more possibly to report greater intensity of defeat, and lower levels of escape potential and social support, compared to the matched controls (Fig. 2.6).

To put the entrapment and defeat elements into context, a study was conducted by Williams et al. (2005) with 56 participants separated into 3 groups; 19 depressed individuals with past suicidal behaviour, 15 depressed individuals without any past suicide experiences, and 22 controls. The model points out that when one fails to

Fig. 2.6 Cognitive processes involved during a means-ends problem solving (MEPS) task to find a solution to a problem

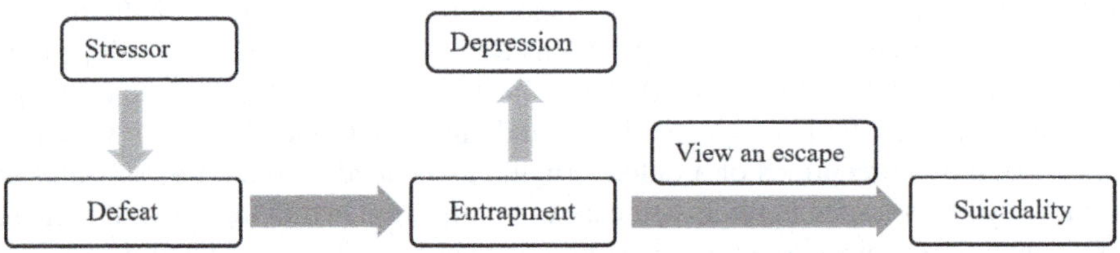

Fig. 2.7 Showing defeat and entrapment in the progression of suicidality in The Cry of Pain model by Williams and Pollock (2001)

figure out alternative ways to resolve problems, it triggers the occurrence of suicidal behaviour. To examine this, interpersonal problem-solving performance was assessed using the Means-Ends Problem solving (MEPS) task before and after a negative mood induction procedure. In an archetypal MEPS task, participants are granted the beginnings and ends of ten vignettes that each describe a problem. As for each problem, participants are required to provide the steps needed to resolve the problem. In other words, they are asked to figure out ideal solutions that can efficaciously associate the problem with the solution (Goddard et al., 1996). Results indicated that in comparison with the other two groups, people with past suicide acts figured out considerably fewer effective problem solutions in the task following negative mood induction. Apparently, this inadequacy in problem-solving and the perceived absence of rescue factors may denote the state of entrapment within the Cry of Pain model, that is, the failure in moving forward because of constrained ability to figure out solutions (Taylor et al., 2011).

Rasmussen et al. (2010) conducted another study that tested the constructs of defeat and entrapment of the Cry of Pain model. It involved 113 patients with past experience of self-harm (36 first-time, 67 repeated incidents) and 37 controls. All individuals completed self-report measures of defeat, entrapment, rescue factors (the measures of perceived social support and positive future thinking), as well as depression, anxiety, and suicidal ideation. Analyses highlighted differences between the three groups on key variables related to the Cry of Pain model. For instance, patients with self-harming experiences reported greater intensity of depression, anxiety, and suicidal ideation, they also reported experiencing higher levels of defeat and entrapment, with fewer rescue factors. In addition, the results indicated that entrapment mediated the relationship between defeat and suicidal ideation, whilst impaired ability to think positively about the future (but not social support) moderated the relationship between total and internal entrapment and suicidal ideation. Therefore, the findings provided further empirical support for the Cry of Pain model.

With reference to the Cry of Pain model in Fig. 2.7, the desire to die as a way to escape painful reality is closely followed by the feelings of entrapment, and when individuals run out of rescue factors. At this stage, individuals may not possess the necessary skills to cope with negative emotions (Rajappa et al., 2011) and redirect the flow of one's own emotions by spontaneous emotional regulation (Miranda et al., 2011). When they immerse in this state for long without being able to figure out alternative solutions, it may increase the desire to conduct a suicide attempt.

With the empirical evidence to support the Cry of Pain model, it is posited that both defeat and entrapment may arise when individuals cannot find an alternative solution to resolve problems and this may eventually give rise to the urge to suicide as the only way out to escape from their agonic conditions (Chat et al., 2010). Likewise, any negative bias about a stressor may also erode an individual's ability to resolve problems associated with the stressor because they may feel negative about their ability and feel pessimistic about the outcome (Pollock & Williams, 2001). This increases negative perceptions of self, others, and the stressor may aggravate the feelings of entrapment because individuals may perceive that there is no way out to the problem and any attempt to try will recurrently result in failure like before. In this entrap situation an individual is likely to view suicide as the only escape route (O'Connor, 2003; Williams, 1997).

In the news extracted below is a real-life example to reflect the dilemma of students feeling defeat and entrapped. In the news, the student stated:—旦學業遇到挫折, 則容易感到沮喪和無所適從, 更可能鑽牛角尖. This is translated as when students face difficulties in school they would easily feel helpless, lost and difficult to find solutions) (Fig. 2.8).

Cha et al. (2010) have offered an explanation for how the feeling of defeat is formed from a cognitive perspective. It is thought that when individuals experience repeated failures and struggles, they may feel hopeless about future outcomes. At this point, information-processing biases are likely to develop (see Fig. 2.9). This is when information is being processed in an illogical manner. For instance, suicidal individuals could selectively attend to, encoding, and retrieving negative information about suicide (Cha et al., 2010). Therefore, individuals may focus more on their own

香港科大新生跳樓死　半年第三宗自殺案

2012年11月18日 第26卷 46期

現時正值大學期中考試，香港科技大學（圖）一名本地潘姓男生於十一月五日在荃灣寓所跳樓自殺，死者是本科一年級新生，就讀數學系。警方在其屋內尋獲一封遺書，內容透露其因不堪學習壓力而自尋短見。香港科技大學世界排名靠前，以課業繁重著稱，今次個案是科技大學近半年來第三宗自殺案例。今年九月二十二日，一位何姓科大本地男生疑因功課壓力跳樓自殺。而在今年五月十四日，一名科大四年級內地豐姓女生在宿舍上吊自殺，遺書透露生活不開心。《明報》報道，有社工表示大學生自殺事件頻發，與升學不易、家人與本人期望過高有關，一旦學業遇到挫折，則容易感到沮喪和無所適從，更可能鑽牛角尖。香港學友社學生輔導中心副總幹事吳寶城認為，新一代青少年多受家庭保護，在抗逆、解決疑難，以致與人相處溝通方面的能力較弱。

中國內地高校有輔導員制度，學生與輔導員聯繫密切，台灣高校則設「學長制」，而在注重個人自由的香港，類似制度並不多見。■

Fig. 2.8 香港科大新生跳樓死　半年第三宗自殺案. (2012, November 18). Retrieved from (Zhoukan, 2012)

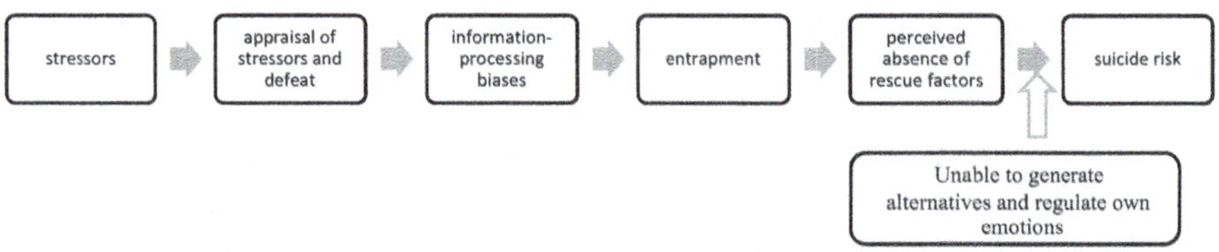

Fig. 2.9 Revised path of suicide by Cha et al. (2010)

losses and failures rather than thinking actively about the solution to these failures. Based on the *schema theory* (Beck & Clark, 1988), if suicidal thought is being rehearsed frequently, the information is activated continuously, forming a stronger memory trace (Baddeley & Hitch, 1992; Baddeley, 2003). This makes the negative information easier to activate and retrieve. In the long term, when the information is expanded, elaborated, and becomes easily accessible, a suicide schema is formed. This is a semantic network comprising interconnecting stimuli, possible responses, and emotionally stored information related to suicide (Johnson et al., 2008; Panagioti et al., 2014).

To investigate the different constructs in the revised path of suicide (Cha et al., 2010), Rajappa et al. (2011) measured six dimensions of emotion regulation (awareness, clarity, non-acceptance, impulse, goals, and strategies) among young adults with varying previous experience of suicidal behaviour. The sample included 17 adults who reported current suicidal ideation, 20 with one past suicide attempt, seventeen with multiple suicide attempts, and 42 healthy controls. Similar to the proposal of the Cry of Pain model, results showed that concurrent suicidal ideation was associated with perceived limited access to effective emotion regulation strategies. Specifically, the non-acceptance of emotional responses was measured by the Difficulties in Emotion Regulation Scale; Gratz & Roemer (2004) significantly predicted suicide risk. Notably, the between-group comparisons revealed that non-acceptance differed significantly only between controls and individuals with multiple suicide attempts but not with the other two groups (with only one attempt). Additionally, Rajappa et al. (2011) suggest that suicidal behaviours are attempts to escape negative emotions when individuals have a lack of rescue factors as proposed by the Cry of Pain model. This is evident in the findings whereby a perceived lack of access to effective regulatory strategies (i.e., lower-scoring on 'Strategies' in the Difficulties in Emotion Regulation Scale; Gratz & Roemer 2004) was associated with an increased level of suicidality. It was suggested that the lack of regulatory strategies may lead an individual to experience emotions as unwanted or behaving impulsively in response to the distress, which in turn increases the risk of an actual suicide attempt.

As suicide schema affects what information an individual pays attention to and how they relate to each other, this may influence individuals by placing greater importance on processing negative rather than positive information. Subsequently, this may increase information processing of emotionally congruent[2] and retrieval of more mood-congruent memories related to suicide. The suicide schema is present in varying degrees of strength among individuals and can be initiated by distressing or innocuous events that appear to be unrelated to suicidal behaviour (Beck & Clark, 1988). While the schema theory emphasizes the role of schemas in creating a processing bias, it is noteworthy that the suicide schema would only be active and influence processing when an individual feels overwhelmingly distressed. In the given situation, the activated schema will trigger suicidal thoughts as an escape strategy, increasing the chance of suicide act (Johnson et al., 2008, p. 65). Marcel Just, a cognitive neuroscientist, a lead author, and a Psychology Professor at Carnegie Mellon University (Ruiz, 2017) stated: "Suicidality isn't that you can't cope with life; it's you've somehow gotten into a pattern of thinking (also known as schema) that leads you to consider suicide."

2.1.3 The Schematic Appraisal Model of Suicide

As the Cry of Pain model merely focuses on suicide risk and does not address any factors that may help individuals to be resilient against suicidal behaviour, the Schematic Appraisal Model of Suicide (SAMS) was proposed as an extension to the Cry of Pain model (Johnson et al., 2008). Both models acknowledge that pre-suicidal individuals may have information processing biases. Examples of such biases are misattribution, incorrect inference, catastrophizing, and misperception of threat. The SAMS (Johnston et al., 2008) is a relatively new approach that attempts to identify the specific processes underlying resilience to suicide. In an extension to the Cry of Pain model, the SAMS explains the role of defeat and entrapment concerning protective

[2] Congruent is a psychological term raised by Bower (2002) to describe emotions, if a person feels happy the retrieval of mood-congruent memories means that he/she is retrieving some positive memories which are consistent with their current mood state.

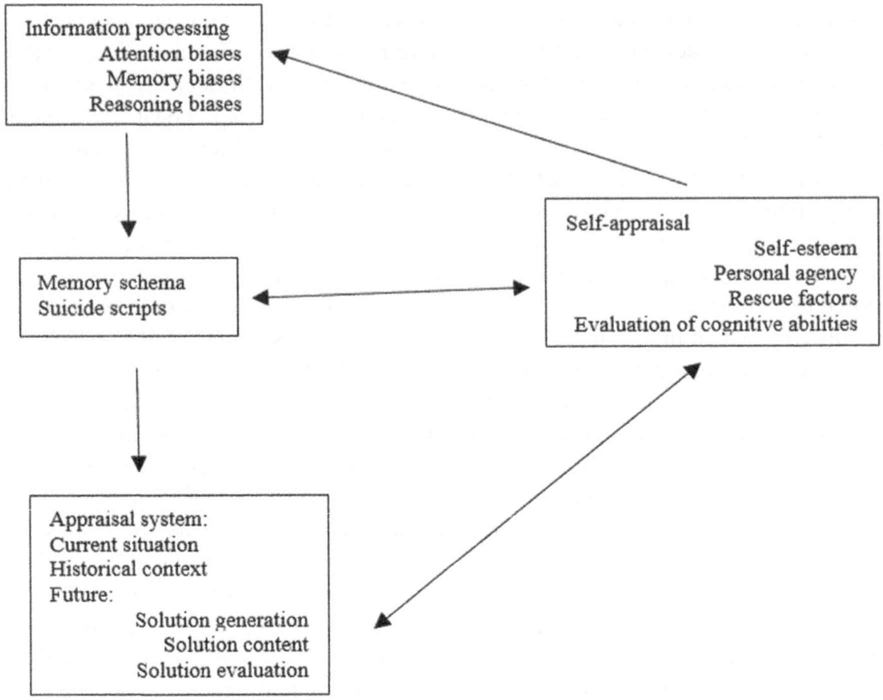

Fig. 2.10 A diagrammatic illustration of the components of the SAMS as described in Johnston et al. (2008)

factors rather than risk factors. It consists of three interacting components; negative information processing biases, the presence of suicide schema, and an appraisal system (see Fig. 2.10).

Similar to the suicide continuum (Potter et al., 2004) outlined in Chap. 1, suicidal behaviour is conceptualized as a series of events from ideation, planning, and intention to act (Johnson et al., 2008). It is posited that suicidal ideation occurs when a suicide schema becomes activated. This may occur in varying degrees of intensity and each time it is activated it will elicit more thoughts of suicide as an escape strategy. It becomes elaborated and associated with a broader range of contexts and affective states (Tarrier et al., 2007). The suicide schema is strengthened by distressing events and information-processing bias whereby the engaged suicidal ideation becomes well established and turns each thought into a more detailed plan of suicide. The critical factor regarding whether individuals proceed to a suicide act or not depends on the third component, the *appraisal system.*

The appraisal includes evaluative judgments that can affect how one views an event or experience (Lazarus & Folkman, 1984). Situation and self-appraisal are two types of appraisal associated with suicidality, upheld by Johnson et al. (2008). Situation appraisal decides if one considers a specific condition to be a threat and if they think they can rescue themselves with possible solutions, or they can't escape from it. Self-appraisal categorizes one's feelings of self-worth. Suicidal people often have little confidence and possess negative thinking of the self, resulting in negative situation appraisal (Johnson et al., 2008). For example, one may appraise an exam as something easy or challenging to deal with. This situation appraisal is also subject to the self-appraisal of being a competent student or not.

Al illustration of how the appraisal can be applied when students overcome problems

An interview conducted with a university student in HK positively expressed that academic achievement is just part of life success, and life should be viewed as a textbook or a journey. In the interview Tiffany, a fourth-year female student of the University of Hong Kong with a double degree in business administration and law used the butterfly as a metaphor to describe the way students overcome some difficult challenges. She said: "If a butterfly wants to fly, it must first experience the painful stage, and then it can break through 「蝴蝶要飛, 都要先經歷痛苦階段, 之後先可以破蛹而出」." (Fig. 2.11).

The vitalness of self-appraisal is depicted in a Johnson et al. (2010) study that examined suicidality levels (as indexed by the SBQ-R) in students who were undergoing pressurized life events. Those who reported low levels of positive self-appraisal revealed elevated suicidal ideation corresponding to the stressor. Contrarily, those who reported moderate or high levels of positive self-appraisal illustrated no elevation in suicidality under pressurized context. This puts forward that positive self-appraisal may protect against suicidality with the existence of environmental risk

Fig. 2.11 If a butterfly wants to fly, it must first experience the painful stage, and then it can breakthrough. Photos from Lai and Cheung (2016). 港大生墮亡同名同齡男生: 勿輕易放棄 [photo]. Retrieved from https://hk.news.appledaily.com/local/daily/article/20160311/19525231

factors. Johnson et al. (2010) deem that positive self-appraisers can adopt an optimistic perspective and hold positive thinking during the pressurized condition. Individuals who execute active efforts may be more resilient to suicidal behaviour in comparison with those with low levels of positive self-appraisal. Remarkably, many of the suicide models, if not all, discussed so far acknowledge that information processing bias and an urge to escape are indispensable in elucidating why one may proceed to more suicidal behaviour.

2.2 How Suicidal Behaviour Is Linked to Cognitive Processing

There is a general assumption that when the brain proceeds to completion in development in early adulthood, all the cognitive abilities should have been fully fostered which are needed to deal with various demands of work, relationships, and academic life (Goldstein & Naglieri, 2013). Some may encounter failure in fostering this efficaciously, which may conjure up negative psychological impacts (Glenn & Nock, 2014). Yet, similar to other cognitive abilities such as language skills and intelligence, cognitive abilities in executive functions form are subject to changes among different individuals. This is indispensable because one's executive function may determine whether a person will proceed from suicidal ideation to planning or from planning to take action in the final stage of a suicide attempt (Glenn & Nock, 2014).

Let's focus on one key aspect of executive function (i.e. attention) and understand how it may relate to suicidal behaviour. In everyday lives, humans are continuously exposed to multimodal sensory stimuli. It is important not only to direct attention and to monitor them but also to make decisions accordingly. When the incoming information from the environment is task-irrelevant, this information can easily interfere with task-relevant cognitive processing. In order to prioritize attention to specific stimuli, it is essential to select the relevant information needed; while inhibiting others in specific situations (Schall et al., 2002). This process is referred to as attentional control (Aarts & Roelofs, 2010; Broadbent, 1958; Treisman, 1960). Lessening and controlling selective attention to relevant information (or sometimes referred to as attentional bias) and inhibiting irrelevant information is called attentional control. This cognitive ability is subject to changes depending on individuals and is under emotional influence (Bower, 1981, 1991; Brosch et al., 2013). It is an essential cognitive aspect in choosing and retaining goal-oriented actions while neglecting task-irrelevant information. Some of the most common cognitive tasks to measure key executive functions are outlined.

Elevated severity of suicidal behaviour has been reported by many studies to be concerning deficits in various dimensions of executive functions, ranging from attentional control, reasoning, problem-solving, planning, monitoring, and inhibition (Burton et al., 2011; Doty, 2012; von Hecker et al., 2013; Imbir & Jarymowicz, 2013; Jollant et al., 2005; Keilp et al., 2012; Løvstad et al., 2016; Loyo et al., 2013;

Fig. 2.12 Example of colour Stroop task

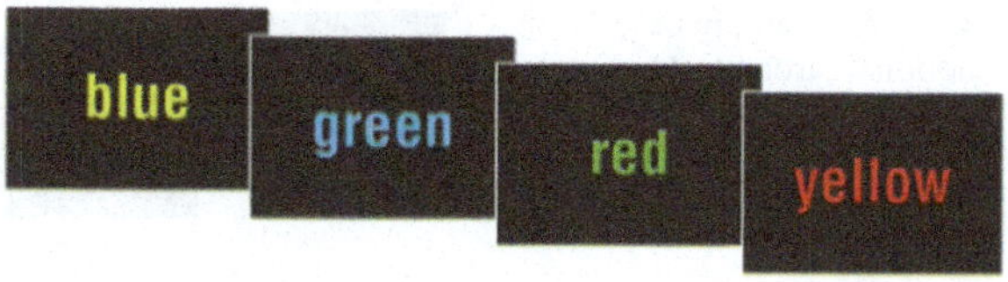

Richard-Devantoy et al., 2017). One of the most developed experimental studies that examined the association between executive functions and suicidality was done by Loyo et al. (2013) using a self-report measure of an individual's own executive functions (BRIEF-A inventory). This record examined individuals' difficulties in various aspects of executive functions. Besides, a series of computerized cognitive tasks was adopted. These consist of colour and emotional Stroop Tests, the Wisconsin Card-sorting task, and the Iowa-type gambling task that measure attentional control, abstract reasoning ability, and decision making respectively. These are commonly used in experimental research to measure executive functions and are described in more detail before exploring the cognitive processing of suicidal behaviour.

2.2.1 The Stroop Task

To measure attentional control, the colour Stroop task (Stroop, 1935) is one of the earliest and most widely used cognitive tasks listed (Ahmed et al., 2015; Williams et al., 1996a, 1996b). In this task, participants are asked to name the colour of printed words that possess either a *congruent* semantic meaning (e.g. the word red printed in red) or *incongruent* semantic meaning (e.g. the word red printed in green, see Fig. 2.12). The task requires the inhibition of automated response (reading the word) to name the colour; therefore it requires selective attention and inhibitory control. Longer response times to incongruent trials reveal difficulties inhibiting an automatic process (known as the Stroop interference effect; Beall & Herbert, 2008; MacLeod, 1991). As for literal adults, reading words is regarded as a spontaneous and automatic process compares to colour identification, therefore, participants must inhibit the prepotent response[3] of reading the word and name the colour of the ink instead (Stroop, 1935). In the *incongruent condition*, reading the word would interfere with naming the colour to a greater extent than in the *congruent condition*. The difference in performance between these two trials is termed the *Stroop interference effect*. Cohen and McClelland (1988) explained that the Stroop interference effect reflects the limited capacity for selective attention and inhibition. More inhibition of the automatic response is required in the incongruent condition, leading to an increase in response times and errors (Algom et al., 2004; Cothran & Larsen, 2008).

[3] Prepotent response is an immediate response that usually have priority over other response tendencies due to virtue of maturational primacy, repetition, practice effect, self-relevance, or positive reinforcement.

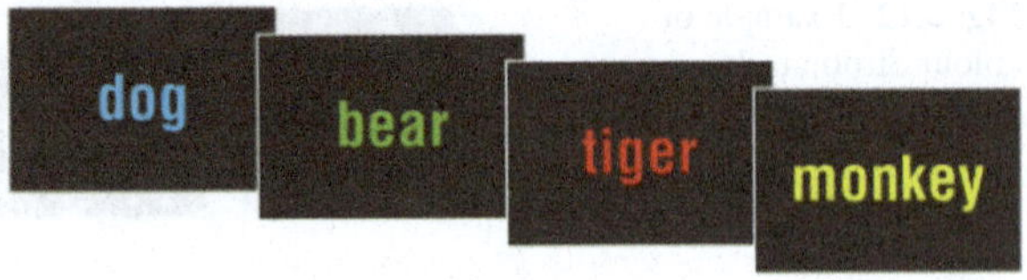

Fig. 2.13 Example of emotional Stroop task

Alongside the Stroop interference effect investigation, researchers further assessed another interference effect called the emotional Stroop effect through the use of the emotional Stroop task. In this task, the emotional information is irrelevant to the task and thus a bias towards this information would limit performance. In the emotional Stroop task findings consistently show slower response times to name the colour of emotional words compared to neutral words (e.g., Ben-Haim et al., 2016; Cothran & Larsen, 2008). The increased response times to emotional stimuli are referred to as *interference* (Cothran & Larsen, 2008) or the *emotional Stroop effect* (Pratto & John, 1991). This is when there is an increased response time to name the colour of emotional words compared to neutral words. Cothran and Larsen (2008) propose that emotional words are more difficult to inhibit than neutral words; therefore naming the colour of these words takes longer.

Algom et al. (2004) argue that attention is allocated to all words but that inhibition of emotional words is more resource-intensive than inhibition of neutral words, therefore resulting in longer response times to these emotional words. In an exploration of attentional bias in clinical populations such as depressed patients (Gotlib & Joormann, 2010; Keilp et al., 2008), a variant of the colour Stroop task called the emotional Stroop task (see Fig. 2.13) is often used (for a review see Williams et al. 1996a, 1996b). It is often reported that anxious and depressed individuals have a bias towards emotional information compared to control groups (Chung & Jeglic, 2015; Imbir & Jarymowicz, 2013). McNeely et al. (2008) explained that this may be driven by difficulties inhibiting distracting information or shifting attention to relevant aspects of a task in patients with affective disorders.

In a modified version of the colour Stroop task an emotional Stroop task was created and this is similar to the colour Stroop task whereby participants are asked to name the colour of words (see Figs. 2.12). As emotional and neutral words are used in the emotional Stroop task, researchers can assess how emotional distraction interferes with colour-naming (see Williams et al., 1996a, 1996b). The task (Cha et al., 2010) was developed to measure one's attentional bias toward certain emotions including suicide-related words. One of the strengths of a behavioural measure is that it can overcome some of the limitations of using self-report measures. As cognitive assessment is based on performance and does not rely on verbal response, it is an objective measure that is considered to be more time- and cost-effective than self-report tools, it is also less prone to respondents' bias. Yet, it is noteworthy that the current development of cognitive assessment used to detect suicide risk is in an early stage and that very few have been tested for their potentials as a screening measure (Cha et al., 2010; Jung & Jeglic, 2016).

Fig. 2.14 Example of Wisconsin card sorting task

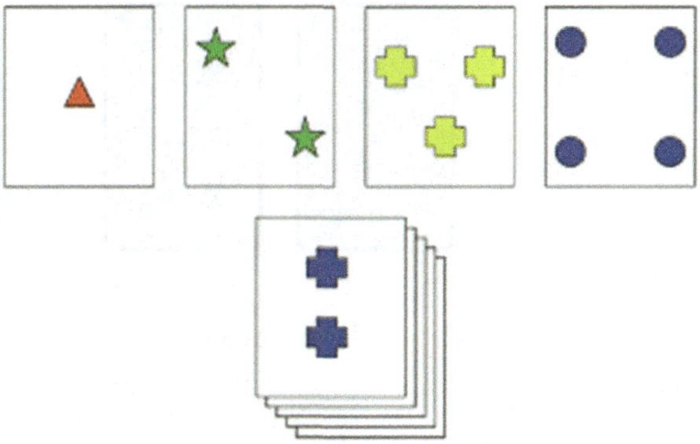

Relating to suicidal behaviour, the emotional Stroop task has also been used to differentiate suicide attempters from those without suicide risk (Jollant et al., 2011). It is considered to be a useful tool to examine the cognitive processes (attention and inhibition) associated with psychopathology (Nock et al., 2010, Williams et al., 1996a, 1996b). For example, the severity of cognitive deficits has been used by Jollant et al. (2011) as indexed by the performance in the Stroop task, to differentiate depressed patients in terms of healthy controls as well as whether they have past suicide attempts. Results depicted that individuals with suicidal behaviour encountered difficulties in conducting the task as they were more sensitive to the interference of negative or suicide-related stimuli.

Aside from attentional control, abstract reasoning, and set-shifting ability other well-established executive functions are common assessed by computerized tasks. In the Wisconsin card sorting task (WCST in Fig. 2.14; Loyo et al., 2013), participants need to categorize cards with reference to various criteria. While the related category varies across trails, task performance is subject to an individual's flexibility in thinking and ability to impede the previously related category.

Another task is the Iowa Gambling Task (IGT) which assesses decision making in a real-life situation; which is another important aspect when someone decides whether to make a suicide attempt or just engage in the thought about it. In the task, participants are required to pick cards from four decks (A, B, C, and D as shown in Fig. 2.15) with the purpose to accumulate as much money as possible by choosing one card at a time. Decks A and B are of higher chance to have immediate wins, yet greater future penalties that lead to a net loss over time (also known as the bad decks). Decks C and D are of lower chances to have immediate wins but smaller future penalties, so that participants accumulate a profit progressively by selecting these decks (also known as the good decks). A greater number of trials (e.g. 150 trials) usually happen. The net score (the number of cards from the bad decks subtracted from the good decks) is the outcome. A positive score implies one's capability in making a good decision, while a lower or negative score depicts poor decision making. Participants can win or lose money with each choice (adopted from Bechara et al. 1999). Some selections are beneficial in the short term (with high

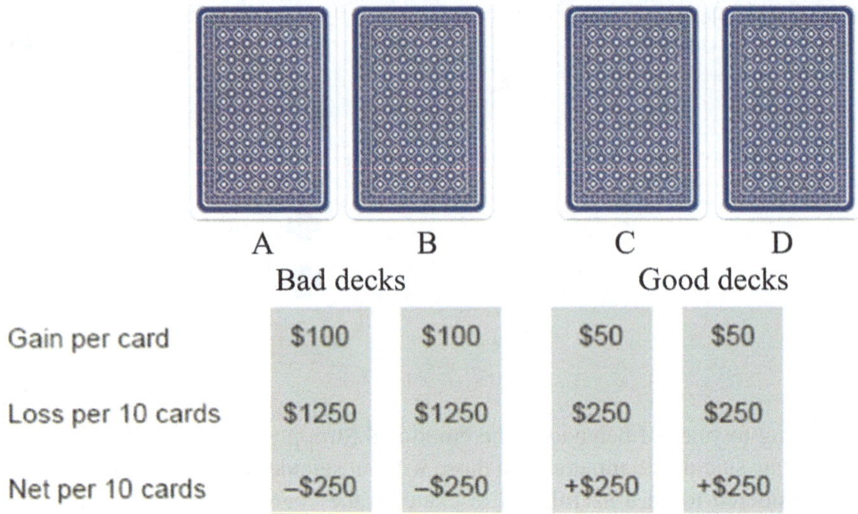

Fig. 2.15 Example of Iowa gambling task

reward), yet detrimental in long term (with higher punishment); other selections have a lower reward in short term yet are beneficial in long term (with lower punishment).

In Loyo et al. (2013) study (Fig. 2.16 for the task paradigm), the sample consisted of 25 suicide attempters with depressive symptoms, 25 non-suicide attempters with depressive symptoms, and 24 non-depressed participants. In comparison with the non-suicide attempters and non-depressed participants, suicide attempters with depression depicted increasing executive function deficits. Apparently, they required a longer time to respond and were less accurate in the colour Stroop task (indicating poor selective attention and inhibition) in comparison with the non-depressed participants. While it was found by Loyo et al. (2013) that suicide attempters also performed worst in the Wisconsin Card-sorting task and the Iowa gambling task, they revealed no betterment in performing the lowa-type gambling task comparing the first and

Fig. 2.16 Experimental paradigm of Loyo et al. (2013) study

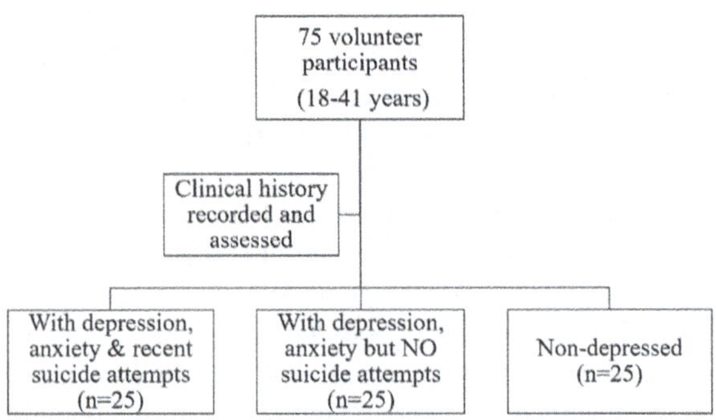

Fig. 2.17 Trail making test

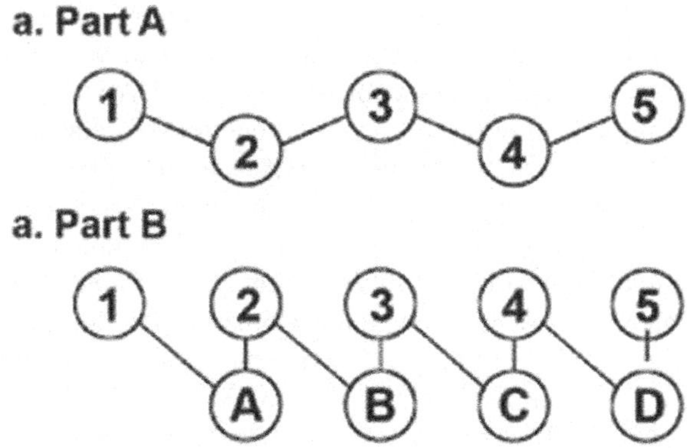

last blocks of trials. This implies comparatively poor decision-making and incapability in improving with practice. This study summarized that people with suicidal propensities may be prone to specific issues with selective attention, inhibition, and decision making. It, therefore, infers that performance in a cognitive task may be one empirical method to identify individuals with dangerous levels of suicidality.

Notwithstanding the evidence developing the relation between various executive functioning aspects and suicidality, a couple of contrasting studies contend that executive function deficits are not associated with suicidality (King et al., 2000; Marzuk et al., 2005), with some results even demonstrating better executive functions in suicidal individuals (Burton et al., 2011, Nangle et al., 2006). For example, it was compared by King et al. (2000) that the neuropsychological performance of depressed patients with the recent incident(s) or attempt to those without. The tasks comprised the Trail Making Test that measures mental sequencing and flexibility, the California Verbal Learning Test measuring verbal learning and verbal fluency, and the Wisconsin Card Sorting Test for reasoning and set-shifting.[4] In general, only the two groups in the Trail Making Test are found different. Participants in this task draw lines as fast as possible to connect a set of dots that comprises number/dots, followed by dots with alternation between numbers and letters. In particular, patients with a recent incident of attempt have a greater likelihood of making more errors and depict damage in cognitive flexibility but not on other dimensions of executive functions (Fig. 2.17).

Contrasting the underpinning evidence for cognitive deficits in suicidal individuals, some findings depicted measures of executive functions as outperformed by suicidal attempters. For instance, it was discovered by Nangle et al. (2006) that capability in problem-solving may correspond to ability in planning and staring of

[4] Shifting is also sometimes called set shifting, both refer to the cognitive ability of updating or changing attention flexibly in response to changes in the environment. In some neuropsychological tests, shifting is measured by having patients to perform according to some rule but then are asked to switch to a new rule. Successful task performance therefore requires the ability to abort the old rule and start applying to a new rule quickly.

behaviour (i.e. to begin a task independently and generate new ideas and problem-solving strategies), which may give rise to the risk of a suicide attempt from a stage of contemplating suicide only. This hypothesis is supported by the evidence that damage in these executive functions is related to the inability in formulating goals and effective planning (Chan et al., 2004). Similar to their estimation, the comparison in performance on the neuropsychological battery[5](a combination of tests that assess a wide array of cognitive skills and functions including memory, attention, or problem solving; Kane, 1991) indicated that participants with at least one-lifetime suicide attempt performed better than participants with suicidal ideation but no history of past attempters on cognitive measures of planning, attention, and verbal fluency. Nangle et al. (2006) explained that the relatively higher executive function measures by suicide attempters may suggest that this group had greater ability to formulate plans and initiate behaviour directed towards a particular goal, including having conducting suicide. In the reflection from these findings, executive dysfunction may not be sufficient to explain the occurrence of suicidal behaviour. It is also important to explore suicidality from a neurobiological perspective as well.

Empirical evidence stemmed from neuroimaging studies indicating particular deficits in executive functions corresponding to frontal brain activity and degrees o suicidality. Goldstein and Naglieri (2013) studied the theoretical and clinical constructs of executive functioning and noted that there is a good connection between PFC and its neighboring brain regions namely the parietal lobes and the midbrain. Such a connection is crucial in regulating and evaluating behaviour that allows individuals to question, develop strategies, and engage in self-monitoring. Clinical studies also illustrated indirect evidence that a range of executive functioning deficits is found when the frontal lobe is impaired. These deficits were formerly indicated to be in relation to suicidal behaviour. For example, distractibility, lack of initiation, impulsive control, and disinhibition (Arria et al., 2009; Goldstein & Naglieri, 2013; Jollant et al., 2011).

To examine the likelihood that executive functions deficits may be associated with suicidal behaviour and depression, Jollant et al. (2007) executed a neurological study with bipolar disorder patients by examining the neural basis of decision making, a cognitive aspect found to impact suicidality. The study included 69 individuals with a history of attempting suicide and depression, 25 patients with depression but no past suicide attempt, and 82 healthy controls to conduct the Iowa Gambling task. This task evaluated decision making by requiring participants to select among cards on four decks, with two favorable decks in which less money is won yet less is lost in long run (resulting in a net gain) and two unfavorable decks in which more money is won yet more is lost in long run (resulting in a net loss). In general, the

[5] A battery is defined as two or more tests that are related by an assessment method. It can give information from combinations and patterns that are derived from the relationships between these tests. Therefore, battery is particularly useful for neuropsychological assessment as it provides information about an individual that cannot be obtained from individual tests used alone (Kane, 1991).

participants are told to win as much money as they can in this task. Repeating their previous findings (Jollant et al., 2005), results indicated that individuals with past suicide attempts performed the worst in the Iowa Gambling Task in comparison with healthy controls and depressed patients with no suicidal behaviour.

Jollant et al. (2007) proposed that this is because of the emotional dysfunctions in suicide attempters that created a decision-making impediment and gave rise to suicidal behaviour. They also pinpointed that the cognitive damage could be ascribed to a decline in the brain region which is essential to decision making. In this regard, Jollant et al. (2010) examined the left lateral orbitofrontal and occipital regions which are vital for making decision under risky contexts. With the neurological correlates of 13 depressed suicide attempters, 12 depressed with no history of attempts, and 25 healthy controls explored whilst they performed Iowa Gambling task, the neurological findings echoed with earlier studies that a decline in activating the lateral orbitofrontal cortex during a decision-making task acts as a neural marker of elevated suicide risk (Wagner et al., 2012; Willeumier et al., 2011). Such convergent findings warrant claims for investigating neurological as well as behavioural traits of suicidal individuals. In conclusion, the cognitive predictors of an individual with suicide risk using cognitive tasks remain difficult, there is a need to find other markers, which could provide more promising and reliable predictions of suicidal behaviour than those currently available. Some recent neurocognitive and functional/structural neuroimaging might shed light in this direction.

Joormann and Gotlib (2010) suggest that excessive worries and contemplation signify anxiety and depression, these characteristics may be the result of impaired inhibitory control because an inability to inhibit negative thoughts may lead to accumulation in the long run which disrupts a person's daily life. To examine the relationship between inhibitory control deficits and suicidality in an experimental setting, response inhibition was measured by Pan et al. (2011) through the use of Go/No-go task in adolescents with a range of suicidality degrees. The capability in executing inhibitory control is vital to allow individuals to respond appropriately and behave according to socially compromised norms. It can also aid suppression of unfavorable thoughts or distractions that are shown concurrently with other essential information. Pan et al. (2011) involved 15 depressed adolescents with past suicide acts, 15 depressed adolescents without past suicide act, and 14 healthy controls. In the Go/No-go task, participants are required to press a button responding to a target stimulus, which signifies "Go", but refrain from pressing the button and do nothing responding to a non-target stimulus, which signifies "No-go". Go trials (when a target is presented) usually occupy 75% of trials in a Go/No-go task to establish a prepotent response that must then be inhibited on the less frequent No-Go trials (Garavan et al., 2002). The number of errors on no-go trials across the whole task for happy and sad faces served as the measures of behavioural inhibition and emotional modulation of this inhibition, respectively (Fig. 2.18).

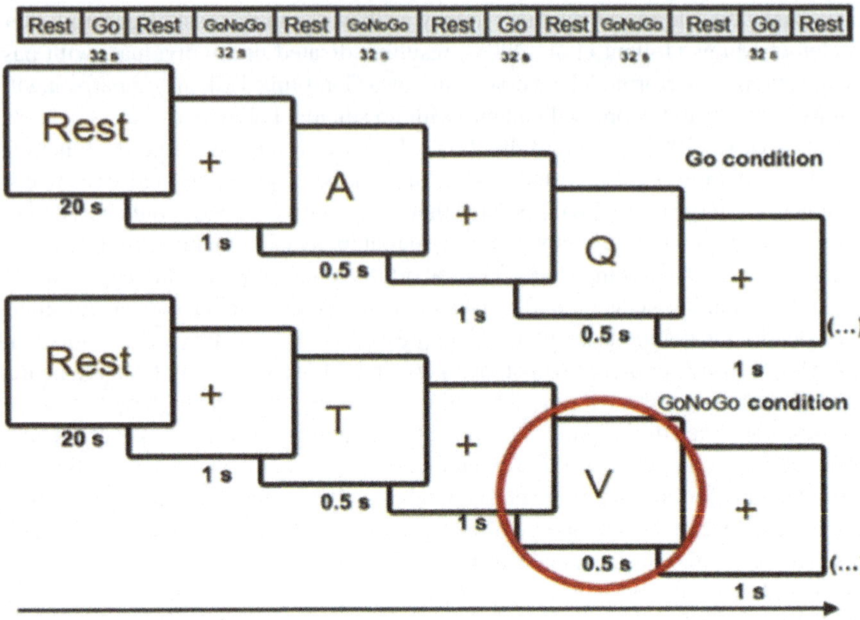

Fig. 2.18 Showing the typical design of a Go/No-go task to measure inhibitory control from Pan et al. (2011)

Participants with activated right anterior cingulate, left insula, and left dorsolateral prefrontal cortex during the task

Among the three groups of participants, no substantial disparity was found in Go/No-Go task performance (both accuracy and response times). The healthy controls in the neuroimaging recordings revealed activation of the prefrontal, anterior cingulate, and parietal cortical regions during the Go/No-Go task (Fig. 2.19). This is typical as the anterior cingulate is an important brain region imperative for inhibitory control (Løvstad et al., 2016). While the depressed individuals without past suicide acts exhibited no difference from the healthy controls regarding the activity in this part, the depressed adolescents with past suicide attempts displayed notably reduced activity. This denotes damages in neural activation during inhibitory control for suicidal individuals and also shows the relationship between cognitive processing and dysfunctional cortical activities. The findings propose that this association may constitute a neurobiological basis for predisposition to suicidal behaviour. It is put forward that suicidal acts link with lateralized frontal cortical activity and thus neurological measures may be adopted to forecast suicidality of individuals beyond the currently used self-report measures (Fig. 2.20).

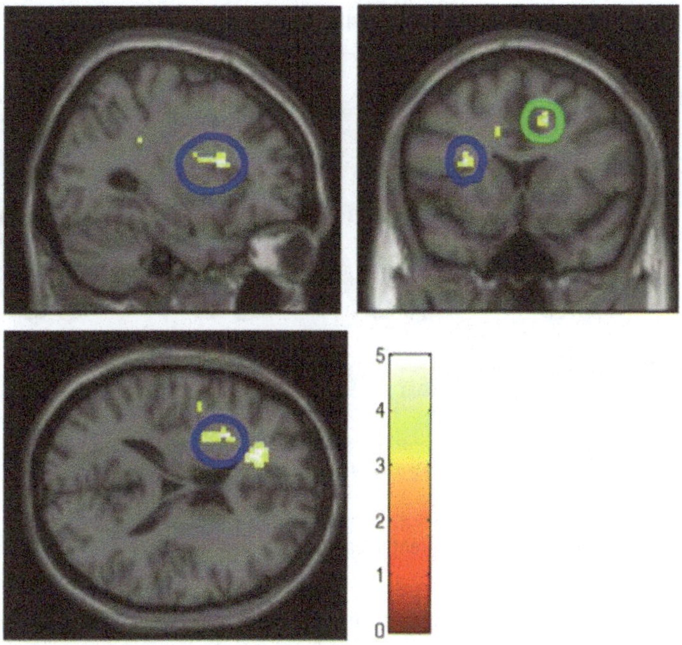

Fig. 2.19 Brain imaging of participants during Go No Go versus Go blocks from Pan et al. (2011)

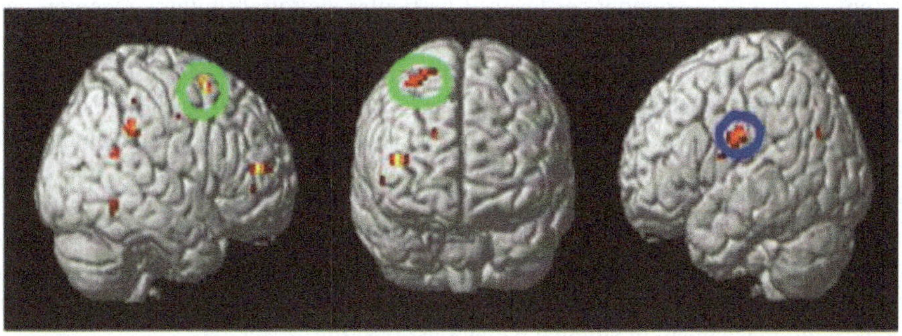

Fig. 2.20 Non-attempters with greater activity than attempters in the right anterior cingulate gyrus (encircled in green) and the left insula (encircled in blue)

2.3 How Suicidal Behaviour Is Linked to Neurobiological Development of the Brain

Other than the use of a self-report questionnaire, a substitute method for examining executive functions objectively has been provided by recent advances in neuroimaging technologies (Clark, 2018). Indeed, neuroimaging has been regarded as one of the most accurate and scientific methods in inspecting the pathophysiology

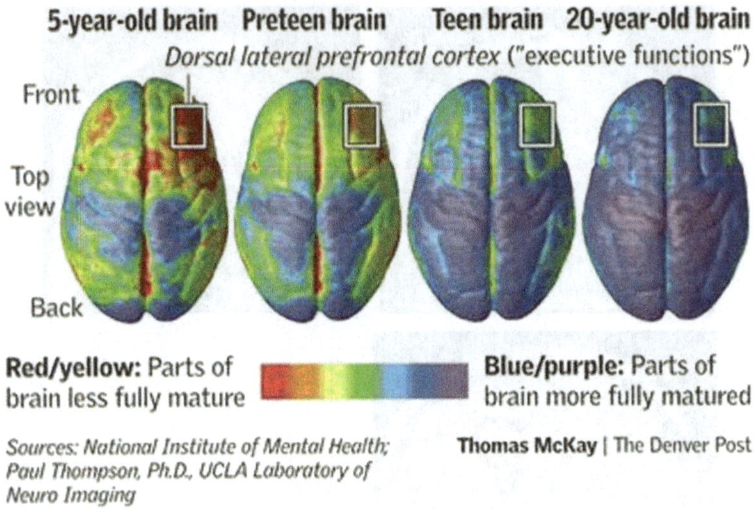

Fig. 2.21 Changes of the brain in different ages. Image from (Clark, 2018)

of psychiatric disorders in the living brain. In this regard, it offers a range of quantitative measures (including morphometry,[6] metabolism, and functional activity). Neuroimaging research of the human brains can predispose if the suicidal act is related to changes in the size or shape of particular brain regions, the functional activity within these regions, or level of particular neurotransmitters, receptors, or key metabolites. As outlined earlier, an individual's biological development determines executive functionability. It starts from infancy and proceeds to rapid development during adolescence and does not reach maturity until early adulthood (Goldstein & Naglieri, 2013). This is underpinned by neuroimaging studies which indicated that the frontal lobes continue white and gray matter development until at least the third decade of life where it reaches the complete stage of development (Johnston et al., 2017). Peak executive functions abilities showed an ongoing brain maturation in individuals ages between 20 and 29 years old (De Luca et al., 2003). As a result, inspecting young adults' brain activities will be advantageous to perceive the underlying mechanism of suicidal behaviours (see Fig. 2.21).

Exploration on the frontal brain region serves as the main source of neurological investigation of executive functions since this is the part that has been discovered as associated with executive functions (Fazakas-DeHoog et al., 2017; Løvstad et al., 2016). The evidence is stemmed from research exhibiting substantial activation in prefrontal regions when participants execute cognitive tasks with the help of executive functions. For instance, the use of fMRI (Functional Magnetic Resonance Imaging) can examine a surge in brain activation of the dorsolateral PFC (dlPFC) during a task that requires executive functions such as attentional control. There has been a

[6] Morphometry refers to the measurement of brain structures and tracking of the changes during development, aging, learning, disease or evolution.

widespread investigation on deficits of executive function by adopting a variety of behavioural and neurological measures in recent years (Baddeley, 1992; Imbir & Jarymowicz, 2013; Løvstad et al., 2016).

Empirical studies support an appreciation for the unique ability of neuroimaging modalities to uncover the multifaceted and riddling nature of suicidal behaviour. These modalities help to understand the relationships between cognitive, emotional, and behavioural components of suicide and altered neuroanatomy and neural function. Neuroimaging studies of the suicidal brain can be divided into three categories; structural imaging (e.g. Magnetic Resonance Imaging; MRI), functional imaging (e.g. fMRI), and molecular imaging. With the current advancement of neuroimaging technologies, researchers and clinicians have successfully pinpointed how the PFC and its distribution network control some executive functions. Some of the common neurological and brain imaging tools are outlined.

2.3.1 Functional Magnetic Resonance Imaging (fMRI)

Among numerous neuroimaging techniques, MRI can evaluate brain function safely, noninvasively, and effectively. fMRI is a very useful technique in mapping and measuring the intensity of human brain activity, providing information on the different functions of the brain, and understanding cerebral pathology (Watson, n.d.). fMRI is easy to use, and the images it produces are very high in resolution, which is the biggest reason clinicians widely favor MRI for measuring brain activity. It works by detecting the changes in blood oxygenation and flow that occur in response to neural activity (Devlin, 2016). The rationale is that when a brain area is more active it will consume more oxygen for meeting the greater demand of blood flow surrounding the active area. fMRI can be used to produce activation maps to indicate which parts of the brain are more involved in a particular mental process. For example, the key predictors for suicidality identified in past research such as inhibition, working memory, and attention are predominantly controlled by the PFC (Baddeley, 2003; Desmyter et al., 2011; Goldstein & Naglieri, 2013; Huntley & Howard, 2010; Marzuk et al., 2005). Other executive function components, including planning and decision-making, correspond to neural pathways within the PFC (Barkley, 2012) (Fig. 2.22).

The PFC has been shown to interact closely with its adjacent brain regions such as the anterior cingulate and the amygdala (Anderson, 2008; Diamond, 2013). Indirect supporting evidence is gleaned from neurological findings using an fMRI study (Hoffmann et al., 2014) that examines brain activations in response to a brief presentation of emotional and neutral word stimuli to participants.

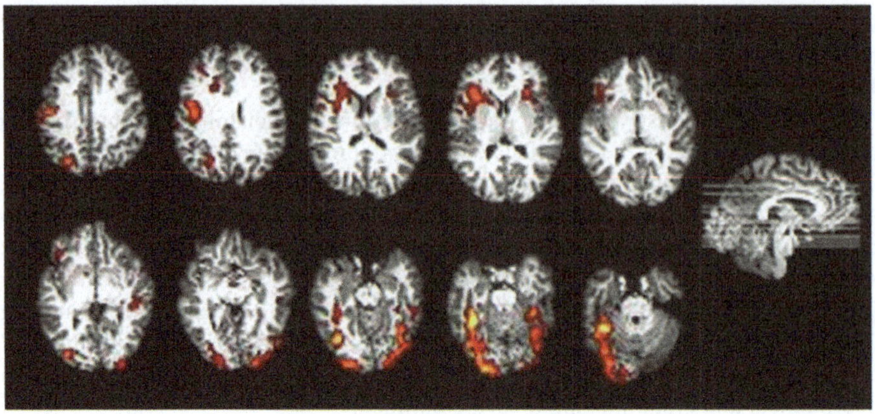

Fig. 2.22 Showing example images of functional magnetic resonance imaging (fMRI)

2.3.2 Structural Magnetic Resonance Imaging

Johnston et al. (2017) have recently implemented neuroimaging data to help identify those most at risk of suicide. It was proposed that the elucidation of neural systems can help to better understand suicidal behaviour and improve suicide prevention. They explored brain development in young adults using MRI on both past suicide attempters (n = 26) or without suicide attempts (n = 42). The MRI is a structural neuroimaging technique that generates an image of neuroanatomical differences between patients and healthy controls. Unlike the fMRI brain-imaging techniques, the MRI examines structural rather than functional abnormalities in patients when compared to the healthy control group (Balcioglu & Kose, 2018). For example abnormalities in volume alterations are found in various brain regions of suicide individuals (e.g. decreased grey and white matter in the PFC, OFC, and hippocampus; Sudol & Mann, 2017).

While in young adulthood, the frontal-limbic system (the neural connection between the frontal region and the limbic system that regulates emotion and impulses) is still under development, neural imaging of these brains may depict the generation of suicidal thoughts and behaviours in young adults (Hathaway, 2017). The findings of Johnston et al. (2017) unveiled that individuals with a past history of suicide attempts revealed comparatively lower activity in the frontal-limbic system, and had less white matter volume (the wiring that provides connections between brain areas) in comparison with healthy controls. The findings also upheld that the frontal cortex of suicide attempters is less functional in regulating the circuitry, which may lead to augmented emotional pain, deficiencies in producing alternate solutions to suicide, and a greater likelihood of acting on suicidal impulses (Johnston et al., 2017). Some ascribed the structural abnormalities to the inability to regulate emotions by the limbic system, difficulties in generating alternate solutions to suicide, and greater risk of having suicidal impulses (Johnston et al., 2017). Consequently, neurological

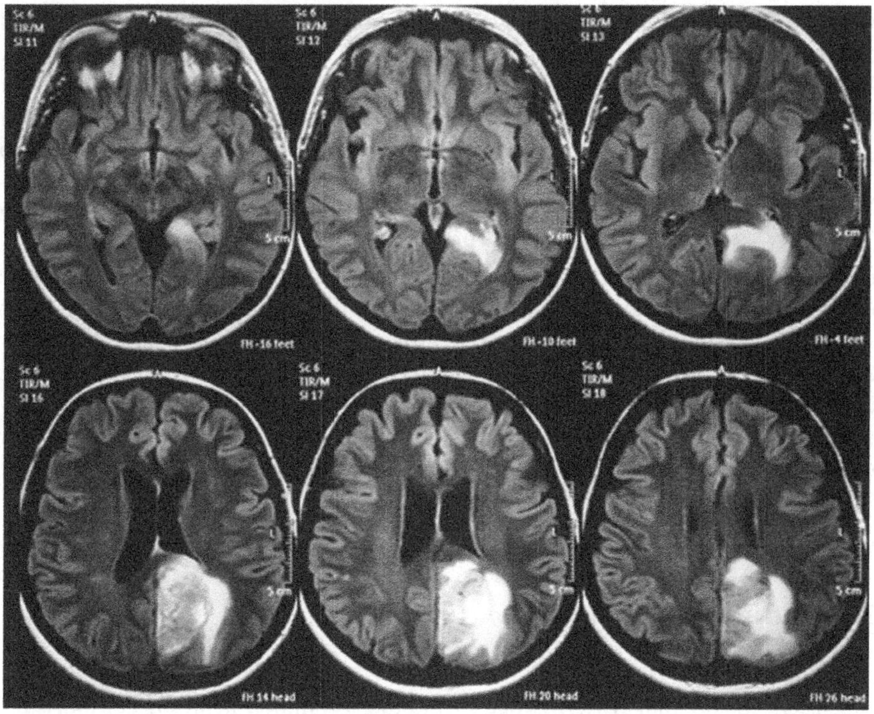

Fig. 2.23 Showing examples of MRI images

deficits in the frontal cortex could reveal the extents of suicidality one is suffering from (Fig. 2.23).

Some researchers specified that the dlPFC and the vlPFC, in particular, are responsible for guiding attention, maintaining the information within the mind, shifting cognitive resources between different sources of information, and inhibiting the processing of task-irrelevant information (Miyake & Friedman, 2012; Ochsner et al., 2012). These cognitive properties are also considered vital for monitoring and minimizing suicidal behaviour (Carter & van Veen, 2007) as response inhibition can help individuals resist the sense of the impulsive act. Such interference control can also aid inhibition of inappropriate and invasive ideas of self-harm (Diamond, 2013). Subsequently, deficits in the neural interactions within the PFC may erode one's ability in coping with emotional turbulence and resolving problems, which may result in aggravation of other symptoms that are frequently found in suicidal patients (e.g. feelings of hopelessness; Desmyter et al., 2011; Jollant et al., 2011).

A selection of functional imaging reports in the suicidal patient has been evaluated by Desmyter et al. (2011). It was discovered that they exhibited damages in executive functions and these damages were exclusive to the prefrontal cortical regions.

With the use of MRI, fMRI, and positron emission tomography (PET)[7] scan, neural deficits of patients were illustrated in the form of reduced volume of grey matter and abnormal metabolism in the PFC. This suggests that suicidal patients differ from healthy individuals with regard to both activity and structure of the PFC. It reveals that suicidal patients are different from healthy individuals concerning both activity and structure of the PFC. In comparison with a control group, the functional neuroimaging measures conducted during resting conditions showed a decline in perfusion (reduced activity) in the PFC of suicidal patients. These deficits were more apparent during cognitive activation such as completing a task that required increased cognitive resources. The findings depict the advantages of the use of brain activation measures as a reliable means to differentiate suicidal patients from healthy controls. Based on finding that individuals may need to recruit left frontal areas when completing inhibitory responses in a task. Failure to do so is linked to inhibitory deficits and the progression of suicidal behaviours. Therefore, the findings show a promising indication that there could be neurological markers for characterizing suicidal behaviour.

2.3.3 *Electroencephalogram (EEG)*

Electroencephalogram (EEG) is one of the most common neurological tools that directly measure brain activities. It is also considered to be relatively inexpensive and widely available compared to other neuroimaging methods for recording electrocortical activity (e.g., fMRI and MRI). In addition, EEG has a long history of measuring rhythmic neural activity in the brain (also referred to as oscillatory states). It can provide high temporal resolution in milliseconds and has been used to measure the effects of health, affective traits, and arousal states on neural activity (Davidson et al., 2004; Urry et al., 2004). The tool consists of many electrodes made of small metal discs with thin wires that are pasted onto the scalp (see Fig. 2.24). These electrodes detect tiny electrical charges that result from brain cells' activity and can also detect abnormalities in brain waves or the electrical activity of the brain (Devlin, 2016). The brain activities detected by the electrodes are then amplified and usually present on a graph of a computer screen, or as a recording printed on paper. Some recent EEG studies (Hatzidaki et al., 2015; Imbir et al., 2015) indicate that there may be a longer response time (indication of more processing cost) for naming the colour of emotional words relative to neutral words.

EEG involves the use of electrodes to measure electrical potential (i.e. cortical activity) on the surface of the scalp. The measures collected, which vary across a range of frequencies from 1 to 30 Hz, are decomposed into distinct frequency bands through a process called Fourier analysis. This helps to decompose the raw EEG

[7] A PET scan is a type of nuclear medicine imaging and is therefore radioactive. It can assess important functions of the brain such as blood flow, oxygen use, and sugar (glucose) metabolism, to help evaluate how well organs and tissue functions.

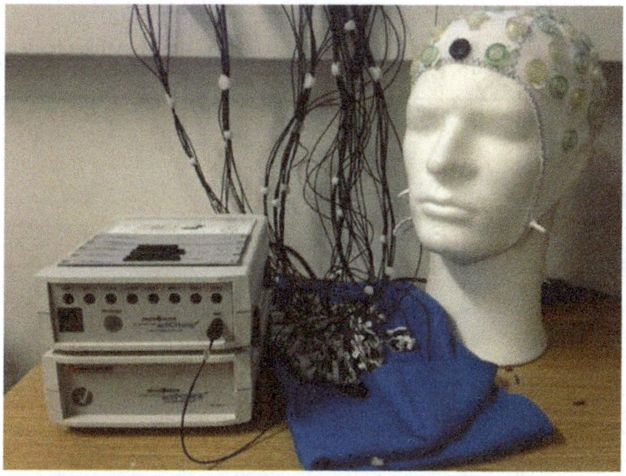

Fig. 2.24 Showing an EEG headset with 128 channels and an *amplifier*. **Adopted from** Centre for Cognition & Decision Making: Facilities (n.d.)

data into various frequency bands (Figs. 2.25 and 2.26) such as delta (0–4 Hz), theta (4–8 Hz), alpha (8–13 Hz), beta (13–20 Hz), and low gamma (30–60 Hz). The power spectral analysis is one of the common methods used to quantify the distribution of each frequency band of an analyzed EEG signal. Changes in the power spectrum give important information about the changes in the constituents of each frequency band, and it thereby reflects a change in cognitive state (Allen et al., 2004; Davidson, 1998). For example, a high-frequency band of beta waves reflects an individual is feeling diligent and alert. Conversely, the alpha measure is also argued to be an effective way to examine asymmetric frontal cortical activity (Coan & Allen, 2004). For instance, alpha (α) frequency bands reflect a relaxed state of wakefulness. An increase in the alpha frequency band reflects a resting state with relatively low levels of cortical activity (Allen et al., 2004). However, when the cortex is active such as when an individual is engaged in a cognitive task, the alpha rhythm is suppressed and the alpha frequency band detected is significantly reduced (Davidson et al., 2000a, 2000b).

2.4 Early Brain Studies Using Neuroimaging

The primary content regarding that deficits in PFC activity may be associated with affective disorders is stemmed from observing patients who had undergone a stroke and were suffering from clinical depression. (Gainotti, 1972; see Harmon-Jones et al., 2010 for a review). In the early studies, some patients with impairment to the left PFC became increasingly depressed, whereas the impairment to the right frontal lesions led to a surge in manic symptoms. Such dissociation was discovered by Schaffer, Davidson, and Sarson (1983) through measurement in cortical activity in patients

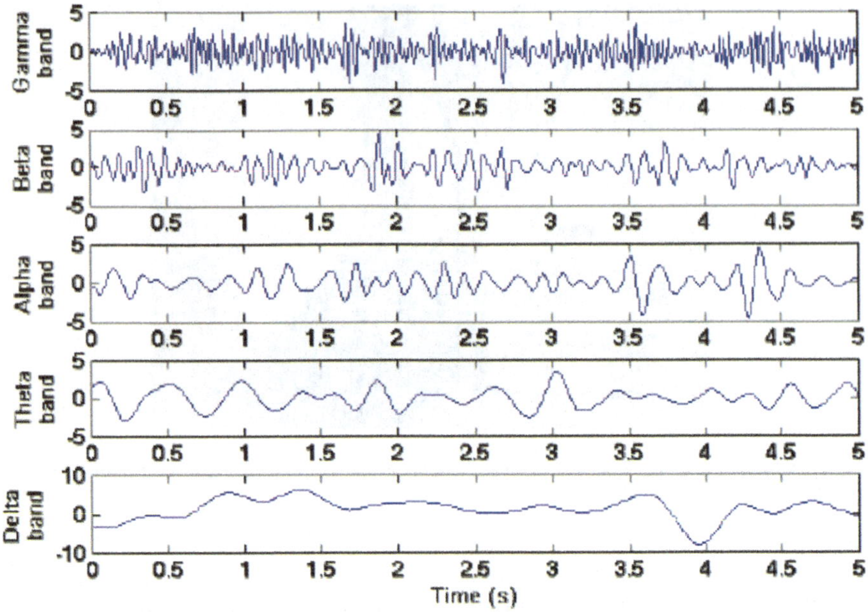

Band	Frequency Range (Hz)	Voltage Level (µV)	Corresponding Brain Activity
Delta	0.5 – 4	20 – 200	Sleeping
Theta	4 – 7	< 20	Dreaming; Meditation
Alpha	8 – 13	30 – 50	Relaxation
Beta	13- 36	5 – 10	Problem solving
Gamma	above 36	5 – 10	Conscious Perception

Fig. 2.25 Comparison of EEG bands from (Abo-Zahhad et al., 2015)

who were suffering from depression. Their objective was to indicate any dissociation (also known as 'asymmetry') of activity that could be used to investigate how various frontal activation patterns may be associated with the severity of the disorder. From then on, the term *brain asymmetry* rapidly emerged and this is often referred to as neurological diversities between the left and right brains or lateralization of brain functions (Tomarken et al., 1992). EEG electrodes were positioned in the frontal and parietal regions of the brain. Echoing the clinical report of Gainotti (1972), patients exhibiting more severe depression symptoms revealed more intense activity in the right in comparison to the left. Notably, this pattern was not found in parietal regions but in frontal regions only.

These findings result in the rapid growth of research in relation to lateralized frontal activation. EEG has also become a common method in measuring the correlates of relative hemispheric dominance (Tomarken, et al., 1992; Tucker, 1981). Since then, research across 30 years has offered support for the association between asymmetric frontal activation and depression (Allen & Kline, 2004; Allen & Reznik,

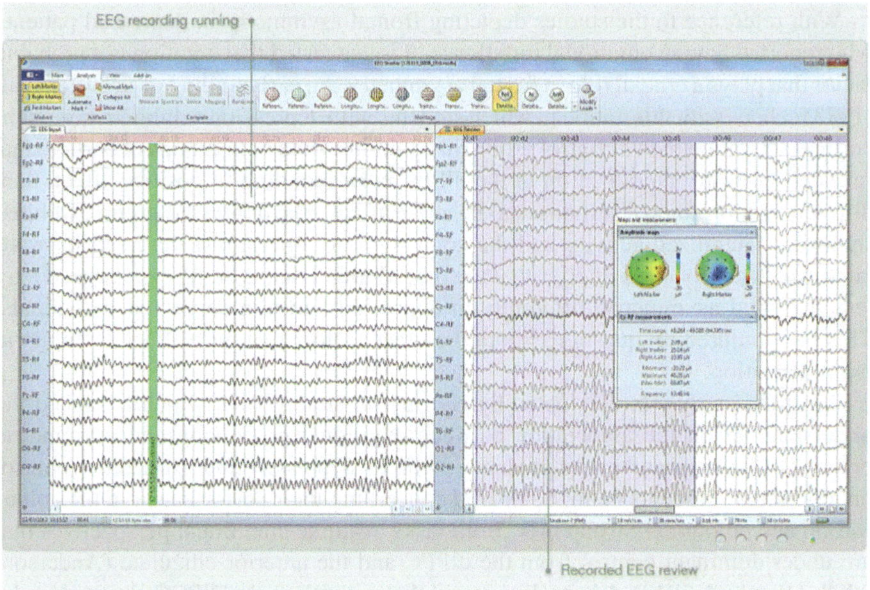

Fig. 2.26 EEG recordings displayed as graph on the computer screen (Bahri et al., 2014). Image from EEG Studio acquisition software (n.d.)

2015; Thibodeau et al., 2006; Tomarken, et al., 1992; Tucker, 1981). Most of the findings reveal that patients with depression history or repetitive depression demonstrate comparatively lower left frontal cortical activity (Gotlib, 1998). This is also referred to as left frontal hypoactivation and corresponds to rightward frontal cortical activity (for reviews, see Davidson et al., 2002). Contrarily, healthy controls depict the opposite pattern, with more intense left frontal cortical activity (Stewart et al., 2010; Thibodeau et al., 2006). It has also been found by Saletu et al. (2010) that the elevated level of right brain activity is also associated with an elevated level of depression reported, which puts forward that brain asymmetry may serve as a potential marker for measuring the severity of disorders in patients.

Notwithstanding the undeniable neurological evidence for frontal asymmetry in depressive samples, some findings are merged, and studies have often revealed non-substantial results (Kemp et al., 2010). For instance, in some findings the EGG activity analysis illustrates that asymmetrical frontal variations in depression are relative rather than absolute (Coan et al., 2006). In other words, it indicates that the frontal cortical activity is subject to changes in various contexts (e.g. resting[8] state versus active state) and is not merely based on the effects of depression.

[8] Resting EEG activity is usually obtained by asking participants to relax and not performing any tasks. There will usually be an equal amount of time having eyes opened and eyes closed during resting state.

With reference to the studies depicting frontal asymmetry in depressed patients who reported having emotional turbulence, it is suggested that emotion is a probable factor that plays a crucial role in frontal asymmetry. An early finding of Schaffer et al. (1983) echoes with this notion in which students with depression exhibited more right cortical activation than a control group. In addition, while both groups of participants revealed leftward lateralization in the dlPFC corresponding to positive affect, they differed in neurological responses to negative affect. The depressed group exhibited rightward lateralized activity and the control group, in contrast, revealed leftward lateralized activity. This implies that the type of affect that is being experienced may lessen frontal asymmetry differently in depressed and non-depressed individuals. This has conjured up questions about the other factors that may affect asymmetric brain activation.

An fMRI study was conducted by Herrington et al. (2010) which advanced the understanding on the association between emotional processing and asymmetric brain activation in university students, with 11 depressed and 18 healthy control undergraduate students being compared concerning their performance in the colour Stroop and emotional Stroop task. Both tasks examine attentional perspectives that are under dominant control from the dlPFC and the anterior cingulate (Anderson, 2008; Diamond, 2013). It was discovered that activity in the dlPFC elevated in the colour Stroop task for trials in which the word was contrasting to the colour (i.e. the word red presented in green font). The surge in cortical activity was also evident during the emotional Stroop task for trails in which negative words were shown. It depicts that constraining automatic responses (reading a word) and constraining negative information was in relation to elevated brain activity in the dlPFC, offering a direct pathway between frontal activity and inhibitory control. Herrington et al. (2010) summarized that there is a presence of frontal asymmetry in depression populations in negative emotional conditions and this reveals particular constraints in managing the negative information processing.

On top of the evidence, more and more neuroimaging studies have examined brain lateralization in response to affective disorders and emotional biases (Auerbach et al., 2015). For example, with the use of EEG measures, it is reasoned by Auerbach et al. (2015) that a negative emotional processing bias was shown in depressed female adolescents ($n = 23$) in comparison with healthy controls ($n = 36$). A face recognition task was conducted with 4 facial expressions presented (happy, sad, fearful, and angry). Participants were required to indicate a specific emotion in each trial as fast as possible. Similar to ample literature, results revealed that the depressed group has a more intense tendency to indicate sad than happy facial expressions. Such a cognitive bias was again categorized by left dlPFC hypoactivity (low activity) in the EEG recordings. They reached a similar conclusion corresponding to Gotlib et al. (2010), that the neural frontal asymmetry in depressed patients correlates with the degree of attention put towards sad emotions and reduced recognition of happiness, thus rightward frontal cortical activation indicates an elevated risk for the persistence of depression

2.4.1 *Theoretical Models and Empirical Findings of Frontal Asymmetry*

The methods of studying frontal asymmetrical activity were originally used to measure "traits" (e.g. depressive traits). Yet, it is contended to be a measure of emotional processing, emotional state, and motivational tendency (n, 1992, 1998). Regarding a critical review of frontal asymmetry by Allen and Kline (2004), Davidson et al. (1979) were among the first to use asymmetric frontal cortical activity to make inferences about asymmetrical brain activity and emotion. They contended that the left hemisphere is prevalent in the positive emotions process while the right is prevalent in the negative emotions process. This reveals that if one has more intense electrocortical activity in the right frontal region, one will tend to emphasize negative emotions and information. Davidson and Fox (1982) echoes with this notion and put forward that patterns of lateralized brain activity can be indicated as early as infancy. With a purpose to examine this hypothesis, they evaluated the activity of 10-month old infants while they watched video recordings comprising happy or sad facial expressions. Activity in frontal and parietal regions was recorded and it was discovered that watching happy facial expressions correlated with elevated activation in the left cortical region (relative to the right) whereas watching sad facial expressions correlates with elevated relative activation in the right. The findings also underpinned Schaffer et al. (1983)'s work that this diverse pattern of activity was only discovered in parietal regions instead of frontal regions (Figs. 2.27 and 2.28).

As of now, the responsivity of depression and emotion has become the emphasis of the literature, and they are well-validated by the associated theoretical models. On top of that, Graae et al. (1996) were among the earliest researchers to examine the association between suicidality and frontal lateralization. They recorded EEG from 16 adolescents with past suicide attempts and compared to 22 healthy controls. The EEG recordings were done during eyes open and eyes closed resting state.

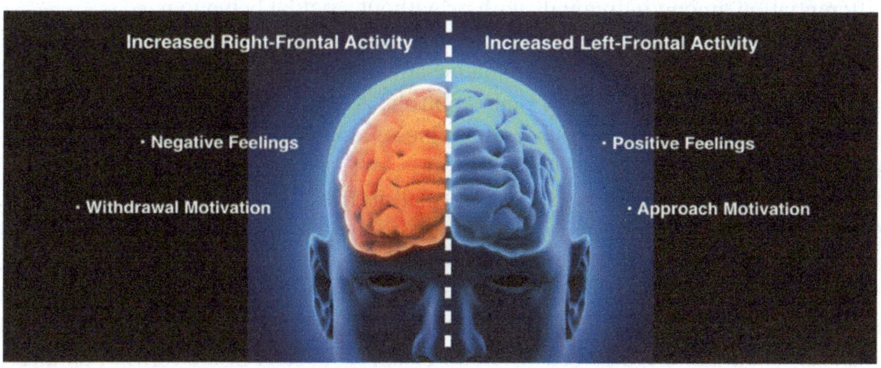

Fig. 2.27 Image from Frontal Asymmetry 101 (2017) $Frontal\ Asymmetry\ Index = \ln\left(\frac{alpha\ power\ right\ F_4}{alpha\ power\ left\ F_3}\right)$

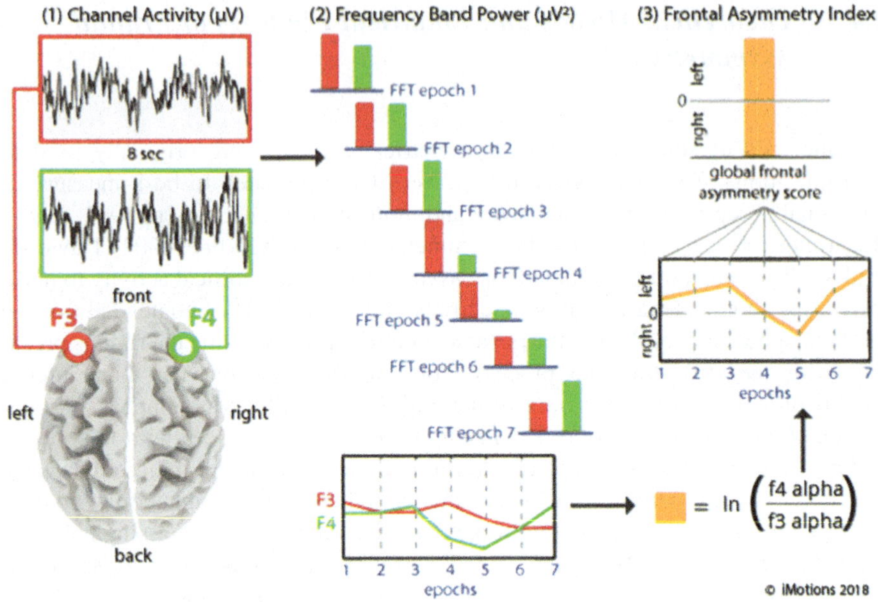

Fig. 2.28 Image from (Frontal Asymmetry 101, 2017)

Results revealed that individuals with a history of attempting suicide varied from healthy controls regarding their levels of frontal brain activity. In particular, the healthy control group had comparatively less activation in the right hemisphere, while a pattern of opposite direction was depicted in suicidal adolescents (exhibiting greater rightward frontal activation). Besides, in comparison with controls, individuals with a history of attempting suicide also illustrated less brain activation in the left hemisphere than the right in the posterior regions (temporal and parietal lobes). It unveils that brain lateralization between the left and the right hemisphere may aid differentiation among individuals with or without suicidal behaviour.

Using event-related fMRI, Jollant et al. (2008) compared the neural activity of previously depressed men with past suicide attempts, previously depressed men with no suicide attempts, and healthy male controls. A series of facial expressions were viewed by all participants, such as happiness, anger, or neutral emotions alongside a memory test on short-term recognition on faces. This test aims to check the ability of participants in processing information from different facial expressions. Among the three groups of participants, only individuals with past suicide attempts revealed varieties in frontal asymmetry when responding to emotional faces (angry, happy, and neutral). In particular, they depicted elevated neural activation in the right lateral orbitofrontal cortex in response to angry faces relative to neutral faces. Jollant et al. reasoned that elevated sensitivity to disapproval (e.g. in the form of an angry facial expression) from another person and a greater tendency to process and act on negative emotions may trigger aggravation in the suicidal behaviour of suicidal individuals. Remarkably, for the other two groups of participants who had no past history of suicidal behaviour, no difference was found during frontal regions activation in response to emotion. This brain laterality may denote vulnerability markers of suicidal behaviour in those with a history of depression. While male participants mostly in middle-age and with past major depressive disorder were particularly recruited, this has cast doubts upon the similarity of the findings to those who may have milder forms of suicidal behaviour but may not be characterized as having a clinical disorder (e.g. a non-clinical student population). Besides, the authors also recognized that their study did not control factors ranging from age, education and did not examine the duration of symptom-free periods in patients.

Notwithstanding the evidence concerning the variations of frontal asymmetry under different emotional and psychopathological contexts in past studies, the existing findings revealed that frontal asymmetry remains unchanged between high and low suicide risk groups. Generally, all participants exhibited leftward frontal cortical activity (more positive alpha symmetric index), disregarding suicidality. In this regard, Kann et al. (2016) also investigated brain lateralization in healthy adults. Likewise, they discovered a substantially greater level of brain activity in the left PFC, specifically, the dorsomedial PFC (dmPFC) and inferior frontal cortex (IFC) when EEG recording was adopted in measuring frontal asymmetry. In comparison with individuals with affective disorders, healthy controls show higher leftward frontal cortical activity than those with evident suicide risk (Stewart et al., 2010; Thibodeau et al., 2006; see Fig. 2.29 for the picture of the meta-analysis).

Thibodeau et al. (2006) tried to reconcile the inconsistent findings in this meta-analysis by investigating the importance of different variables including, gender, age, resting EEG strength, and scalp site. It was found that all of these variables influenced the effect size across the different studies. Notably, they specified that when examining resting frontal asymmetry, it is better to take EEG recordings of shorter periods (e.g. 2 min). This is based on the comparative analysis that shorter recording periods were associated with larger effects on frontal asymmetry. Thibodeau et al. (2006) explained that this is possibly due to the more enriching emotional state that is elicited at the beginning of an experimental condition shortly after the presentation of the emotional stimuli. When the recording was taken for a longer duration at rest, the emotional state may have worn off. Taking note of Thibodeau et al.'s (2006) meta-analysis. Aside from the duration of EEG recordings, it is noted that asymmetry can be affected by a number of factors. Thibodeau et al. also noted that age is an important factor in moderating frontal asymmetry, with younger participants showing more variations in frontal cortical activations than older participants. This may have affected the impact of depression on frontal asymmetry. Regarding the EEG frontal activity that was taken during the resting state, Coan et al. (2006) have questioned the reliance on using resting EEG data as a stable measure of individual traits. Instead, they argued that frontal EEG should be measured in specific situational contexts (i.e. under situations that require more emotional and cognitive demands) to assess an individual's capacity to respond emotionally. They also disputed that consideration of dispositional trait alone may not be sufficient to account for changes in frontal

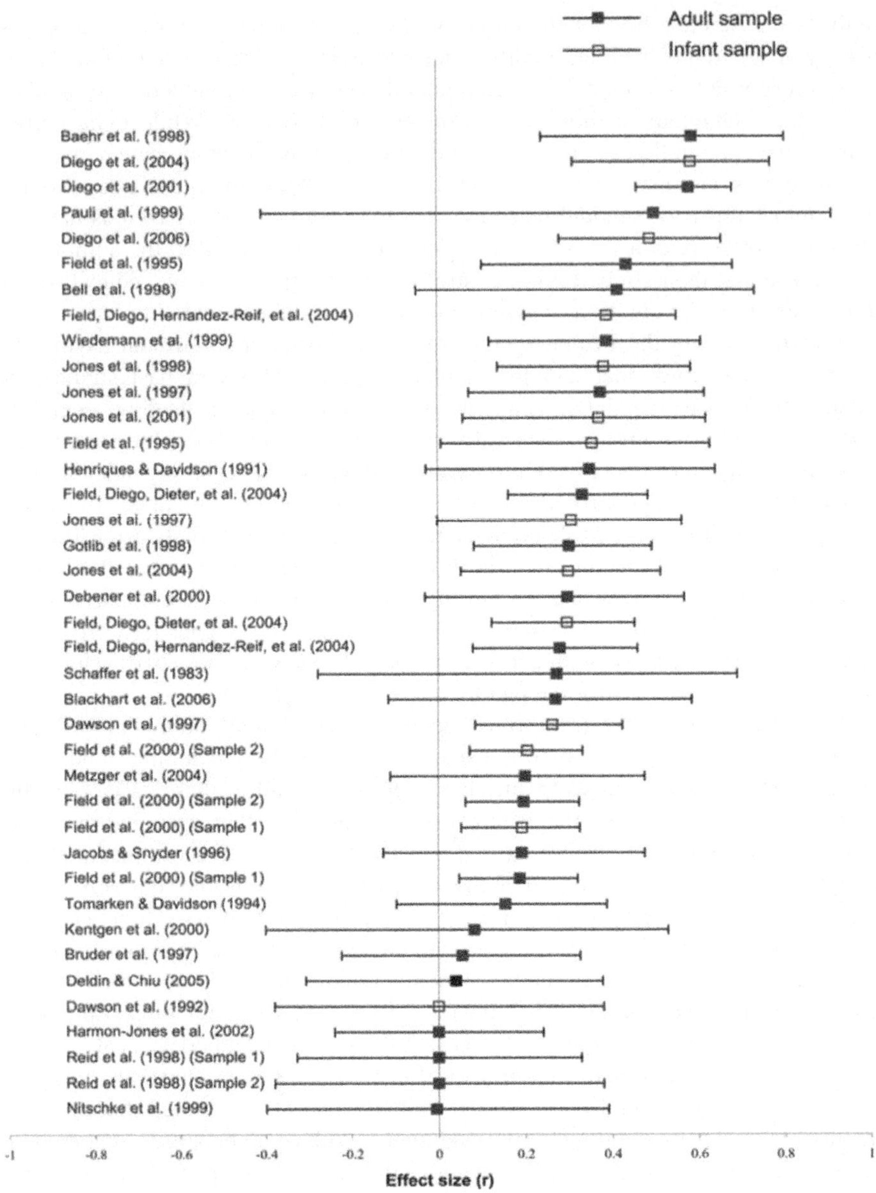

Fig. 2.29 Forest plot representing weighted effect sizes (r) and 95% confidence intervals for depression studies in the meta-analytic database. From (Thibodeau et al., 2006)

asymmetry. Therefore, other variables may influence frontal alpha asymmetry in relation to suicidality.

References

Abo-Zahhad, M., Ahmed, S. M., & Abbas, S. N. (2015). A new EEG acquisition protocol for biometric identification using eye blinking signals. *International Journal of Intelligent Systems and Applications, 7*(6), 48. https://doi.org/10.5815/ijisa.2015.06.05.

Ahmed, S., Bittencourt-Hewitt, A., & Sebastian, C. (2015). Neurocognitive bases of emotion regulation development in adolescence. *Developmental Cognitive Neuroscience, 15*, 11–25.

Algom, D., Chajut, E., & Lev, S. (2004). A rational look at the emotional Stroop phenomenon: A generic slowdown, not a Stroop effect. *Journal of Experimental Psychology: General, 133*(3), 323–338. https://doi.org/10.1037/0096-3445.133.3.323.

Allen, J. J., & Kline, J. P. (2004). Frontal EEG asymmetry, emotion, and psychopathology: The first, and the next 25 years. *Biological Psychology, 67*(1–2), 1–5. https://doi.org/10.1016/j.biopsycho.2004.03.001.

Allen, J. J., & Reznik, S. J. (2015). Frontal EEG asymmetry as a promising marker of depression vulnerability: Summary and methodological considerations. *Current Opinion in Psychology, 4*, 93–97.

Allen, J. J., Urry, H. L., Hitt, S. K., & Coan, J. A. (2004). The stability of resting frontal electroencephalographic asymmetry in depression. *Psychophysiology, 41*(2), 269–280. https://doi.org/10.1111/j.1469-8986.2003.00149.x.

Anderson, P. J. (2008). Towards a developmental model of executive function. In V. Anderson, R. Jacobs, & P. J. Anderson (Eds.), Neuropsychology, neurology, and cognition. *Executive functions and the frontal lobes: A lifespan perspective* (pp. 3-21). Philadelphia, PA, US: Taylor & Francis.

Arria, A. M., O'Grady, K. E., Caldeira, K. M., Vincent, K. B., Wilcox, H. C., & Wish, E. D. (2009). Suicide ideation among college students: A multivariate analysis. *Archives of Suicide Research: Official Journal of the International Academy for Suicide Research, 13*(3), 230–246. https://doi.org/10.1080/13811110903044351.

Auerbach, R. P., Stewart, J. G., Stanton, C. H., Mueller, E. M., & Pizzagalli, D. A. (2015). Emotion processing biases and resting EEG activity in depressed adolescents. *Depression and Anxiety, 32*(9), 693–701. https://doi.org/10.1002/da.22381.

Baddeley, A. (1992). Working memory. *Science, 255*(5044), 556–559.

Baddeley, A. (2003). Working memory: Looking back and looking forward. *Nature Reviews Neuroscience, 4*(10), 829–839. https://doi.org/10.1038/nrn1201.

Baechler, J. (1979). *Suicides*. Basic Books.

Bahri, Z., Abdulaal, S., & Buallay, M. (2014, January). Sub-band-power-based efficient brain computer interface for wheelchair control. In *2014 World Symposium on Computer Applications & Research (WSCAR)*, (pp. 1–7). IEEE.

Balcioglu, Y. H., & Kose, S. (2018). Neural substrates of suicide and suicidal behaviour: From a neuroimaging perspective. *Psychiatry and Clinical Psychopharmacology, 28*(3), 314–328. https://doi.org/10.1080/24750573.2017.1420378.

Barkley, R. (2012). Assessing executive functioning as an extended phenotype. *The ADHD Report, 20*(2), 1-6.

Baumeister, R. (1990). Suicide as escape from self. *Psychological Review, 97*(1), 90–113. https://doi.org/10.1037//0033-295x.97.1.90.

Beall, P., & Herbert, A. (2008). The face wins: Stronger automatic processing of affect in facial expressions than words in a modified Stroop task. *Cognition & Emotion, 22*(8), 1613-1642. https://doi.org/10.1080/02699930801940370.

Bechara, A., Damasio, H., Damasio, A. R., & Lee, G. P. (1999). Different contributions of the human amygdala and ventromedial prefrontal cortex to decision-making. *The Journal of Neuroscience, 19*(13), 5473-5481. https://doi.org/10.1523/jneurosci.19-13-05473.1999.

Beck, A., & Clark, D. (1988). Anxiety and depression: an information processing perspective. *Anxiety Research, 1*(1), 23-36. https://doi.org/10.1080/10615808808248218.

Ben-Haim, M. S., Williams, P., Howard, Z., Mama, Y., Eidels, A., & Algom, D. (2016). The emotional Stroop task: assessing cognitive performance under exposure to emotional content. *Journal of Visualized Experiments, 112*, e53720. https://doi.org/10.3791/53720.

Bower, G. H. (1981). Mood and memory. *American Psychology, 36*, 129–148. https://doi.org/10.1037/0003-066X.36.2.129.

Bower, G. H. (1991). Mood congruity of social judgements. *Emotion and social judgements* (pp. 31–53). Pergamon.

Brosch, T., Scherer, K., Grandjean, D., & Sander, D. (2013). The impact of emotion on perception, attention, memory, and decision-making. *Swiss Medical Weekly, 14*, 143–152. https://doi.org/10.4414/smw.2013.13786.

Burton, C., Vella, L., Weller, J., & Twamley, E. (2011). Differential effects of executive functioning on suicide attempts. *Journal of Neuropsychiatry, 23*(2), 173–179.

Carter, C., & van Veen, V. (2007). Anterior cingulate cortex and conflict detection: An update of theory and data. *Cognitive, Affective, & Behavioral Neuroscience, 7*(4), 367-379. https://doi.org/10.3758/cabn.7.4.367.

Cha, C., Najmi, S., Park, J., Finn, C., & Nock, M. (2010). Attentional bias toward suicide-related stimuli predicts suicidal behaviour: Correction. *Journal of Abnormal Psychology, 119*(4), 874–874. https://doi.org/10.1037/a0021512.

Chung, Y. & Jeglic, E. (2015). Use of the modified emotional Stroop task to detect suicidality in college population. *Suicide and Life-Threatening Behavior, 46*(1), 55-66. https://doi.org/10.1111/sltb.12174.

Clark, A. (2018, February 11). What are executive functioning skills and why do they matter? *Educational Connections Tutoring and Test App*. Retrieved from https://www.ectutoring.com/executive-functioning-skills-matter.

Coan, J., & Allen, J. (2004). Frontal EEG asymmetry as a moderator and mediator of emotion. *Biological Psychology, 67*(1–2), 7–50.

Coan, J., Allen, J., & McKnight, P. (2006). A capability model of individual differences in frontal EEG asymmetry. *Biological Psychology, 72*(2), 198–207.

Cothran, D., & Larsen, L. (2008). Comparison of inhibition in two timed reaction tasks: The colour and emotion Stroop tasks. *The Journal of Psychology, 142*(4), 373–385.

Davidson, R. J. (1998). Anterior electrophysiological asymmetries, emotion, and depression: Conceptual and methodological conundrums. *Psychophysiology, 35*, 607–614.

Davidson, R. J., & Fox, N. A. (1982). Asymmetrical brain activity discriminates between positive and negative affective stimuli in human infants. *Science, 218*, 1235–1237.

Davidson, R. J., Jackson, D. C., & Kalin, N. H. (2000a). Emotion, plasticity, context, and regulation: Perspectives from affective neuroscience. *Psychological Bulletin, 126*(6), 890–909. https://doi.org/10.1037//0033-2909.126.6.890.

Davidson, R., Marshall, J., Tomarken, A., & Henriques, J. (2000b). While a phobic waits: Regional brain electrical and autonomic activity in social phobics during anticipation of public speaking. *Biological Psychiatry, 47*(2), 85–95.

Davidson, R. J., Pizzagalli, D., Nitschke, J. B., & Putnam, K. (2002). Depression: Perspectives from affective neuroscience. *Annual Review of Psychology, 53*, 545–574.

Davidson, R. J., Schwartz, G. E., Saron, C., Bennett, J., & Goleman, D. J. (1979). Frontal versus parietal EEG asymmetry during positive and negative affect. *Psychophysiology, 16*, 202–203.

Davidson, R. (2004). What does the prefrontal cortex "do" in affect: perspectives on frontal EEG asymmetry research. *Biological Psychology, 67*(1-2), 219-234.

De Luca, C. R., Wood, S. J., Anderson, V., Buchanan, J., Proffitt, T. M., Mahony, K., & Pantelis, C. (2003). Normative data from the Cantab. I: development of executive function over the lifespan.

Journal of Clinical and Experimental Neuropsychology (Neuropsychology, Development and Cognition: Section A), *25*(2), 242-254. https://doi.org/10.1076/jcen.25.2.242.13639.

Desmyter, S., Van Heeringen, C., & Audenaert, K. (2011). Structural and functional neuroimaging studies of the suicidal brain. *Progress in Neuro-Psychopharmacology and Biological Psychiatry, 35*(4), 796–808. https://doi.org/10.1016/j.pnpbp.2010.12.026.

Devlin, H. (2016). What is functional magnetic resonance imaging (fMRI)? *Psych Central.* Retrieved on October 29, 2018, from https://psychcentral.com/lib/what-is-functional-magnetic-resonance-imaging-fmri/.

Diamond, A. (2013). Executive functions. *Annual Review of Psychology, 64*(1), 135–168.

Doty, L. (2012). Executive function and memory/cognition changes. *Florida Department of Elder Affairs Alzheimer's Disease Initiative.* Retrieved from http://alzonline.phhp.ufl.edu/en/reading/executivefxlatest.pdf.

Fazakas-DeHoog, L., Rnic, K., & Dozois, D. (2017). A cognitive distortions and deficits model of suicide ideation. *Europe's Journal of Psychology, 13*(2), 178-193. https://doi.org/10.5964/ejop.v13i2.1238.

Gainotti, G. (1972). Emotional behavior and hemispheric side of the lesion. *Cortex, 8*(1), 41-55. https://doi.org/10.1016/s0010-9452(72)80026-1.

Glenn, C. & Nock, M. (2014). Improving the short-term prediction of suicidal behavior. *American Journal of Preventive Medicine, 47*(3), 176-180.

Goddard, L., Dritschel, B., & Burton, A. (1996). Role of autobiographical memory in social problem solving and depression. *Journal of Abnormal Psychology, 105*(4), 609-616. https://doi.org/10.1037//0021-843x.105.4.609.

Goldstein, S., & Naglieri, J. A. (2013). *Handbook of executive functioning.* Springer.

Gotlib, I. (1998). EEG alpha asymmetry, depression, and cognitive functioning. *Cognition & Emotion, 12*(3), 449–478.

Gotlib, I. H., Hamilton, J. P., Cooney, R. E., Singh, M. K., Henry, M. L., & Joormann, J. (2010). Neural processing of reward and loss in girls at risk for major depression. *Archives of General Psychiatry, 67*(4), 380–387. https://doi.org/10.1001/archgenpsychiatry.2010.13.

Gotlib, I. H., & Joormann, J. (2010). Cognition and depression: Current status and future directions. *Annual Review of Clinical Psychology, 6*(1), 285–312. https://doi.org/10.1146/annurev.clinpsy.121208.131305.

Graae, F., Tenke, C., Bruder, G., Rotheram, M.-J., Piacentini, J., Castro-Blanco, D., Leite, P., & Towey, J. (1996). Abnormality of EEG alpha asymmetry in female adolescent suicide attempters. *Biological Psychiatry, 40*(8), 706–713.

Gratz, K. L., & Roemer, L. (2004). Multidimensional assessment of emotion regulation and dysregulation: Development, factor structure, and initial validation of the Difficulties in Emotion Regulation Scale. *Journal of Psychopathology and Behavioral Assessment, 26*, 41-54.

Gross, J. J., & John, O. P. (2003). Individual differences in two emotion regulation processes: implications for affect, relationships and well-being. *Journal of Personality and Social Psychology, 85*, 348–362. https://doi.org/10.1037/0022-3514.85.2.348.

Harmon-Jones, E., Gable, P.A., & Peterson, C.K. (2010). The role of asymmetric frontal cortical activity in emotion-related phenomena: a review and update. *Biological Psychology, 84*(3), 451–62.

Hathaway, B. (2017, January 31). Brain circuits may reveal which young people are likely to commit suicide. *Yale News.* Retrieved from: https://news.yale.edu/2017/01/31/brain-circuits-may-reveal-which-young-peopleare-likely-commit-suicide.

Herrington, J. D., Heller, W., Mohanty, A., Engels, A. S., Banich, M. T., Webb, A. G., & Miller, G. A. (2010). Localization of asymmetric brain function in emotion and depression. *Psychophysiology, 47*(3), 442–454. https://doi.org/10.1111/j.1469-8986.2009.00958.x.

Hoffmann, M., Mothes-Lasch, M., Miltner, W., & Straube, T. (2014). Brain activation to briefly presented emotional words: Effects of stimulus awareness. *Human Brain Mapping, 36*(2), 655-665. https://doi.org/10.1002/hbm.22654.

Huntley, J. D., & Howard, R. J. (2010). Working memory in early Alzheimer's disease: A neuropsychological review. *International Journal of Geriatric Psychiatry, 25*(2), 121–132. https://doi.org/10.1002/gps.2314.

Imbir, K., & Jarymowicz, M. (2013). The effect of automatic versus reflective emotions on cognitive control in antisaccade tasks and the emotional Stroop test. *Polish Psychological Bulletin, 44* (2), 137–146.

Imbir, K. K., Jarymowicz, M. T., Spustek, T., Kuś, R., & Żygierewicz, J. (2015). Origin of emotion effects on ERP correlates of emotional word processing: The emotion duality approach. *PLOS ONE, 10* (5), e0126129. https://doi.org/10.1371/journal.pone.0126129.

Johnson, J., Gooding, P., & Tarrier, N. (2008). Suicide risk in schizophrenia: explanatory models and clinical implications, The Schematic Appraisal Model of Suicide (SAMS). *Psychology and Psychotherapy: Theory, Research and Practice, 81*(1), 55-77.

Johnson, J., Gooding, P., & Tarrier, N. (2008). Suicide risk in schizophrenia: Explanatory models and clinical implications, The Schematic Appraisal Model of Suicide (SAMS). *Psychology and Psychotherapy: Theory, Research and Practice, 81*(1), 55-77.

Johnston, J. A., Wang, F., Liu, J., Blond, B. N., Wallace, A., Liu, J., Landeros- Weisenberger, A. (2017). Multimodal neuroimaging of frontolimbic structure and function associated with suicide attempts in adolescents and young adults with Bipolar disorder. *American Journal of Psychiatry, 174*(7), 667-675. https://doi.org/10.1176/appi.ajp.2016.15050652.

Jollant, F., Bellivier, F., Leboyer, M., Astruc, B., Torres, S., Verdier, R., Castelnau, D., Malafosse, A., & Courtet, P. (2005). Impaired decision making in suicide attempters. *American Journal of Psychiatry, 162*(2), 304–310.

Jollant, F., Lawrence, N., Olié, E., Guillaume, S., & Courtet, P. (2011). The suicidal mind and brain: A review of neuropsychological and neuroimaging studies. *The World Journal of Biological Psychiatry, 12*(5), 319–339.

Jollant, F., Guillaume, S., Jaussent, I., Bellivier, F., Leboyer, M., Castelnau, D., Courtet, P. (2007). Psychiatric diagnoses and personality traits associated with disadvantageous decision-making. *European Psychiatry, 22*(7), 455-461.

Jollant, F., Lawrence, N. S., Olie, E., O'Daly, O., Malafosse, A., Courtet, P., & Phillips, M. L. (2010). Decreased activation of lateral orbitofrontal cortex during risky choices under uncertainty is associated with disadvantageous decision-making and suicidal behavior. *NeuroImage, 51*(3), 1275-1281. https://doi.org/10.1016/j.neuroimage.2010.03.027.

Jollant, F., Lawrence, N. S., Giampietro, V., Brammer, M. J., Fullana, M. A., Drapier, D., … Phillips, M. L. (2008). Orbitofrontal cortex response to angry faces in men with histories of suicide attempts. *American Journal of Psychiatry, 165*(6), 740-748. https://doi.org/10.1176/appi.ajp.2008.07081239.

Joormann, J., & Gotlib, I. H. (2010). Emotion regulation in depression: Relation to cognitive inhibition. *Cognition & Emotion, 24*(2), 281–298. https://doi.org/10.1080/02699930903407948.

Kane, R. L. (1991). Standardized and flexible batteries in neuropsychology: An assessment update. *Neuropsychology Review, 2*(4), 281-339. https://doi.org/10.1007/bf01108849.

Kaplow, J. B., Gipson, P. Y., Horwitz, A. G., Burch, B. N., & King, C. A. (2014). Emotional suppression mediates the relation between adverse life events and adolescent suicide: implications for prevention. *Prevention Science: The Official Journal of the Society for Prevention Research, 15*(2), 177–185. https://doi.org/10.1007/s11121-013-0367-9https://biblio.ugent.be/publication/361667/file/597651.pdf.

Keilp, J., Gorlyn, M., Oquendo, M., Burke, A., & Mann, J. (2008). Attention deficit in depressed suicide attempters. *Psychiatry Research, 159*(1–2), 7–17.

Keilp, J. G., Grunebaum, M. F., Gorlyn, M., LeBlanc, S., Burke, A. K., Galfalvy, H., Oquendo, M. A., & Mann, J. J. (2012). Suicidal ideation and the subjective aspects of depression. *Journal of Affective Disorders, 140*(1), 75–81.

Kemp, A., Griffiths, K., Felmingham, K., Shankman, S. A., Drinkenburg, W., Arns, M., Bryant, R. (2010). Disorder specificity despite comorbidity: Resting EEG alpha asymmetry in major depressive disorder and post-traumatic stress disorder. *Biological Psychology, 85*(2), 350-354.

Lai, M. T., & Cheung, P. S. (2016). 港大生墮亡同名同齡男生: 勿輕易放棄 [photo]. Retrieved from https://hk.news.appledaily.com/local/daily/article/20160311/19525231.

Lau, C. W. (2016, March 16). 分析: 香港為何學生自殺事件不斷. Retrieved from https://www.bbc.com/zhongwen/simp/china/2016/03/160318_ana_hong_kong_youth_suicide.

Law, K. M. (2016). 墮斃港大文學院男生 遺書「未能做得完美」 [photo]. Retrieved from https://hk.on.cc/hk/bkn/cnt/news/20160310/bkn-20160310002646786-0310_00822_001.html?eventid=402882b0533bcabd01535b747d3d6cb1&eventsection=hk_news.

Lazarus, R. S., & Folkman, S. (1984). *Stress, appraisal, and coping*. New York, NY: Springer.

Loyo, L. M. S., Martínez-Velázquez, E. S., & Ramos-Loyo, J. (2013). The influence of emotions on executive functions in suicide attempters. *Suicidology, 4*(1), 42–55.

Løvstad, M., Sigurdardottir, S., Andersson, S., Grane, V., Moberget, T., Stubberud, J., & Solbakk, A. (2016). Behaviour rating inventory of executive function adult version in patients with neurological and neuropsychiatric conditions: Symptom levels and relationship to emotional distress. *Journal of the International Neuropsychological Society, 22*(6), 682–694.

MacLeod, C. (1991). Half a century of research on the Stroop effect: An integrative review. *Psychological Bulletin, 109*(2), 163–203. https://doi.org/10.1037/0033-2909.109.2.163.

Marzuk, P. M., Hartwell, N., Leon, A. C., & Portera, L. (2005). Executive functioning in depressed patients with suicidal ideation. *Acta Psychiatrica Scandinavica, 112*(4), 294-301. https://doi.org/10.1111/j.1600-0447.2005.00585.x.

Miranda, R., Gallagher, M., Bauchner, B., Vaysman, R., & Marroquín, B. (2011). Cognitive inflexibility as a prospective predictor of suicidal ideation among young adults with a suicide attempt history. *Depression and Anxiety, 29*(3), 180–186.

Miyake, A., & Friedman, N. P. (2012). The nature and organization of individual differences in executive functions. *Current Directions in Psychological Science, 21*(1), 8–14. https://doi.org/10.1177/0963721411429458.

Nangle, J., Clarke, S., Morris, D. W., Schwaiger, S., McGhee, K., & Donohoe, G. (2006). Neurocognition and suicidal behaviour in an Irish population with major psychotic disorders. *Schizophrenia Research, 85*(1-3), 196-200. https://doi.org/10.1016/j.schres.2006.03.035.

Nock, M. K., Park, J. M., Finn, C. T., Deliberto, T. L., Dour, H. J., & Banaji, M. R. (2010). Measuring the suicidal mind: implicit cognition predicts suicidal behavior. *Psychological Science, 21*(4), 511-517. https://doi.org/10.1177/0956797610364762.

Ochsner, K. N., Silvers, J. A., & Buhle, J. T. (2012). Functional imaging studies of emotion regulation: a synthetic review and evolving model of the cognitive control of emotion. *Annals of the New York Academy of Sciences, 1251*, 1–24. https://doi.org/10.1111/j.1749-6632.2012.06751.x.

O'Connor, R. C. (2003). Suicidal behaviour as a cry of pain: Test of a psychological model. *Archives of Suicide Research, 7*(4), 297–308. https://doi.org/10.1080/713848941.

Pan, L. A., Batezati-Alves, S. C., Almeida, J. R. C., Segreti, A., Akkal, D., Hassel, S., Lakdawala, S., Brent, D. A., & Phillips, M. L. (2011). Dissociable patterns of neural activity during response inhibition in depressed adolescents with and without suicidal behaviour. *Journal of the American Academy of Child and Adolescent Psychiatry, 50* (6), 602–611.e3. https://doi.org/10.1016/j.jaac.2011.03.018.

Potter, L., Silverman, M., Connorton, E., & Posner, M. (2004). *Promoting mental health and preventing suicide in college and university settings*. Presented at the Center for Mental Health Services, Substance Abuse and Mental Health Services Administration, U.S. Department of Health and Human Services: SPRC: Suicide Prevention Resource Center. Retrieved from: http://www.sprc.org/sites/sprc.org/files/library/college_sp_whitepaper.pdf.

Pratto, F., & John, O. P. (1991). Automatic vigilance: the attention-grabbing power of negative social information. *Journal of Personality and Social Psychology, 61*(3), 380-391. https://doi.org/10.1037//0022-3514.61.3.380.

Preventing suicide: A Global imperative. (2014). *World Health Organization*. Retrieved from http://apps.who.int/iris/bitstream/handle/10665/131056/9789241564779_eng.pdf;jsessionid=969F67939D60B3E3E0C962C06CEF30E2?sequence=1.

Rajappa, K., Gallagher, M., & Miranda, R. (2011). Emotion dysregulation and vulnerability to suicidal ideation and attempts. *Cognitive Therapy and Research, 36*(6), 833–839. https://doi.org/10.1007/s10608-011-9419-2.

Rasmussen, S. A., Fraser, L., Gotz, M., MacHale, S., Mackie, R., Masterton, G., … O'Connor, R. C. (2010). Elaborating the cry of pain model of suicidality: Testing a psychological model in a sample of first-time and repeat self-harm patients. *British Journal of Clinical Psychology, 49* (1), 15–30. https://doi.org/10.1348/014466509x415735.

Reich, J. W., Newsom, J. T., & Zautra, A. J. (1996). Health downturns and predictors of suicidal ideation: an application of the Baumeister model. *Suicide and Life-Threatening Behavior*, *26*, 282-291.

Richard-Devantoy, S., Yang, D., Gustavo, T., & Fabrice, J. (2017). Attentional bias toward suicide-relevant information in suicide attempters: A cross-sectional study and a meta-analysis. *European Psychiatry, 41*(1), 101–108. https://doi.org/10.1016/j.eurpsy.2017.02.471.

Ruiz, R. (2017, November 1). How your brain responds to certain words might predict your suicide risk? *MashableAsia.* Retrieved from https://mashable.com/2017/10/31/suicide-risk-words-neuroscience/#DGysk6qN8gqY.

Saletu, B., Anderer, P., & Saletu-Zyhlarz, G. (2010). EEG topography and tomography (LORETA) in diagnosis and pharmacotherapy of depression. *Clinical EEG and Neuroscience, 41*(4), 203–210.

Schaffer, C. E., Davidson, R. V., & Saron, C. (1983). Frontal and parietal electroencephalogram asymmetry in depressed and nondepressed subjects. *Biological Psychiatry, 18*, 752–762.

Shneidman, E. S. (1984). Aphorisms of suicide and some implications for psychotherapy. *American Journal of Psychotherapy, 38*, 319–328.

Stewart, J., Silton, R., Sass, S., Fisher, J., Edgar, J., Heller, W., & Miller, G. (2010). Attentional bias to negative emotion as a function of approach and withdrawal anger styles: An ERP investigation. *International Journal of Psychophysiology, 76*(1), 9–18.

Stroop, J. R. (1935). Studies of interference in serial verbal reactions. *Journal of Experimental Psychology, 18*, 643–662. https://doi.org/10.1037/h0054651.

Sudol, K., & Mann, J. (2017). Biomarkers of suicide attempt behaviour: Towards a biological model of risk. *Current Psychiatry Reports, 19* (6). https://doi.org/10.1007/s11920-017-0781-y.

Tarrier, N., Gooding, P., Gregg, L., Johnson, J., & Drake, R. (2007). Suicide schema in schizophrenia: The effect of emotional reactivity, negative symptoms and schema elaboration. *Behaviour Research and Therapy*, *45*(9), 2090-2097. https://doi.org/10.1016/j.brat.2007.03.007.

Taylor, P., Gooding, P., Wood, A., Johnson, J., & Tarrier, N. (2011). Prospective predictors of suicidality: defeat and entrapment lead to changes in suicidal ideation over time. *Suicide and Life-Threatening Behavior*, *41*(3), 297-306. https://doi.org/10.1111/j.1943-278x.2011.00029.x.

Thibodeau, R., Jorgensen, R. S., & Kim, S. (2006). Depression, anxiety, and resting frontal EEG asymmetry: A meta-analytic review. *Journal of Abnormal Psychology, 115*(4), 715–729. https://doi.org/10.1037/0021-843x.115.4.715.

Tomarken, A. J., Davidson, R. J., Wheeler, R. E., & Kinney, L. (1992). Psychometric properties of resting anterior EEG asymmetry: Temporal stability and internal consistency. *Psychophysiology, 29*(5), 576–592. https://doi.org/10.1111/j.1469-8986.1992.tb02034.x.

Tucker, D. (1981). Lateral brain function, emotion, and conceptualization. *Psychological Bulletin, 89*(1), 19-46.

Urry, H. L., Nitschke, J. B., Dolski, I., Jackson, D. C., Dalton, K. M., Mueller, C. J., Davidson, R. J. (2004). Making a life worth living: neural correlates of wellbeing. *Psychological Science*, *15*, 367–372.

Von Hecker, U., Sedek, G., & Brzezicka, A. (2013). Impairments in mental model construction and benefits of defocused attention. *European Psychologist*, *18*(1), 35-46.

Wagner, G., Schultz, C. C., Koch, K., Schachtzabel, C., Sauer, H., & Schlösser, R. G. (2012). Prefrontal cortical thickness in depressed patients with high-risk for suicidal behavior. *Journal of Psychiatric Research*, *46*(11), 1449-1455. https://doi.org/10.1016/j.jpsychires.2012.07.013.

Willeumier, K., Taylor, D. V., & Amen, D. G. (2011). Decreased cerebral blood flow in the limbic and prefrontal cortex using SPECT imaging in a cohort of completed suicides. *Translational Psychiatry*, *1*(8), e28-e28. https://doi.org/10.1038/tp.2011.28.

Williams, J. M. G. (1997). *Cry of pain*. Penguin.

Williams, J. M. G., Barnhofer, T., Crane, C., & Beck, A. T. (2005). Problem solving deteriorates following mood challenge in formerly depressed patients with a history of suicidal ideation. *Journal of Abnormal Psychology, 114*, 421–431.

Williams, J. M., Ellis, N. C., Tyers, C., Healy, H., Rose, G., & Macleod, A. K. (1996a). The specificity of autobiographical memory and imageability of the future. *Memory & Cognition, 24*(1), 116–125. https://doi.org/10.3758/bf03197278.

Williams, J. M., Mathews, A., & MacLeod, C. (1996b). The emotional Stroop task and psychopathology. *Psychological Bulletin, 120*(1), 3–24. https://doi.org/10.1037/0033-2909.120.1.3.

Williams, J. M. G., & Pollock, L. (2001). Psychological aspects of the suicidal process. *Understanding suicidal behaviour: The suicidal process approach to research, treatment and prevention* (pp. 76–94). John Wiley.

Yazhou Zhoukan. (2012). 香港科大新生跳樓死 半年第三宗自殺案 (p. 26). Retrieved from https://www.yzzk.com/cfm/content_archive.cfm?id=1363610650665&docissue=2012-46.

Chapter 3
Existing Suicide Prevention Programmes and Assessments in Hong Kong

Suicide prevention efforts require coordination and collaboration among multiple sectors of society, both public and private, including health and non-health sectors such as education, labor, agriculture, business, justice, law, defense, politics, and the media ("Preventing suicide," 2014). These efforts must be comprehensive, integrated, and synergistic, as no single approach alone can impact a complex issue such as suicide. For this reason, many suicide research units have been set up and also there are academic courses that focus on suicide prevention. To provide practical help, non-specialized health professionals are being used to improve the assessment of suicidal behaviours, for example, self-help groups of bereaved families have been established in many places, and trained volunteers are helping with online and telephone counseling (Education Bureau, 2018). Typical national strategies in HK comprise a range of prevention strategies such as surveillance, means restriction, media guidelines, stigma reduction, raising public awareness, and training for health workers, educators, police, and other gatekeepers. They also usually include crisis intervention services and postvention. For example, they can improve response to and care for those affected by suicide and suicide attempts. Provide supportive and rehabilitative services to persons affected by suicide attempts.

For suicide prevention to be effective, there should be objectives designed to
Source from ("Preventing suicide," 2014)

- enhance surveillance and research;
- identify and target vulnerable groups;
- improve the assessment of suicidal behaviour;
- promote environmental and individual protective factors;
- increase awareness through public education;
- improve societal attitudes and beliefs and eliminate stigma towards people with exhibit suicidal thoughts and behaviours;

E. Ong, *Early Identification and Intervention of Suicide Risk in Chinese Young Adults*,
https://doi.org/10.1007/978-981-16-7641-3_3

- reduce access to means of suicide;
- encourage the media to adopt better policies and ethical practices toward reporting suicide
- support individuals bereaved by suicide.

3.1 Structure of Suicide Prevention Programs: The 3-Tier Support Model from (Education Bureau, 2018)

In 2014 WHO has composed the 3-tier support model to target different types of students in need of suicide prevention service and how to reduce suicide risk (Fig. 3.1)

Interventions

Currently, the evidence-based interventions for suicide prevention in Hong Kong are organized in a theoretical framework adapted from the *3-Tier Support Model* by the WHO ("Preventing suicide," 2014). The types of interventions are categorized into three categories: ***Universal, Selected,*** **and** ***Indicated prevention***.

"**Universal**" prevention strategies target to reach the entire population to maximize access to health care, promote mental health, reduce the harmful use of alcohol, limit access to the means for suicide or promote responsible media reporting. It also aims to strengthen social support and alter the environment, which may serve as protective factors against suicide. "**Selective**" prevention strategies are designed

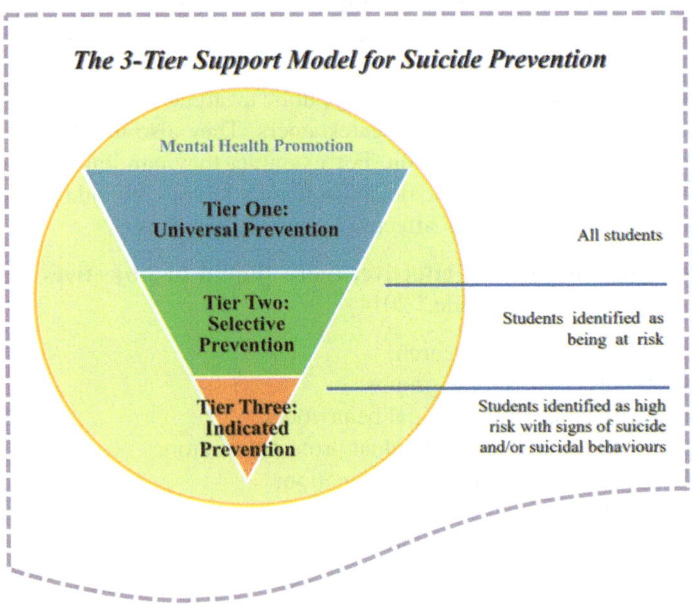

Fig. 3.1 Adapted from World Health Organization (2014). Preventing suicide: A global imperative

more specifically for the vulnerable groups within a population based on characteristics such as age, sex, occupation, or family history. This may include individuals suffering or have suffered from trauma or abuse, family conflict or disaster, refugees and migrants, and bereaved by suicide. These people are identified as targets because while they may not currently express suicidal behaviours at this moment, they may be at an elevated level of biological, psychological, or socioeconomic risk. Therefore training "gatekeepers" could assist the vulnerable and offer helping services. "**Indicated**" prevention strategies target specific vulnerable individuals within the population. They are the group who often shown early signs of suicide potential or who have made a suicide attempt ("Preventing suicide," 2014).

Given the multiple factors involved and the many pathways that lead to suicidal behaviour, suicide prevention efforts require a broad multi-sectoral approach that addresses the various population and risk groups and contexts throughout the life course. Figure 3.2 listed out some of the common risk factors and then shows how they align with the three groups. It should be noted that these linkages are not finite, but are rather context-driven. In relation to the list of risk factors identified by WHO (2018, p. 20), strategies to counter these risk factors are grouped into three groups as in Fig. 3.2. These may include community support, follow-up for those leaving healthcare facilities, education and training for health workers, and improved identification and management of mental and substance use disorders ("Preventing suicide," 2014). Prevention can also be strengthened by encouraging protective factors such as strong personal relationships, a personal belief system, and positive coping strategies.

3.2 Universal Strategy

3.2.1 Restricting the Means for Suicide

Suicides are preventable causes of death and an effective strategy for preventing suicides and suicide attempts is to restrict access to the most common means (Yip et al., 2012). These include restricted access to pesticides, firearms, and certain medications. Indeed, the CSRP has run several pioneer programmes for suicide prevention in HK, and its impact has been widely recognized. From 2003 to 2012, these multi-pronged population-based suicide prevention programmes have successfully contributed to HK's suicide rate reduction of 32%. These include research, education, and training as well as means restriction, which aims to empower and educate the community to prevent suicide. It has successfully transformed the university's knowledge, through advocacy, into concrete changes in society, such as speeding up the installation of platform doors by MTR Corporation and the practice adopted by supermarkets of putting warning labels on charcoal packs and removing charcoal from open selves. The programme also contributes to enhancing the mental wellness of disadvantaged groups and school children. It reaches out to disconnected

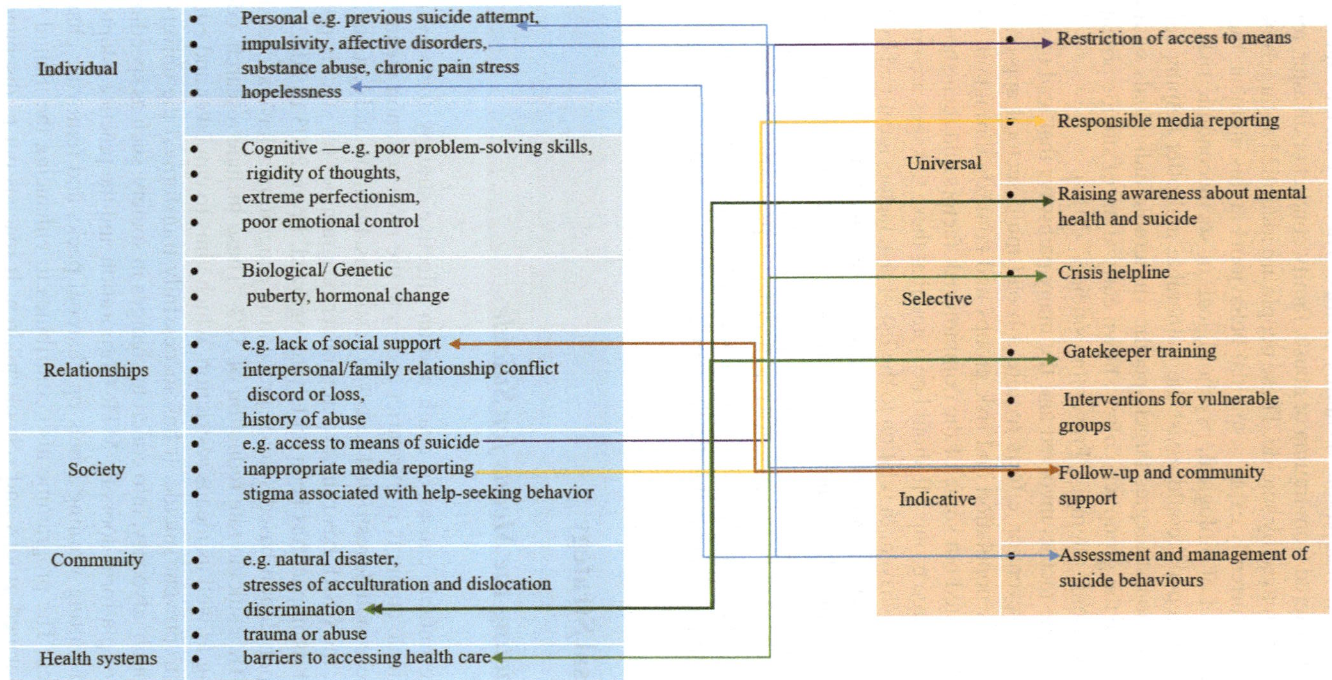

Fig. 3.2 How risk factors for suicide aligned with the current *interventions,* Lines reflect the relative importance of interventions at different levels for different areas of risk factors from ("Preventing suicide," 2014)

Fig. 3.3 Installation of platform doors by MTR Corporation

youth through social media and dedicated websites. Through its outstanding accomplishment in community engagement, the Centre has been identified as a local and regional knowledge hub in suicide research and prevention (Fig. 3.3).

Empirical studies reported that many suicide cases happened at the critical time when the attempters were going through intense impulsiveness, especially in Asia, therefore, restriction of access to lethal means of conducting suicide is typically effective for the impulsive types. In 2002, The Hong Kong Mass Transit Railway (MTR) Corporation have built glass screen doors along the entire platform to separate the platform from the railway in order to prevent intentional and accidental falling onto the railway tracks (Law et al., 2009). Following the installation of screen doors the suicide incidents by jumping onto the railway tracks has significantly reduced from 38 cases between 1997 and 2001 to 7 cases between 2003 and 2007. With such success in prevention, similar practices have also been adopted in high-rise shopping malls.

Aside from the installation of barriers, Yip et al. (2010) have also conducted comparative studies in limiting access to charcoal bags in supermarkets, one of the most popular methods of suicide. By enlisting the help of all supermarkets where charcoal packs were removed from the open shelves of major retail outlets, the numbers of suicide cases were compared longitudinally for one year across two districts, Tuen Mun and Yuen Long, where charcoal used to be sold openly. From June 2006 to July 2007, the rates of charcoal burning suicides fell sharply in Tuen Mun, by 53.8%, but similar results were not seen in Yuen Long. These results were compared with the overall drop in HK's suicide rate during the same period, which was 5.7%. The results demonstrated the effectiveness of means restriction as a suicide prevention strategy and were reported in major local and international newspapers

Fig. 3.4 Images from http://www.mindmap.hk/restriction/control-charcoal-sales-and-save-lives/

and published in the British Journal of Psychiatry and Lancet. They concluded that removing the charcoal packs from the shelves in grocery stores was a simple but effective way of suicide prevention. By making customers ask shop assistants for charcoal, a barrier to access was created. The tactic of limiting easy access to charcoal made the potential suicide attempters think twice. After its implementation, within the intervention region, the suicide rate by charcoal burning was significantly reduced by 66.7% within 12 months (Cheng et al., 2014). It was concluded that the exercise of access limitation can significantly hinder individuals from imminent impulsive suicides (Fig. 3.4).

3.3 Universal Strategy

3.3.1 Responsible Media Reporting

There are many misconceptions about suicide, and the media can play a role in dispelling various myths (see Fig. 3.5 for the most common myths about suicide). According to the Department of Mental Health and Substance Abuse World Health Organization (2008), the factors that lead an individual to suicide are usually multiple and complex, and should not be reported in a simplistic way. Media professionals recognize the importance of language in conveying nuanced meanings. The language which conveys that suicide is a significant public health problem will serve to educate the community. Such language should not sensationalize suicide. Terms like 'increasing rates' should be used in preference to hyperbolic phrases like 'suicide epidemic', and caution should be exercised in using the word 'suicide' in headlines. The language that misinforms the public about suicide or normalizes it should be avoided (Au et al., 2004). Out-of-context use of the word 'suicide'—e.g., 'political suicide'—may serve to desensitize the community to its gravity. Terms like

Myth 1
Students who talk about suicide do not mean to do it and they just want to seek attention.

Fact 1
Talking about suicide can be a plea for help and it can be the final warning in the progression towards a suicide attempt. We must seriously take every precaution when our students talk about suicidal ideation, intent or plan.

Myth 2
People who have attempted suicide once seldom make a second attempt.

Fact 2
Past suicide attempts are a major risk factor for suicide death. Up to 50% of individuals who die by suicide have made at least one previous attempt (Chehil & Kutcher, 2012). All suicide attempts must be treated as though the individual has the intent to die. Do not dismiss a suicide attempt as simply being an act to gain attention. This is why it is very important to provide continuous support for individuals with a history of suicide attempts.

Myth 3
Most suicides happen suddenly without warning.

Fact 3
In Hong Kong, about 74% of children aged below 18 who conducted suicide had expressed their suicidal thoughts implicitly or explicitly before actual attempts (Child Fatality Review Panel, 2015). Thus, it is important for us to know the warning signs of suicidal behaviours so that we can develop a higher level of sensitivity towards students at risk.

Myth 4
A marked and sudden improvement in the mental state following a crisis indicates the suicide risk is over.

Fact 4
In the three months following an attempt, a student is still at the highest risk of completing suicide. A sudden improvement could only mean an apparent lifting of the problems, that is, the person has decided to conduct suicide and feels relieved because of this decision. It is of great importance to provide intensive support continuously and monitor the student closely following a crisis.

Myth 5
Suicide is always hereditary.

Fact 5
Suicide involves complex interaction between an individual's risk factors and protective factors. Genetics may relate to one's predisposition to psychiatric illness, which is a risk factor for suicidal behaviour. Family history of suicide is also a high risk factor for suicidal behaviour. Members of family share the same emotional environment and the completed suicide of one family member may well give other family members a message that suicide is an option for solving problems.

Myth 6
Children do not conduct suicide since they do not understand the consequence of death and are cognitively incapable of engaging in a suicidal act

Fact 6
Although rare, children do conduct suicide; and hence, any suicidal gesture, at any age, should be taken seriously. They may have a distorted perception of their actual life situation and the solutions available for them to cope with the difficulties they are facing. They may perceive suicide as a means to make people feel sorry, to show how much they love someone, to escape from a stressful situation, etc.

Fig. 3.5 Common myths and facts about suicide from (resource handbook for school, 2017, p. 8) 'unsuccessful suicide' imply that death is a desirable outcome and should not be used; alternative phrases such as 'non-fatal suicide attempt' are more accurate and less open to misinterpretation. The phrase 'conducted suicide' should not be used because it implies criminality, thereby contributing to the stigma experienced by those who have lost a loved one to suicide and discouraging suicidal individuals from seeking help. Rather, one should refer to 'completed suicide'. Suicide remains a criminal offense in some countries around the world.

Media reporting has been consistently shown to impact suicidal behaviour of individuals. For example, suicide incidents described in much detail in social media have been associated with a risen number of imitated suicide cases especially young adults who may be more vulnerable to engaging in imitative suicidal behaviours. Therefore, WHO (2008) has made recommendations on how to publicize responsible media reports that could serve as educational material for the public, supporting those at risk and helping to reduce suicide rates. In relation to this, much research had been done in an attempt to understand the phenomena of contagious or imitative suicide acts. It was repeatedly found that media reporting of suicide has an important role in this (e.g., Gould et al., 2014; Niederkrotenthaler et al., 2010). Specifically, the magnitude of the rise in suicides following a suicide incident was found to be proportional to the amount, duration, and prominence of media coverage (Gould et al., 2003). Dramatic headlines and more prominently placed suicide stories in the newspapers were associated with more significant increases in subsequent suicide rates (Gould & Lake, 2013).

According to the Final Report by the Committee on Prevention of Student Suicides. (2016), apart from the amount and prominence of news coverage, Gould and Lake (2013) found that national suicide rates were higher in countries where media attitudes on suicide portraits a more accepting perspective or that suicidal behaviour was glamorized and romanticized in the news. On the contrary, suicide rates were lower in countries where media report portraits negative consequences of suicide and portrayed the suicide victims and their acts in terms of psychopathology and abnormality. Similar patterns were observed in local research conducted by the CSRP that suicide spates often coincided with extensive and sensational media coverage. Based on the data recently collected by the CSRP from January 2015 to June 2016, there existed an association between the amount of media reporting of student suicide and the number of a student suicide death. Specifically, media reporting was most extensive and prominent in March 2016 with the occurrence of student suicide spate. With concerted effort to alert the media, a salient reduction of substantial or sensational media reporting had been noticed, which corresponded with a drastic decrease in student completed suicide. A 75% drop from 18 cases from January to April 2016 to 4 cases in May to August 2016 was reported by the Committee on Prevention of Student Suicides. Despite that, local media had been noted to report younger suicides more extensively whilst under-representing late-life suicides (Fu et al., 2011), it was thus a matter of concern that such misrepresentation and disproportionate news coverage could trigger imitative suicidal behaviour of the youth who were especially vulnerable to the copycat effect (Final report by Conductee on Prevention of Student Suicides, 2016). It was also worth noting that oversimplifying the causes of suicide, i.e. attributing suicide to a particular cause, could lead vulnerable individuals to accept that suicide was a way to solve their problems. However, local research on suicide news reporting indicated that account of risk factors in newspapers was often inaccurate (Cheng & Yip, 2012). In sum, media takes on an important role in minimizing harm and the risk of suicide contagion by responsibly reporting suicides, educating the public about risks for suicide, and shaping attitudes towards positive coping strategies (Gould, 2001; WHO, 2000)

WHO media reporting recommendations for suicide news include from (Chu et al., 2018):

- Acknowledge the link between suicide and mental disorders like depression;
- Discuss possible impacts on survivors and victim's families in terms of psychological suffering and stigma;
- Avoid language that sensationalizes or normalizes suicide;
- Avoid presenting suicide as a solution to problems;
- Avoid prominent placement like the front page, boxes, or similar;
- Avoid undue repetition of stories about suicide;
- Avoid explicit description of the method;
- Avoid labeling any sites as hot spots for suicide;
- Word headlines carefully;
- Avoid photographs or video footage of the deceased, the means, or the scenes;
- Show due consideration for people bereaved by suicide and respect their privacy;
- Provide information about where to seek help.

Avoid prominent placement and undue repetition of stories about suicide

Prominent placement and undue repetition of stories about suicide are likely to generate imitative behaviours than more subtle presentations. Therefore rather than placing suicide stories on the front page or at the top of an inside page, any newspaper reports should ideally be located on the inside pages and towards the bottom of the page Department of Mental Health and Substance Abuse World Health Organization (2008). Similarly, broadcast stories about suicide should be presented in the second or third break of television news, and further down the order of radio reports, rather than as the lead item. These stories should not be overly repeated or updated as these may elicit more suicidal behaviours, and caution should be exercised in this regard.

Avoid explicit description of the method used in a completed or attempted suicide

When reporting suicide incidents, a detailed discussion of the method used in a given completed or attempted suicide should be avoided. Any details may be used as a step-by-step description for vulnerable individuals to imitate the act (Department of Mental Health & Substance Abuse World Health Organization, 2008). For example, in reporting a suicide by drug overdose, the detail in terms of the nature, quantity, or combination of drugs taken, or how they were procured should never be disclosed. Particular caution should be exercised when the method of suicide is unusual. While this may appear to make the death more newsworthy, reporting the method may prompt other people to use this means. One classical example of a contagious suicide act was the reporting of the suicide case by using charcoal burning. In October 1998, a 38-year-old woman in Hong Kong conducted suicide by burning barbecue charcoal in a small, sealed bedroom to create a carbon monoxide chamber. The media vividly portrayed this method for killing oneself as a painless and non-violent way to end one's life. At that time, the media portrayal of charcoal-burning suicides has not adhered strictly to WHO's guidelines on presenting suicide news, the innovative method of suicide attempt was described in great detail. Moreover, the newspaper reports have conveyed an implicit message that charcoal-burning is an easy, painless, and effective means of ending one's life, especially in the face of business failure or insurmountable debts' (Au et al., 2004). As a result, this method of suicide has rapidly developed into an alarming regional trend. Since 2000, they have had more and more people dying of charcoal burning and they have never seen that before. It has only happened since the case in Hong Kong.'

Capture passage of the news

"When Jessica Choi Yuk-Chun sealed the windows and doors of her bedroom, lit charcoal in a barbecue grill and then lay down to die in her village house in Sheung Shui in November 1998, she cannot have imagined the appalling repercussions of her lonely death"

Following the 'popularity' of using charcoal as a means for suicide, in 2014, the CSRP observed increasing popularity of suicide using gas among teenagers in Hong Kong. This retells how the method of suicide has been wrongly promoted by using charcoal-burning, which used to be rare, has become one of the most common methods of suicide in just a few years (Who cares wins, 2017). For the media, many newspaper offices have learned from the previous lessons and are now willing to adapt to the recommendations of removing details describing the method of suicide involving gas. For online media, major search engines and social media platforms also agreed to delete information and messages that promote suicide, provide local hotline suicide prevention hotline to those who search for suicide using gas, and encourage them to seek help (Fig. 3.6).

Avoid providing detailed information about the site of a completed or attempted suicide

Sometimes a location to carry out the suicide act may build a reputation for becoming a 'suicide Hot Spot'—e.g., a bridge, a tall building, a cliff, or the MTR platform where suicide attempts have consistently occurred. In this case, more attention should be taken to media reporting to avoid over-promoting such locations as suicide Hot Spot. For example, reporters should avoid using sensationalist language to describe these places or avoid overplaying the number of incidents (Fig. 3.7).

Word headlines carefully

Headlines are designed to attract the reader's attention by giving the essence of the story in as few words as possible. However, the word 'suicide' should be avoided in the headline together with avoidance in explicit reference to the method or site of

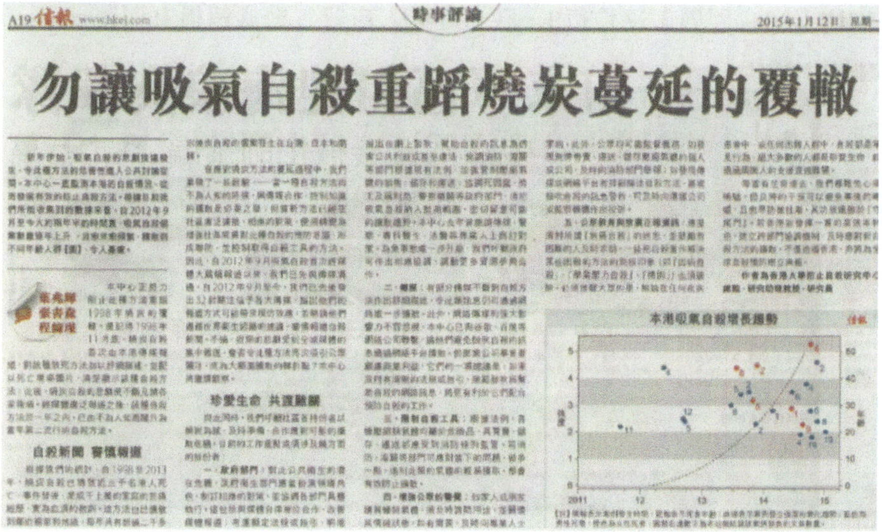
A19 信報 www.hkej.com 時事評論 2015年1月12日

勿讓吸氣自殺重蹈燒炭蔓延的覆轍

自殺新聞 警惕報道

珍愛生命 共建關懷

本港吸氣自殺增長趨勢

Fig. 3.6 Images copied from (Who cares wins, 2017), 葉兆輝, 張書森, 程綺瑾 (2015 年1月12日) 。勿讓吸氣自殺重蹈燒炭蔓延的覆轍。信報。來源: http://www1.hkej.com/dailynews/commentary/article/969136/勿讓吸氣自殺重蹈燒炭蔓延的覆轍

Fig. 3.7 Image from (Oriental daily, 2016)

Fig. 3.8 Picture from Lui and Leung (2017)

the suicide. Exercise caution in using photographs or video footage should also be noted (Department of Mental Health & Substance Abuse World Health Organization, 2008) (Fig. 3.8).

Avoid photographs or video footage of the scene of a given suicide

It is particularly important not to state the location or method too clearly to the reader or viewer in social media. If visual images are used, explicit permission must be given by family members. In addition, pictures of an individual who has died by suicide should not be used. These images should not be prominently placed and should not glamorize the individual. Also, suicide notes should not be published (see Fig. 3.9 for the inappropriate reporting in the South morning post) (Fig. 3.10).

Show due consideration for people bereaved by suicide

Individuals who have experienced the death from the suicide of a loved one are vulnerable and are working through grief and related issues. Therefore, extra caution should be taken when interviewing someone who has been bereaved by suicide because these people may be at heightened risk of suicide themselves. Their privacy should be respected at all times.

Provide information about where to seek help

Very often in news reporting suicide, there is Information about the options for seeking help. These are usually specific help sources but might sometimes include general physicians, other health professionals, and community resources, and telephone helpline services. Listing available help sources will provide immediate

Fears for Hong Kong students after fifth suicide at Chinese University since start of academic year

PUBLISHED : Sunday, 06 March, 2016, 12:51am
UPDATED : Monday, 14 March, 2016, 12:05pm

COMMENTS: 21

A third-year Chinese University medical student took her own life yesterday – the fifth suicide at the Sha Tin institution in the six months since the start of the academic year.

Fig. 3.9 Retrieved from the press (*South China Morning Post, 2016*)

avenues of support for individuals who are distressed or prompted to consider self-harm due to the story (Figs. 3.11 and 3.12; Table 3.1).

In an interview with Mr. Tsang (2018), the executive director of the Samaritan Befrienders association, he commented that the young people of this generation had lost the sense of trust with others. They often like to turn to social media to express their feelings rather than speaking directly to someone they know. This may be a problem because a growing number of internet sites have been shown to provide in-depth guidance on suicide methods, smoothen suicide pacts, give overt accounts of celebrity cases of suicides, and illustrate graphic images of people who have passed away from suicide. On top of that, fictional depictions of suicide on the big and small screen and stage may affect the public's perspectives of suicidal behaviours. It is out of the scope of this resource to address those responsible for the content of websites, films, television soap operas, or stage plays which are areas warranting further attention. Yet, this resource may be of good use for other forms of media as well.

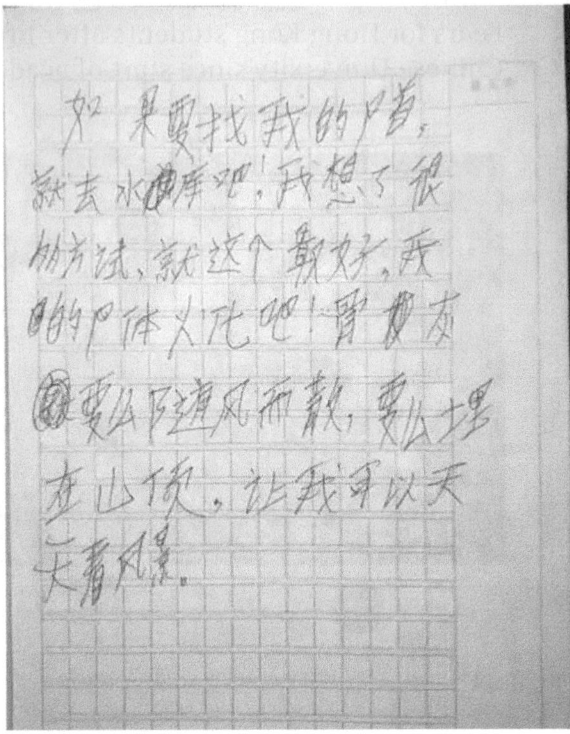
如果要找我的尸首，
就去水库吧！我想了很
多方法，就这个最好，我
的尸体火化吧！骨灰
要么随风而散，要么埋
在山顶，让我可以天
天看风景。

Fig. 3.10 Showing published suicide note left by the boy before suicide on South morning post from (Li, 2016)

3.4 Universal Strategy

3.4.1 Raising Awareness About Mental Health via the Use of Social Media

Along with the rising use of social media in youth, it is suggested that message delivered through this medium is the most effective means of communication among young people. As mentioned earlier, it was indicated that adolescents prefer to express their emotional distress and suicidal thoughts through social media sites (CSRP newsletter, 2016). Therefore, utilizing the internet as an online platform, such as instant online chat rooms, can help identify those who are currently suffering from emotional distress, thus reaching out to those who find it difficult to express their feelings. To achieve these aims, suicide prevention programmes have collaborated with Facebook, the Hong Kong Youth Federation Groups, The Samaritans and Save the Children Hong Kong to work closely with Initium Media in order to establish a website supporting HK students. Specifically, the Samaritans are well established in offering services for young people in both HK and other countries worldwide, the 9th Young Samaritans Peer Support Programme (YSPSP) is set up in HK that is centered around group enhancement. This collaboration aims to promote good

Left top: 2016 年 3 月 5 日，22 歲中大醫學院女生，疑因學業問題在粉嶺寓所墮樓身亡
Right top: 2015 年 12 月 15 日，22 歲中大男生突由西環寓所墮樓亡。

(a) (b)

(c) (d)

Left bottom: 2016 年 1 月 20 日，21 歲中大城市研究課程女生，疑因學業及情緒問題在沙田校園墮樓亡。
Right bottom: 2015 年 11 月 19 日，18 歲中大英文系女生，疑因學業壓力情緒受困，在香港仔寓所墮樓亡。

Fig. 3.11 **a**, **b**, **c**, **d**, Copy from *本學年20宗學生自殺 大學生佔8宗* [photograph]. (2016). Retrieved from (on.cc, 2016). 2015年11月4日, 21歲樹大輔導及心理學系女生, 疑因學業及情緒問題, 在筲箕灣墮樓亡。2015年11月3日, 21歲理大電子及資訊工程學系男生, 疑因家事問題在沙田寓所墮樓亡。2015年9月7日, 21歲中大教育文憑男生, 疑憂慮學業問題, 在慈雲山寓所墮斃。

practices of social media engagement with vulnerable youth. It was also proposed that raising awareness in the school population can help reduce inappropriate use of communication platforms of information technology (I.T.), e.g., cyberstalking and cyberbullying. Students can act as gatekeepers to stop and report these undesirable behaviours.

Collaboration with social media is therefore deemed favorable for mental health promotion, gatekeeper training, provision of counseling services, and development of suicide prevention tools. Nevertheless, social media platforms should be more frequently used in schools to raise awareness about mental health among students. Since 2006, CSRP has been implemented a school-based mental health enhancement program, "The Little Prince is Depressed", for secondary school

Fig. 3.12 With the development of social media and online forums, more and more young people choose to vent their emotions online. Photo from (Lau, 2016)

Table 3.1 Summarizing the number of online media outlets and social network service (SNS) providers who acted in response to CSRP letter of concern (Who cares wins, 2017)

Media outlets and SNS	Actions after receiving CSRP letter of concern	Potential effect size (no. of viewers from unique IP addresses on average)
Apple Daily	• Removed problematic animation news from their official website • Display local suicide prevention hotlines when people search suicide-related keywords in Hong Kong, Taiwan, and mainland China	1,666,860 every day
Google	• Removed a blog that contained detailed instructions on suicide	1.17 billion every month
Baidu	• Removed a website archive that contained detailed instructions on suicide using gas from their search results • Removed topics relating to suicide using gas from their forums • Display local suicide prevention hotlines when people search suicide-related keywords in mainland China	64,475,433 every day
YouTube	Removed problematic animation news about suicide using gas	Billions every day

Fig. 3.13 "The Little Prince is Depressed" and "The Adventures of DoReMiFa" (DoReMiFa 歷險記, n.d.)

students (see Fig. 3.13). This programme aims to enhance students understanding in managing stress and depression, identify thinking errors, improve anger management and communication skills. Following the program, a web-based mental health programme called "Professor Gooley & the Flame of Mind" was launched in 2012 for HK secondary school students and parents. For the younger student population, a similar mental health promotion programme named "The Adventures of DoReMiFa" (DoReMiFa 歷險記, n.d.) was similarly launched. This programme targets primary school students and aims to enhance student's understanding of emotional health, thus strengthening their social problem-solving skills and communication skills.

In 2017, the CSRP has collaborated with Youtuber (e.g. Aumen produced a short film called "The Last Day" in Fig. 3.14) to encourage teenagers and young adults to seek help in a desperate situation. The film features a message to say goodbye to someone on 'the last day' of bitterness and welcome a brand-new day with hope (Who cares wins, 2017). After first releasing the film on social media platforms (YouTube and Facebook on May 4, 2017), the number of views for this film has shot up to 98,000 within 1 month and many positive comments were received in June 2017 (see Table 3.2). The online survey also received 108 responses in total. Notably more than half of the respondents were adolescents under 25 years old. Based on the

(a) (b)

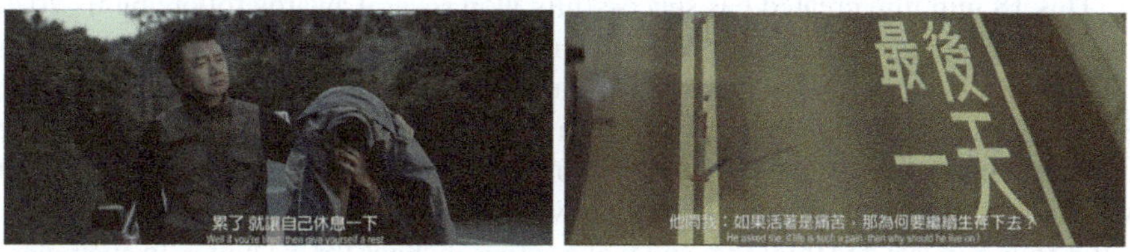

Fig. 3.14 The short film called "The Last Day", Image taken fromhttps://www.youtube.com/user/csrphku

Table 3.2 Questions extracted from the survey regarding perception of the film "The Last Day"

Questions in the survey	Percentage of respondents choosing 'agree' or 'strongly agree' (%)
1. Raise my awareness of suicide prevention	83.0
2. Enhance my understanding of people with suicidal thoughts	85.8
3. Allow me to pay more attention to people around me showing any signs of suicide	75.9
4. Allow me to be more accepting towards people with suicidal tendencies and mental health issues	88.7
5. Encourage me to share my thoughts and feelings with others or to seek help more willingly when emotionally distressed or suicidal	75.2
6. Encourage me to actively seek help from professionals or community service organizations more	61.0
7. Encourage me to accept help from others more willingly when emotionally distressed or suicidal	74.3
8. Allow me to know more about mental health and suicide prevention	83.2

Adopted from (Who cares wins, 2017)

survey response, it was alarming to note that nearly half of the respondents indicated that they have had suicidal thoughts in the past 12 months. Regardless of having suicidal thoughts or not, the majority of respondents agreed the film raised their awareness of help-seeking and improved their attitudes towards suicide prevention.

Back in the old days, educational films or TV programmes do not attract much attraction to the audience, most were developed by the Educational Bureau in HK without much passion. However, this situation has changed in recent years whereby education and destigmatization programmes such as 'StoryTaler' are more often used to story sharing of people's mental health challenges. One recent and successful example is a film produced named 'Daffodil' (Fig. 3.15c), which was created by Nicola Fan and her team.

This 18 min film created has successfully won several awards following its 2020 release including the best short film cinematography at the 2019 European Cinematography Awards, and was in the official selection for the 2020 Vancouver Asian Film Festival. The film centered around a young woman's internal struggle as she comes to terms with the suicide of her estranged mother. The director Fan said that she wanted to use the story to express how loss forces us to realize what we have, retune our mindset and thinking, and make active changes for the better. In awareness of the stigmatization of mental health issues, Fan hopes her film will influence others to become more open-minded in having honest conversations. In fact, she said that

Fig. 3.15 An image of the film 'Daffodil' taken from https://www.scmp.com/lifestyle/health-wellness/article/3140446/mental-health-movie-indieflix-about-womans-struggle-cope

immediately after private screenings of the film, audience members came up to her privately and shared very personal stories "I see the film as a great medium to dive into topics that are often too hard or too awkward to start with friends," she says. "It's easier than to talk about how to make changes and move on from there." She says that as a university student, she did her best to support her friend who lost his mother, but now that she's older, she has learned to be less intimidated about starting a conversation about mental health.

Some responses after watching the film include (adopted from Who cares wins, 2017):

> The film mentioned that many suicidal people felt they did not belong to this world, nor the world needed them. I have experienced all these personally, and I am glad that I made it through with the support from my family. Without them, I may have already pushed myself into a dead-end.
>
> There aren't many local films on this topic. I really appreciate the producer's hard work and sincerity. The narrator can engage the audience, and the production team did a wonderful job in casting.
>
> Able to portray the suicidal thoughts and feelings.
>
> I would personally recommend this to school teachers as teaching material. Thank you very much for the hard work. It is difficult to put my appreciation of this video into words. A good piece should be made known to the public. Nice script and great actors!

The CSRP organizes the "WeCare" website to provide extensive information such as risk factors, protective factors, warning signs, statistics, intervention suggestions about suicide to the general public. The name of this website implies that CSRP cares about the community and, at the same time, urges members of the community to care for others, as suicide prevention requires the participation of everyone in our society. The WeCare website offers ways of preventing suicide and follow-up suggestions; thus providing interactive online inquiry service. The CSRP also collaborated with Facebook and implemented various mental health educational programmes to develop students' positive attitudes and values. They have released a booklet called

Fig. 3.16 "I'm Here to Support!" booklet and Relaxing dashboard for DSE students from. Sources from (CSRP newsletter, 2016)

"I'm Here to Support!" (「有困難, 我撐你!」) which outlines some suicide prevention tips. With social media such as Facebook, the underlying theme "Connect" is promoted to students. It carries the aim which is to connect everyone in Hong Kong's society and encourage them to cherish life and always have faith that the best is yet to come.

Besides raising public awareness and equipping the community with crucial knowledge on suicide prevention, the booklet provides information on the warning signs of suicide and the necessary skills needed when communicating with suicide individuals. To address students going through DSE exams who may be incredibly distressing and depressing, the CSRP collaborates with Initium Media to establish a dashboard to support students who have just received their DSE results [see Fig. 3.16 from CSRP newsletter (2016)]. The dashboard is developed with the aims to enhance the mental well-being of students, and to raise public awareness on mental well-being and suicide prevention. It provides a platform for students to relieve stress and feel relax through several mini-games and breathing exercises. The site also featured a video with encouraging messages by various famous artists and graphics from well-known illustrators (CSRP newsletter, 2016).

3.5 Selected Strategy

3.5.1 Crisis Helplines

Crisis helplines are public call centers that are available to anyone who may not prefer social support or professional care through other means. Compared to face-to-face talk, helplines are useful to a wider population or target certain vulnerable groups. In HK helplines are considered to be effective in engaging seriously suicidal individuals and in reducing suicide risk among callers during the call session and subsequent weeks. In other countries like Belgium, phone and crisis helpline services have been shown to be cost-effective strategies for suicide prevention. One of the most well-known Samaritans offers services in person or via the phone on an individual basis that provides a one-to-one opportunity to express a concern. By talking and active listening, the service aims to let individuals find solutions for their problems, which is consistent with an individualist view. Although helplines provide a quick, practical, and widely implemented way to help reduces suicide risk, the lack of evaluation from these conversations means that it remains inconclusive in terms of its effectiveness in reducing suicide rates ("Preventing suicide," 2014).

- **The Samaritans** 香港撒瑪利亞防止自殺會 (www.samaritans.org.hk) is a 24 h hotline for people who are in emotional distress and want to talk to someone. Calls are confidential and can be made in English, Cantonese or Mandarin. The multi-Lingual Suicide Prevention Hotline: 2896 0000 or 2389 2222. There is also **The Samaritan Befrienders Hong Kong** (http://www.sbhk.org.hk/hotline_service.php?lang=en)
- **Suicide Prevention Services** 生命熱線 (www.sps.org.hk) provides a 24 h hotline and a Youth Link number. They promote "Caring, Listening, Acceptance and Companionship": 2382 0000 (青少年生命專線 Youth Link: 2382 0777)
- **Caritas Family Crisis Support Centre** 明愛向晴軒 (http://fcsc.caritas.org.hk) is a 24 h hotline that provides immediate counseling support to those going through a crisis: 18,288
- **24 h Hospital Authority Psychiatric Hotline** 醫管局精神健康專線 (http://ipep.hk/en/community_resources/HA-24-7-hotline) is a psychiatric hotline that allows people to get in touch with medical staff through the Hospital Authority hotline: 2466 7350
- **Tung Wah Group of Hospitals CEASE Crisis Centre** 東華三院芷若園 (http://ceasecrisis.tungwahcsd.org/intro.html) Persons in need are encouraged to call their Crisis Centre hotline which is manned by registered social workers: 18,281
- **Breakthrough** 突破機構 (https://www.breakthrough.org.hk/contact.xhtml) is a non-profit making organization providing cultural and educational services for young people: 2632 0000
- Hotline Service by the **Social Welfare Department** 社會福利署熱線服務 (https://www.swd.gov.hk/tc/index/site_pubsvc/page_family/sub_listofserv/id_department/) provide counseling, support, and advice and arrange appropriate follow up services for those in need: 2343 2255
- **Hong Kong Federation of Youth groups** 香港青年協會 (青協) provides 'Youth-line' hotline for children and youth aged 6 to 24 (http://mcc.hkfyg.org.hk/page.aspx?corpname=mcc&i=6445)

  and also 'uTouch Online Outreach' Counselling Service' that provides online counseling via http://www.utouch.hk/27778899
- **HKJC Centre for Suicide Research** and Prevention's page: www.depression.edu.hk

- **The Mental Health Association of Hong Kong** provides an online counseling service via mobile Apps called 'Counseline'. The service operates Monday to Friday 2:00 p.m.–10:00 p.m. (http://www.mhahk.org.hk/chi/sub2_1_service_1_4.htm)
- **The Boys' and Girls' Clubs Association of Hong Kong** sets up Nite Cat Online and Nite Cat Chat Room. This is an online counseling service from Monday and Friday 6:00 p.m. to 10 p.m. (http://nitecat.bgca.org.hk/ and Nite Cat Chat Room: http://nitecat.bgca.org.hk/) WhatsApp: 9726 8159 / 9852 8625.
- **Social Welfare Department Hotline Service** hotline: 2343 2255 (http://www.swd.gov.hk/en/index/site_pubsvc/page_cps/sub_application/) Monday to Friday 9:00 a.m. to 5:00 p.m.

3.6 Selective Strategy

3.6.1 Gatekeeper Training

The importance of having gatekeeper training may be expressed through the repeated tragic incidents of student suicide cases in schools where many of the warning signs have gone unnoticed. One example is shown in Fig. 3.17 whereby a 17-year-old student died from jumping down the building of a shopping mall. The student (Mei) has also left a suicide note to express how he suffered from an unsatisfactory life, substantial academic as well as peer pressure. Following the tragic incident, his brother reported some unusual acts of Mei yesterday, including writing letters to classmates, transferring his most beloved items (e.g., camera and rug sack), and wishing his class teacher to disseminate his letters one day later. Although Mei's brother acknowledged that he and his family have great responsibility for the incident, he reasoned that this suicide case did not arise from a sudden impulse. He believed that if the school or class teacher could detect something unusual happening with Mei earlier, the incident could have been avoided. In response to this, the school teacher explained that she did not open those letters immediately due to confidentiality issues.

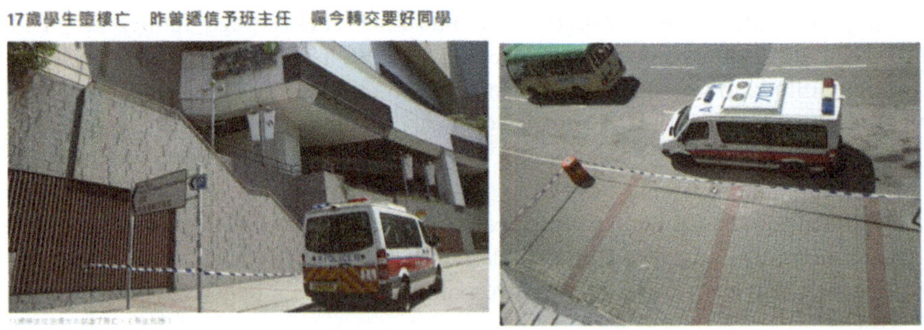

Fig. 3.17 The 17-year-old student died in the building yesterday and sent a letter to the class teacher

From this case, it reflects the importance of having gatekeeper training which may help educators or others to identify any early signs of problems as suicide prevention.

Since teachers and school personnel are not mental health professionals, having gatekeeper training to increasing knowledge on their own roles and limitations before talking with the student can be a useful way to gate keep the identification of those with suicide risks. These educators should always be clear about their roles and limitations before talking to the students (resource handbook for school, 2017, p. 12) (Table 3.3).

The suicide incident reported in Fig. 3.17 reflects that there is a niche to improve educators' awareness of their students' behaviours. One of the best locations for training efforts has been considered to be schools because adjustment of student emotions and behaviours is vital to educational outcomes (Katz et al., 2013). Likewise, in a supportive school ambience, students have a higher chance of having better access to credible mental health information and services (Husky et al., 2011). What's more, it has been discovered that school-based student gatekeeper training (the purpose of developing the knowledge, attitudes, and skills to identify and refer at-risk youth; Kalafat, 2003) is efficacious in enhancing students' knowledge upon suicidality. (Cusimano & Sameem, 2011; Robinson et al., 2013). However, some critics have suggested that these knowledge gains in identifying their suicide peers are not particularly meaningful, as high levels of pretraining knowledge are often found (Shaffer et al.,1991). Indeed, aside from training the educators, school-based student training programmes aimed to enhance students' awareness of suicidal behaviours in their peer groups. However, although a representative review of evaluations has reported high levels of knowledge prior to training, it was shown that students who attended the workshop often express discomfort and anxiety over not knowing what to do when faced with self-harming peers (Muehlenkamp et al., 2010). One reason for the discrepancy between pretraining knowledge and confidence in assisting at-risk peers may be due to the assessment of knowledge gained from these programmes which is vastly based on using multiple-choice or true/false measures (Labouliere et al., 2015). The design of such forced-choice measures has long been criticized for only testing surface-level knowledge rather than the ability to accessing knowledge relevant for problem-solving in real-world situations (Simkin & Kuechler, 2005). Therefore it is argued that the high levels of knowledge are artifacts of methodology rather than true measures of students' ability to interact effectively with suicidal peers. Once again this highlights the assessment of suicide risk as well as assessment of suicide prevention knowledge are in need of substantial revision and improvement.

Table 3.3 Advice for educators when talking to students

Talking with students is about	Talking with students is NOT about
✓ Showing your concerns and letting them know they are not alone	× Trying to handle the issues alone without seeking support from other staff
✓ Helping them work through or resolve minor concerns	× Solving all the problems for them
✓ Linking them to professional help if issues are complex	× Trying to make a diagnosis or 'treating' their mental health problems

Examples of strategies given to teachers to get connected with students	
Selecting the right time and place	Avoid choosing a time when the student is emotionally charged by distress or anger. Allow time for a student to settle emotions that might arise from the discussion. Choose a place where you can have a private conversation with the student but additional support from other adults is available if necessary
Active and reflective listening	Listen patiently to what the student is saying and reflect on what you have heard to show you correctly understood what the student had said and make them feel accepted
Being non-judgmental	Try not to express your own opinions, jump to conclusions, or argue with the student whether their views are right or wrong. Try to view the problems in their context will help you show empathy to the student,
Acknowledging student's feelings	Acknowledge what the student is facing and convey that you are taking it seriously. It should precede and is more important than giving alternatives or directives
Initiating the Conversation	• Building rapport and expressing your concerns. Let the student know that you have initiated the conversation because you care and worry about them Using open-ended questions to invite the student to talk more about their situation • Understanding the motives of student's suicidal behaviours—Students may have different motives, such as to terminate or escape from pain, to stop burdening others, to atone, revenge or accuse, hoping to reunion with the deceased, or to have a new start in life, etc • Acknowledging the difficulty of talking about the issues

Retrieved from resource handbook for school (2017, p. 12)

3.7 Selective Strategy

3.7.1 Interventions for the Vulnerable Group

Over the last 40 years, there is an increase in mental healthcare resources, and major advances in suicide prevention have become more widely available (Klein et al., 2011; Pedersen & Paves, 2014; Pompeo, 2014), these include cognitive-behavioural therapies (CBT) and workshops. Aaron Beck and Gregory Brown developed the CBT for suicidal patients. This therapy consists of basic skills training such as state-dependent learning. The rationale for the training is from the idea that when a person is suicidal, they are in a state of over-arousal, as evident by many who reported prolonged periods of insomnia and restlessness as some of the main immediate warning signs for suicide (Firestone, 2013). The CBT approach was initially implemented in the military by Dr. David Rudd, a lead researcher in the area of suicide who has recently developed a specialized time-limited CBT approach to treat suicidal military personnel. Rudd's model considered preventing suicide as a shared responsibility between patient and therapist. The treatment helps people learn tools to develop their ability to notice and label their emotions, as they get activated into the suicidal state. They develop personalized strategies to calm themselves and keep themselves safe.

Rudd et al. (2015) presented his study at the American Psychological Association Convention regarding his suicide intervention which consisted of 12-session of Brief CBT. In his study, he recruited 76 active-duty Army soldiers at Fort Carson, Colo., with a history of attempted suicide or who have experienced suicidal ideation with intent, with past suicide attempts. There was a promising finding of a 60% reduction in the reattempt rate for his participants. It was postulated that in the CBT session, suicide attempters could learn skills in a non-activated state just as well as the others, but the problem arises when they are triggered as suicidal individuals become unable to access these skills. Therefore, one primary purpose of the CBT is to induce the suicidal state during the therapy session and essentially training one's ability to implement different skills that have been learned but have difficulty applying when they are in the suicidal mode. Although the therapist is to help individuals through the induced suicidal state, they need to demonstrate the ability to calm themselves down when triggered and survive on their own (Firestone, 2013). Therapy continues until they can do this on their own.

Another related therapy that shares some similarities of the cognitive-behavioural components with the CBT has emerged after CBT. It is an empirically supported intervention named Dialectical Behavioural Therapy (DBT) developed by Linehan et al. (2015). It aims to directly target suicidal behaviour and consists of multiple components: individual therapy, skills training, telephone coaching, and a therapist consultation team. According to Linehan et al., (2015), DBT emphasizes individual psychotherapy and group skills training classes to help people learn and use new skills and strategies to develop a life that they experience as worth living. These

Fig. 3.18 Image retrieved from ("What is Dialectical Behaviour Therapy (DBT)?", n.d.)

skills include skills for mindfulness,[1] emotion regulation, distress tolerance, and interpersonal effectiveness. DBT has a history of being used to treat women with personality disorders, who engaged in suicidal behaviour. One of the core elements of DBT is teaching skills that help individuals to regulate their negative emotions, it also aims to build skills that help to stay strong and to build a life that is worth living for. In DBT, the client and the therapist work together to set goals that are meaningful to the client ("What is Dialectical Behaviour Therapy (DBT)?", n.d.). Often this means they work on ways to decrease harmful behaviours and replace them with effective, life-enhancing behaviours. There are usually five components in a standard programme which differs from many psychotherapies that consist of just one mode or aspect of treatment (such as individual therapy). Each component or mode of treatment is intended to meet a specific function (see Fig. 3.18). It has been shown to be effective in reducing suicide attempts and self-harm.

In HK, there is a comprehensive establishment of suicide prevention services that is developed from the basis of CBT and DBT, for example, The CSRP has introduced problem Solving Skills Training and Mentorship Programme for people with difficulties in emotions, behaviours, or academic issues. These programmes were inspired by the rationale of CBT and aim to enhance the knowledge and skills that students acquire. It also strives for encouraging students to solve problems by themselves with mentor' support (CSRP, 2017). Likewise, Samaritans organizes the Young Peer Support Programme (YSPSP) that also aims to train students in giving social support to peers with emotional distress (Samaritans Hong Kong, 2018). Through a six-month programme with workshops and outdoor life-skills training, the participants develop their own, and peers' personal and group capacities to attain emotional well-being. In the year April 1, 2011–March 31, 2012, 68 student ambassadors completed the training and reached out to about 6500 peers through the school activities they organized (The Samaritans, 2017).

[1] Mindfulness is a practice of meditation where an individual becomes fully aware and present of this one particular moment.

3.8 Indicated Strategy

3.8.1 Follow-up and Community Support

Communities play a critical role in suicide prevention as they provide social support to vulnerable individuals by helping with follow-up care, fighting stigma, and supporting those bereaved by suicide. New Life Psychiatric Rehabilitation Association is one of the most established Community centers. The Wellness Centre (TWC) in Tin Shui Wai was established in 2009 with service points extended to Sham Shui Po, Yau Tsim Mong, Sha Tin, Kwai Chung, Tuen Mun, and Islands Districts in the following year (The Wellness Centre, n.d.). These integrated Community Centres for Mental Wellness have now been extended to all 18 districts in Hong Kong. These centers collectively serve more than 6600 members a year providing district-based and integrated community support services. The service team includes social workers, occupational therapists, nurses, mental health education officers, peer support workers[2], and programme workers. The community support service aims to provide comprehensive and recovery-oriented services to local residents, assistance and follow-up services for people with mental health problems as well as supporting families and carers in relation to those with mental concerns. The community support also promotes education in social inclusion, harmony, and well-being in the neighborhood. They have a common slogan which is "instill hope for a better life".

According to (The Wellness Centre, n.d.), Community support service consists of:

- **Counselling Service**

  The service consists of a professional staff team giving casework counseling and outreaching home visits, thus helping service users cope with their mental health and life challenges, actualizing self-directive in their journey of recovery, and leading a fulfilling life in the community.
- **Wellness Programs**

  Various interest classes, social recreational programs, therapeutic and support groups are offered to those who need to improve their psychological well-being, physical, social and transcendental dimensions.
- **Community Education**

  Exhibitions, talks, and activities in the community are regularly held to promote well-being to the public and to increase understanding of mental health. All have the common aims of advocating for anti-stigma and collaborating with district partners to build an inclusive society.

---

[2] A peer support worker is a person who has recovered to a great degree from a mental health challenge that he/she is now able to share with others who are undergoing similar problems, and support them in the recovery journey.

- **Vocational Planning and Development**

  Pre-vocational, on-the-job support, and community living skills training are offered to those in recovery and help prepare individuals to work according to one's own abilities and potentials.

In terms of the suicide prevention programmes and services that are launched by internationally-known providers such as the Samaritans. The YSPSP youth programme by Samaritan aims to train up secondary school students to provide peer support to peers in distress. The programme consists of outdoor activities and a series of workshops about listening skills, depressions, and deliberate self-harm and suicide issues. The student will spread the word in their own schools by organizing school-based awareness programs. (e.g., "Youth Programme"—Samaritans Hong Kong, 2018 and the "We Care" program, (https://wecare.csrp.hku.hk). The design of this programme is likely to emerge from the idea that suicidal individuals often confide in peers who may be ill-equipped to respond to these disclosures (Elzy et al., 2012; Kalafat & Elias, 1994). Thus, training adolescents to recognize suicide warning signs in their peers and take responsible action could dramatically increase the identification of youth at risk for suicidal behaviour (Elzy et al., 2012; Katz et al., 2013; Labouliere et al., 2015).

Since 2005, the Social Welfare Department (SWD) has been subventing the Suicide Crisis Intervention Centre (SCIC) of the Samaritan Befrienders Hong Kong to provide different dedicated services including outreaching, crisis intervention, intensive counseling services, etc. to persons beset with suicidal problems ("LCQ12: Prevention of child and youth suicide," 2015). The SCIC works on the cyber services of regular blog search to identify blog authors with suicidal thoughts in recent years. Under the Web-engagement Service, forums, email-boxes, and chat rooms have been set up to reach out to internet users, especially young users with suicidal ideation to facilitate their ventilation of negative emotions, and help them gain emotional support, and deter their ideations of conducting suicide. Besides, case stories and videos are uploaded to promote a positive life attitude, and information on related social services was provided to the service users. In the light of the service demand, SWD has increased the subvention for SCIC since 2014–15 and the Web-engagement Service will be regularized and incorporated into SCIC's regular service until now.

3.9 Indicated Strategy

3.9.1 Assessment of Suicidal Behaviours by Identifying Warning Signs of Suicide Attempt

Some common warning signs of suicide risk retrieved from Substance Abuse & Mental Health Services Administration, 2012) include:

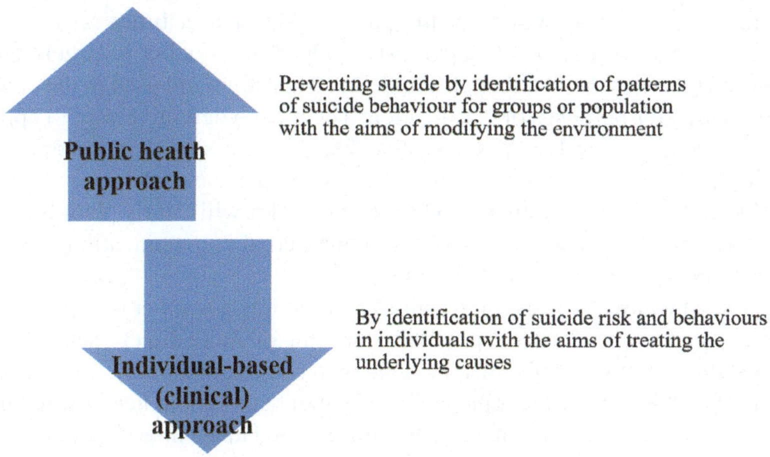

Fig. 3.19 Two Approaches to assessing suicide risk by Shum (2016)

- Disclosing suicidal thoughts or intentions on self-harm, or having possible plans conceived, via conversation, online messages/comments or at home, etc.
- Threatening to conduct a suicide act
- Searching for methods of suicide, and/or how to undergo such methods
- Attempting to gather the materials needed for carrying out the suicide (e.g. buying charcoal packs)
- Dealing with matters of a post-mortem nature (e.g. writing a suicide note, giving away personal belongings to others)
- Feeling hopeless or despair about the future.
- Drastic changes in emotions and life habits
  - Feeling depressed
  - Feeling irritable and agitated
  - Becoming violent
  - Having sleeping and/or eating problems
  - Clear self-isolation; unwilling to connect with people
  - Lack of care for their hygiene and appearance
  - Excessive drinking and/or drug abuse.

It is noted that individuals displaying the number of signs reflect the degree of risk of suicide (Fig. 3.19).

3.9.1.1 Qualitative Assessment—The Interview Setting

Assessment in the form of an interview would usually take place in a quiet room where the chances of being disturbed are minimized ("Assessment of suicide risk in people with depression," n.d.). During the interview, the assessor (usually a counseling psychologist) will meet the patient alone but at times also invite the family/carers/friends, together as appropriate. Open questioning is largely encouraged during the assessment although some closed questions are used in the consultation progresses for purposes of clarification. There is no definitive way to approach enquiring about suicide but it is essential that this is assessed in anyone who is depressed. In recent years it is becoming more common that interview assessment can be conducted by telephone rather than face-to-face. This will clearly place limitations on the assessment procedure (e.g. access to non-verbal communication). However, the principles of assessment are the same.

The assessment will consist of questions surrounding a number of topics, starting with more general questions and gradually focusing on more direct ones, depending on the patient's answers. This must be done with respect, sympathy, and sensitivity. It may be possible to raise the topic when the patient talks about negative feelings or depressive symptoms. Common areas that are explored in the interview may include:

- Are they feeling hopeless, or that life is not worth living?
- Have they made plans to end their life?
- Have they told anyone about it?
- Have they carried out any acts in anticipation of death (e.g. putting their affairs in order).
- Do they have the means for a suicidal act (do they have access to pills, cutter?
- If you think about suicide, do you have a particular mental picture of what this might involve?
- Is there any available support (family, friends, carers...)?

Sometimes the assessment can be conducted in the form of focus group interviews. Patients will introduce the topic without prompting, while others may be too embarrassed to admit they may have been having thoughts of suicide. However the topic is raised, it is important for the counselor to ask careful and sensitive questions. For example, broach suicidal thoughts should be explored in the context of questions about mood symptoms or link this into an exploration of negative thoughts (e.g. "It must be difficult to feel that way—is there ever a time when it feels so difficult that you've thought about death or even that you might be better off dead?"). Another approach counselors often used is active and reflective listening where counselors will reflect back to the patient observations of their non-verbal communication (e.g. "You seem very down to me". "Sometimes when people are very low in the mood they have thoughts that life is not worth living: have you been troubled by thoughts like this?"). It is important to pay attention to non-verbal cues and intuitive feelings about a person's level of risk. There is no definitive way to approach enquiring about suicide but it is essential that this is assessed in anyone who is depressed (Ghasemi et al., 2015).

Since the COVID-19 pandemic in 2020, there has been a significant surge of individuals seeking online counseling. In light of this, ***Open Up***; an artificial intelligence implemented online platform, was developed by University of Hong Kong expert to help young people in distress. The system was first launched in 2018 and provides synchronous online counseling and crisis intervention service using the text-based

Fig. 3.20 An AI implemented online platform: Open Up, Image obtained from https://www.scmp.com/news/hong-kong/health-environment/article/2167376/open-hong-kongs-first-24/7-counselling-platform

support service. The main target age group is 11–35 yearls old and they can be evaluated quickly in terms of their suicide risk, and whether timely intervention is required. With the assistance of algorithms, all chat conversations are automatically recorded and annotated to develop algorithms for categorizing and screening users.

Four possible outcomes of suicide risks are generated: crisis, high, medium, or low. Followed from this, different intervention approaches will be recommended for different levels of risk to and linking users with appropriate connected care (Fig. 3.20) (Table 3.4).

Some commonly questionnaires not directly related to suicidal behaviours

- Subjective happiness scale (Nan, 2014)
- General Health Questionnaire (Goldberg, 1997)
- The Positive and Negative Affect Schedule (PANAS; Watson et al., 1988)
- Perceived stress scale (Cohen, 1994)
- Depression Anxiety Stress Scale (Lovibond & Lovibond, 1995)
- Mental Health Knowledge Schedule (Evan-Lacko, 2010) (Fig. 3.21).

3.9.2 Concerns with the Existing Approach in Assessing Suicide Risk

3.9.2.1 Traditional Questionnaires Are Questionable

While a diverse range of research in the field of suicidal behaviour has been conducted, suicide prediction and prevention are still intricate since suicide itself is an exceedingly personal and sensitive issue (Nock et al., 2010). People who undergo suicidal behaviour may refrain from discussing related issues with others as sharing

Table 3.4 List of current suicide assessment measures for young adults from (Ghasemi et al., 2015)

Existing self-report measures of suicidal thoughts and behaviour	Details
Paykel's questionnaire (Paykel et al., 1974)	5 items about suicidal thoughts and attempts
Modified Scale for Suicidal Ideation (MSSI; Miller et al., 1986)	• 18 items Suicidal ideation that contains 13 items from the SSI and 5 additional items • This is a revised version of the Scale for Suicidal ideation (SSI; Beck et al., 1979)
Suicidal Ideation Questionnaire, Reynolds. (SIQ; Reynolds, 1987)	• 30 items on specific thoughts and cognitions about suicide and death • to assess suicidal ideation in adolescents
The Suicidal Ideation Scale (SIS; Rudd, 1989)	• 10 items on the severity or intensity of suicidal ideation • Each item is scored from 1 ("Never or none of the time") to 5 ("Always or a great many times") according to how often the respondent felt or behaved during the past year • The total score ranges from 10 to 50
Adult Suicidal Ideation Questionnaire, Reynolds. (ASIQ; Reynolds, 1991)	• 25 items on the current level of suicidal ideation and behaviour in adults • The ASIQ yields a total score, ranging from 0 to 150
The Scale for Suicidal ideation (SSI; Beck & Steer, 1979)	• 21 item assessing suicidal ideation (e.g., the current intensity of patients' specific attitudes, behaviours, and plans to conduct suicide • 3-point scale ranging from 0 to 2 • The ratings for the first 19 items are summed to yield a total score, ranging from 0 to 38
Beck Scale for Suicidal ideation (BSSI; Beck & Steer, 1991)	• 21-item for detecting and measuring the current intensity of the patients' specific attitudes, behaviours, and plans to conduct suicide during the past week • These ratings are summed to yield a total score ranges from 0 to 38 • Individual items assess characteristics such as wish to die, desire to make an active or passive suicide attempt, duration and frequency of ideation, sense of control over attempting, number of deterrents, and amount of actual preparation for a contemplated attempt

(continued)

Table 3.4 (continued)

Existing self-report measures of suicidal thoughts and behaviour	Details
Suicide Probability Scale (SPS; Cull & Gill, 1988; 1995)	• 36 items on attitudes/behaviours related to suicide risk and suicidal ideation • the measure of current suicidal ideation, hopelessness, negative self-evaluation, and hostility • the item on a 4-point scale ranging from 1 ("None or a little of the time") to 4 ("Most or all of the time") three summary scores: A Suicide Probability Score, a total weighted score, and a normalized T-score. The Suicide Probability Score can be adjusted to reflect different a priori base rates for particular clinical populations • 4 clinical subscales: Hopelessness, Suicidal Ideation, Negative Self-Evaluation, and Hostility
Suicidal behaviours Questionnaire, Linehan. (SBQ; Linehan, 1981; 1996)	• 34 items measuring suicidal thoughts and past attempts
Positive and Negative Suicidal ideation (PANSI; Osman et al., 1998)	• 10 items on the frequency of protective and negative risk dimensions of suicidal ideation • A 20-item self-report measure of positive and negative thoughts related to suicide attempts • Respondents rate each item during the past two weeks using a 5-point Likert scale, ranging from 1 ("none of the time") to 5 ("most of the time") • 2 scales measured: positive and negative Ideation
Suicidal behaviours Questionnaire-Revised (SBQ-R; Osman et al., 2001)	• 4 items on about suicidal thoughts and past attempts
Columbia Suicide Severity Rating Scale (C-SSRS; Posner et al., 2008)	• 23 items on suicide-related ideation and behaviour and intensity of the ideation • 4 major constructs rated by the patient: severity of SI, the intensity of SI, suicidal behaviour, and lethality
Brief Symptom Rating Scale (BSRS-5; Lung et al., 2008)	• 5 item on suicidal ideation
Suicide Opinion Questionnaire (SOQ; Domino et al., 1982)	• 100 items on attitudes towards suicide
Suicide Attitude Questionnaire (SUIATT; Diekstra, 1985)	• 63 items on perceptions on suicide, and circumstances leading to suicidal ideation
Multi-Attitude Suicide Tendency Scale (MAST; Orbach et al., 1991)	• 30 items to evaluate conflicting attitudes related to life and death • The domains of attitudes assessed with the MAST include attraction to life, repulsion by life, attraction to death, and repulsion by death

(continued)

Table 3.4 (continued)

Existing self-report measures of suicidal thoughts and behaviour	Details
MAST-II (Cashin, 2012)	• 24-item to include the same general constructs as with the original MAST • The MAST-II differs from MAST as it includes both risk and protective factors
Suicide Attitudes and Attribution Scale (SAAS; Sorjonen, 2002)	• 36 item on suicidal act and suicides' character
Attitudes Toward Suicide Scale (ATTS; Renberg & Jacobsson, 2003)	• 61 items with 5 sections – experience of suicidal problems among significant others, – attitudes toward suicide in the general population – life satisfaction and suicidal expressions, – related demographic data, suicide causes and – means of prevention
Attitude Towards Suicide Scale (ATSS; Eskin, 2004)	• 24 items on right to conduct suicide or whether suicide is a sign is mental illness, also refers to social aspects, such as communication around the topic of suicide
HK version of the Chinese Attitude toward Suicide Questionnaire (CASQ-HK; Sing Lee et al., 2007)	• Has 3 parts – Part A composed of 73 statements about attitudes toward suicide – Part B includes 12 statements about 12 difficult scenarios – Part C contains 13 items about socio-demographic characteristics, presence of serious suicidal ideation before a suicidal attempt, and knowing someone who attempted or conducted suicide previously
The scale of public attitudes about suicide (SPAS; Li et al., 2011)	• 47 item assessing knowledge about suicide and 7 specific attitudes about suicide • cover attitudes about the preventability of suicide, ability to control tendency toward suicide, approving or disapproval of suicide, having empathy with the suicide conductor, objective(s) of a suicidal act, considering suicide as a social problem, and differences between suicide attempt and successful suicidal act

(continued)

Table 3.4 (continued)

Existing self-report measures of suicidal thoughts and behaviour	Details
Self-Monitoring Suicidal ideation Scale (SMSI; Clum & Curtin, 1993)	• Three-item to assess the strength, duration, and level of control relative to suicidal ideation • measure the intensity and duration of ideation and level of control in making a suicide attempt daily • The intensity of the ideation item ("Today I have had thoughts of making an actual suicide attempt") uses a 4-point scale ranging from 0 ("none") to 3 ("strong"). The duration of the ideation item ("Today I have thought about making an active suicide attempt") employs a 5-point scale ranging from 0 ("not at all") to 4 ("continuously"). The control over suicidal ideation item ("Today I have felt that the control I have over making an active suicide attempt was") uses a 4-point scale ("strong; no doubt I had control") to 3 ("absent; no sense of control")

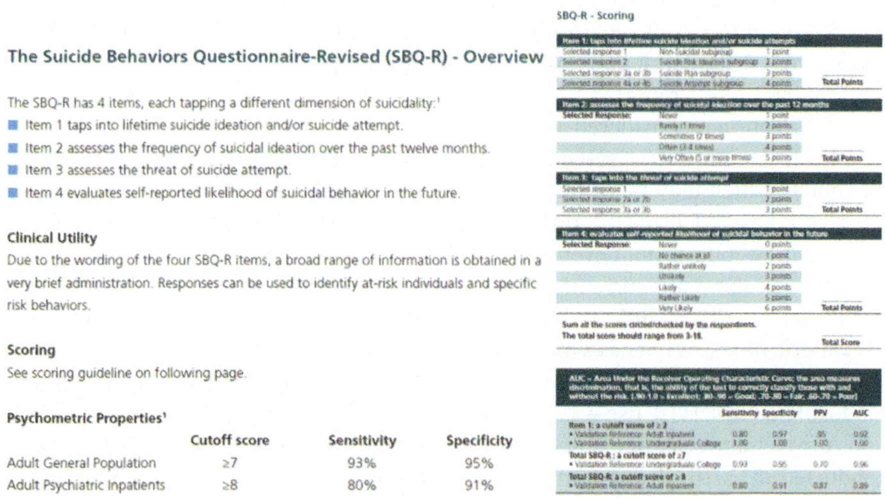

Fig. 3.21 An example of suicide assessment by a self-report method

feelings and thoughts may be very likely to ignite a sense of stigmatization. This can also adversely obstruct the prediction of suicidality because assessments hugely rely on self-report measures and clinical interviews (Wilson, 2009). In other words, clinicians have to rely on individual self-disclosing information regarding their current suicidal ideation, suicide plans, and any history of past suicide attempts. In that sense, the data may not reflect the whole picture of the situation (Mann & Currier, 2007) in case one is unwilling to report their intentions. Chances are that they may intentionally hide or deny their tendency to conduct suicide to prevent intervention or hospitalization (Nock et al., 2010).

Jamie Zhong Zheng, a clinical psychologist for schools in HK commented that many schools have asked students to do mental health questionnaires on a regular basis, but this could be a problem in effectively exploring emotional support needs of students ("數碼同學會: LULIO 推手機遊戲測抑鬱幫助學生對抗逆境," 2016). "The questionnaires are long and boring and many students have submitted a blank questionnaire showing a lack of interest in responding." Secondly, Jamie reasoned that many secondary school students are not fully aware of their psychological state of mind. "Students sometimes deliberately provide "false" answers possibly due to the stigmatism in having emotional problems since discussing this is a sensitive topic and has been considered as a taboo."

With the substantial number of survey instruments available, several potential confounding factors can affect self-report rates of suicidal ideation and suicide attempts ("Preventing suicide," 2014). For instance, different terms and definitions may be implicated by different instruments, there is also diverse literacy level of the population, the specific wording used in the questionnaire, the length of the questionnaire, the interpretation (i.e. the exact meaning and implications) of the wording in the local language, the time frame considered, etc. These could all contribute to issues in interpreting findings of measuring suicidal behaviours, especially when comparing them across different demographic or cultural groups. Some researchers cautioned that comparing self-reported rates of suicidal ideation across groups is challenging as suicidal ideation is considered a fleeting, fluctuating experience that is not observable by others. Comparison of self-reported lifetime rates of suicidal ideation and suicide attempts—which may be of limited value in assessing the current risk of suicide—are also confounded by the different ages of respondents and by recall biases in remembering long-distant events.

Although there are currently ample data on those who have received help from healthcare providers, little is known about the profiles of suicide individuals with psychiatric illnesses but have made no contact with psychiatric services prior to their death. To explore this, Law et al. (2010) conducted a study whereby a Behavioural model of health service use was applied to identify factors associated with the utilization of psychiatric service among suicide individuals. Based on the CSRP research conducted in 2010, it was found that among the 313 responses through telephone survey there was a low percentage of youth who had actually seek for professional help. A comparison was made between those who had (n = 52; 43.7%) versus those who had not made any contact (n = 67; 56.3%) with a psychiatrist during the final six months prior to death. A sample of 119 deceased cases aged between 15 and 59 with at least one psychiatric diagnosis assessed by the Structured Clinical Interview for DSM-IV-TR (SCID I) was selected from a psychological autopsy study. Results revealed that the non-contact group was much larger in number than the contact group and that usual individual-based suicide prevention efforts could hardly reach them. For this reason, both universal and strategic suicide prevention measures need to be explicitly developed in non-medical settings to reach out to this non-contact group in order to achieve better suicide prevention results (Fig. 3.22, Law et al., 2010) and Fig. 3.23 (2013) showing that only 7% of youth would seek formal help whilst 28% would not seek any form of help at all (Committee on Prevention of Student Suicides, 2016).

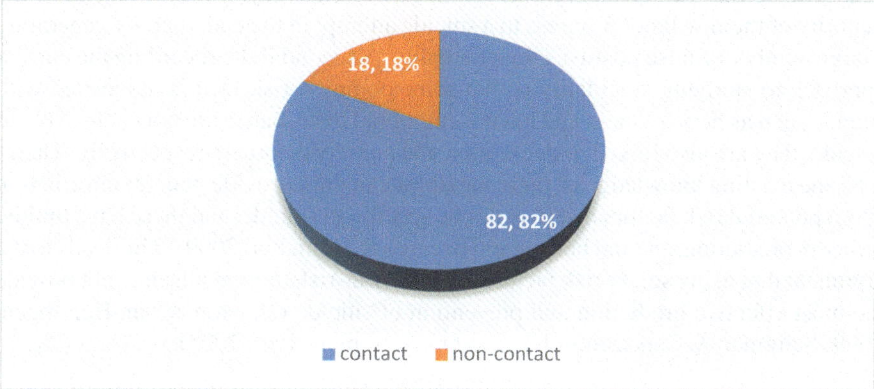

Fig. 3.22 The majority of the suicide population has not made contact with any psychiatric service before they conducted suicide (Law et al., 2010), ***Contact group—substantial attention, Non-contact group – 62 to 86%*** (Anderson et al., 2000; Law et al., 2010; Manchester 2006)

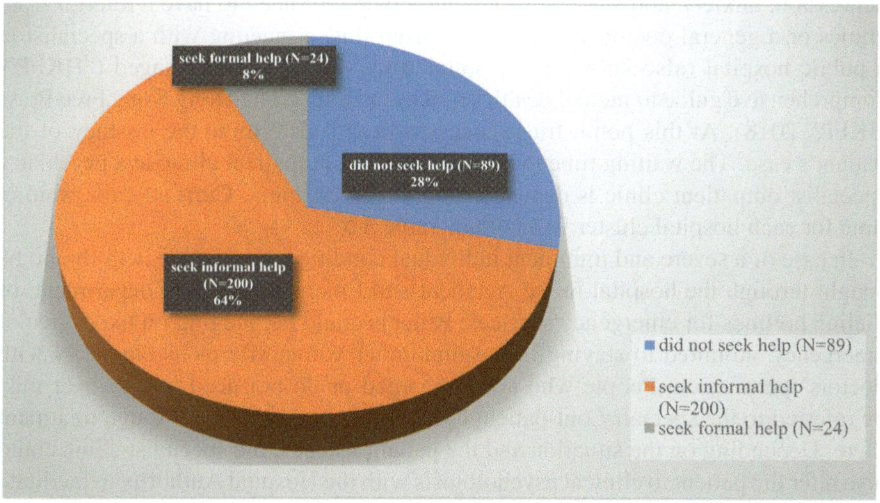

Fig. 3.23 Of help-seeking behaviour in youth (2013), Data picture from Final report by Committee on Prevention of Student Suicides (2016)

Although the use of a risk-based approach within the empirical and epidemiological research has helped to identify important variables to predict suicide progression, there is concern over the approach which often identifies a large number of individuals who may be at risk of suicide. For example, approximately 20% of the young adult population who has experienced suicidal ideation and more than 10% reported having depressive symptoms were identified as being at risk of suicide each year (Hawton & van Heeringen, 2009, Hogan & Kennedy, 2011).). However, the majority of them will not progress to a suicide attempt in the end, thereby generating a large number of false positives for suicidality. A second issue regarding the current approach to studying suicidality is that some common risk factors associated with suicide such as hopelessness and having emotional disturbance are not exclusively to suicide, they are also linked to depression and anxiety disorders respectively. Therefore, the existing knowledge of these variables can only provide general information about potential risk factors that may not be specific to suicide, and these have limited utility in predicting suicidal behaviour (Brenner & Homaifar, 2009). This leads to the argument that using solely risk factors to identify at-risk individuals may not provide the most effective prediction and prevention of suicide (Hawton & van Heeringen, 2009; Seligman & Csikszentmihalyi, 2000; Seligman et al., 2005).

3.9.2.2 Waiting Times

In HK if a person wishes to receive medical assistance for mental health issues (e.g. depression, anxiety, and suicidal behaviours) they will need to have a referral from clinics or a general doctor first. Followed from this, a meeting with a specialist at a public hospital (also known as Hospital Authority) will be arranged ("HKFP's comprehensive guide to mental health services in Hong Kong|Hong Kong Free Press HKFP," 2018). At this point, triage assessment will determine the urgency of the patient's case. The waiting time to be referred to an outpatient clinic at a psychiatry specialist outpatient clinic is dependent on this assessment. Currently, the waiting time for each hospital cluster is shown in Table 3.5.

In case of a severe and imminent individual condition, immediate help should be sought through the hospital in the Accident and Emergency (A&E) department, or dialing hotlines for emergency services. Patients could be, judging on the degree of emergency, admitted to staying in hospital either voluntarily or involuntarily with doctors' permission. People who are discharged or do not need to stay over may be referred to the specialist out-patient clinics and continue to go through treatment there. Depending on the situation and the patient's needs, the specialist clinic could also refer the patient to clinical psychologists with the Hospital Authority to facilitate recovery. According to the HK Hospital Authority (HA) website, if an individual is located in the New Territories East area and is considered to be a "stable case", the waiting times can be as long as 127 weeks, though 90% of new case bookings is shorter than this ("HKFP's comprehensive guide to mental health services in Hong Kong | Hong Kong Free Press HKFP," 2018).

Table 3.5 Waiting times (in weeks) for new case booking at psychiatry special out-patient clinic (1 April 2017–31 March 2018)

	Hospital clusters						
	HK East	HK West	Kowloon Central	Kowloon East	Kowloon West	New Territories East	New Territories West
Urgent case	1	1	1	< 1 week	< 1 week	1	< 1 week
Semi-urgent case	3	3	5	3	3	4	4
Stable case	45	118	81	117	78	127	96

Notes Urgent case represents those under Priority 1 category, Semi-urgent case represents those under Priority 2 category and Stable case represents those under routine category

From ("HKFP's comprehensive guide to mental health services in Hong Kong | Hong Kong Free Press HKFP," 2018)

Similar to the situation in HK, the National Health Service[3] (NHS) in the UK has also reported that long waiting times for hospital admission or referral for service when having suicidal thoughts and behaviours (Mind, 2010). Indeed, thousands of individuals with past histories of suicide attempts need to have long waiting times before receiving psychological treatments. Specifically, in April 2010, the We need to talk coalition reported that one in 10 patients are waiting for more than a year just to be assessed for treatment, and one in six had attempted suicide while on a waiting list. Although those with more severe risks of suicide are waiting less than six months from referral to treatment, one in five reported having to wait over a year to receive treatment and one in 10 has been waiting over two years to receive treatment. The We need to talk coalition (2010) from (We need to talk: Getting the right therapy at the right time, n.d.) found that long waiting times not only reduce the effectiveness of therapy but also reduce the chance of getting people back to work. Therefore, the cost of long waiting times should not be underestimated as it can have devastating, exacerbating mental distress and negative impact on lives. The survey responses also revealed that long waiting times impede relationships of suicide individuals with others attributing to family breakdown, social isolation, homelessness, financial problems, job losses[4]and, more suicide attempts.

Some of the personal quotes from individuals suffering long waiting times in the UK

[3] The National Health Service (NHS) is the publicly funded national healthcare system for England under government administration. Virtually the entire population is covered, and health services are free except for certain minor charges.

[4] Losing a job, home foreclosure and financial uncertainty lead to an increase in the risk of suicide through comorbidity with other risk factors such as depression, anxiety, violence and the harmful use of alcohol (111). Consequently economic recessions, as they relate to cases of individual adversity through job or financial loss, can be associated with individual suicide risk (112).

> I had a complete breakdown, was unable to work, and was hospitalized. If therapy had been available when I needed it, I believe I could have been helped to manage the illness and not reach the stage where everything fell apart.
>
> I was placed on a waiting list. Six months later, I decided to refer myself to a private therapist, which has worked out well. About a year later, I received a letter from the unit apologizing for the delay and asking if I still wanted to be considered for therapy. Thankfully, I'm doing so much better with my new therapist. I'm glad to say I didn't have to go back to the NHS provider. I'm so grateful that my parents can afford private therapy. Otherwise, I think I would probably be dead now.

Waiting times can have a devastating impact on a person's life. They can exacerbate mental distress and cause relationships to break down, jobs to be lost, people to be isolated and, in extreme cases, lead to suicide attempts. But far too many people are still waiting far too long to receive treatment. Less than two-thirds of people with severe mental health problems are offered evidence-based psychological therapies. Below are some of the statements captured from (We need to talk: Getting the right therapy at the right time, n.d.)

> In the end, I fell apart and had to go down the massively expensive private route (a big struggle for us). Why could the NHS not have helped me when I was seriously unwell? I realize how very fortunate I have been to have had some access to private healthcare. I can't bear to think where I'd be if I'd been completely dependent on the NHS. It really shouldn't be this way in a country where healthcare is meant to be available to everyone based on clinical need and not ability to pay.
>
> I was not considered in enough need – it's a very sad state of affairs when you have to be much, much worse or suicide before you will be taken as someone 'in need'... well, I'm on my way there…
>
> Having to wait for therapy and not getting the help I needed nearly caused me to lose my life. It exacerbated the despair and it exacerbated the hopelessness I was feeling. I didn't bond with my son for 10 months and I feel so sad that I've lost that early part of his life. I've lost a year and a half of my own life, I've had to give up a job and a career that I loved and I've had to give up my financial stability now that I'm on benefits.

3.9.3 What Can We Do While We Wait?

With the increasing ubiquity of using mobile phones and apps in the digitized world today, there is a recent development of suicide interventions to improve access and availability of e-interventions at a relatively low-cost, convenient, and discreet way compared to the traditional intervention of seeing counseling (Larsen et al., 2017). The apps may have valuable applications as suicidal ideation and suicide risk change rapidly. Therefore, easy access to high-quality resources may be lifesaving in such imminent situations especially for those who experience barriers to seek help. Indeed, 85% of the young adults in the U.S. own a smartphone these days, of which 75% of these users have accessed health information through this device (Smith, 2015). In a survey conducted by Torous et al. (2014), 69% of respondents and 80% of those aged 45 years or younger indicated a desire to use a mobile app to track their mental health. This has inspired the development of more apps for people to manage their mental health and even as a means of suicide prevention (Torous et al., 2014).

> If we don't all mobilize to work together to make connections in the bid to fight suicide, according to IASP, the number of people who die by suicide is expected to reach a staggering 1.5 million per year by 2020 – shocking statistics which we are hoping can be reduced through empowering people with direct access and connection to professional assistance for those in crisis. From (World suicide, 2014)

3.9.3.1 Recent Mobile Tools for Suicide Prevention

With technology and social media becoming an indispensable part of the young generation at a very early age, it can be enlightening yet alarming at the same time since it can expose adolescents to social pressures and behaviours that trigger suicidal intentions (World suicide, 2014). These young people often feel detached from society, so they use this App to help cultivate their sense of connection with society, instead of isolating themselves from help or hope as they maneuver their emotional turmoil. This serves as an essential tool to provide young people with speedy access to resources and services if necessary Dovel (2016) (Fig. 3.24).

In awareness of the changing trend where adolescents prefer to stay connected with their peers or online friends rather than with their authoritative figures such as parents and teachers, many suicide prevention organizations have widely implemented social media (Facebook, WhatsApp) in their programmes Pao (2018). For example, Samaritan's suicide prevention has launched two new online platforms in

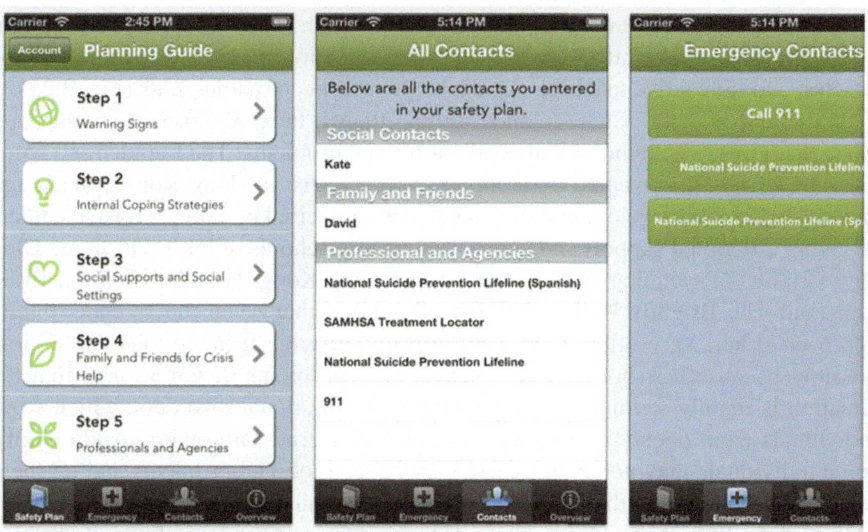

Fig. 3.24 Suicide prevention app aims to reach a wider population from Dovel (2016) and (O'Connell, 2013)

Fig. 3.25 Showing how "Chat 窿" allows anonymous communication and lifetube

August 2018, namely a mobile app "Chat 窿" (https://chatpoint.org.hk/) and the life education platform Lifetube to enable more young people in need to get support. The "Chat 窿" offers an anonymous way for people to talk directly to social workers that contrasts with the traditional way of face-to-face counseling. The platform service began to serve the public on August 22, 2018, and the service time was from 6 to 1 am on Monday to Friday, and from 8 pm on Saturday and Sunday to 1 am on the following day to support. The "Chat 窿" also has a mood log whereby users can evaluate their mood every day on a scale from 1 to 10 use, with 1 being the lowest. For those who have been depressed for many days, the programme will automatically pop up prompts and images that aim to have a "cheer up" effect. Users can also use the hotline to talk to volunteers on the phone. Aside from "Chat 窿", Life tube is launched by the Samaritan's suicide prevention which is the first cross-institutional online life education platform to promote life education. It consists of film, photos, articles, and interactive teaching materials for students or adolescents (Fig. 3.25).

Differed to both the "Chat 窿" and Lifetube, there is the emergence of a mobile app game that aims to help individuals with emotional problems. The founder of a game named LULIO was invented by a clinical psychologist in Hong Kong 5 years ago (Jamie, 2012). The development of this game was inspired by Jamie's related careers of giving emotional support and counseling among schools in HK ("Dr. Jamie Chiu 趙千媄博士—Psychologist and Therapist in Hong Kong. Founder of Good Brain Labs and The Brightly Project," 2019). She noted that when the students finally approached her. Very often, they were already suffering from serious depression, possibly because it is not easy to disclose their problems. It is reasoned that the situation is mainly stemmed from the stigma of emotional disorders, which stops individuals from openly discussing emotional concerns with others. Additionally, some individuals may not even realize they have emotional problems and let these emotions accumulate to the state where seeking assistance is a must. Moreover, Jamie criticized the current screening of suicide using interviews and questionnaires which are not useful and accurate ways to assess student psychological well-being state (Lau, 2016). When it comes to highly sensitive questions such as *Have you ever*

Fig. 3.26 The use of mobile apps to characterize individuals with depression and suicidal ideation, LULIO pushes mobile games to measure depression to help students fight against adversity, Digital Alumni Association: ("Dr. Jamie Chiu 趙千媄博士—Psychologist and Therapist in Hong Kong. Founder of Good Brain Labs and The Brightly Project." 2019)

thought about Suicide, many of them will refuse to answer or give a false answer. In light of these issues, Jamie suggests that it is necessary to identify students with depression and provide appropriate assistance and support to the channel, this is the reason why the mobile game LULIO was developed as an aim to offer alternative measures for depression ("數碼同學會: LULIO 推手機遊戲測抑鬱 幫助學生對抗逆境," 2016).

About LULIO, two more games have been developed to measure cognitive flexibility, an aspect related to how well one can get out from the state of entrapment mentioned in Chap. 2. The game named Hangry Planet assesses cognitive ability whereby players select the appropriate food to feed the planet, but the game rules will change every trial. The score reveals how long it takes for players to adapt to new rules. Jamie said that the games series consists of five to six games, each playing two to three minutes. The whole set can be completed within ten minutes and provides a quick, easy, and fun way to collect mental health data such as cognitive flexibility, coping strategy, reward versus risk, and personal perspective (Altosaar, 2016) (Fig. 3.26).

3.9.3.2 Apps Could Save Lives in the UK

The implementation of mobile apps to help prevent suicide is becoming more common, especially in countries where suicide rates are rising. For example, in Northern Ireland where suicide rates have doubled in the last 15 years, a not-for-profit, potentially life-saving, crisis App named "Here2Help" has been developed. This mobile app has been downloaded more than 2000 times since its launch and it mainly aims to connect those in crisis or those supporting someone in crisis, to support organizations. It is designed for emergencies when someone requires immediate crisis support or for friends, families, or even strangers who are faced with the dilemma of assisting someone in crisis (World suicide, 2014). The App has the

it allows users to interact. However, the general limitation of these apps is that there is a lack of privacy policies, locking and protecting of the content which could be a concern especially for suicidal individuals. These have impeded user's confidence in using these apps (Larsen et al., 2016).

References

A resource handbook for school. (2017). Retrieved from education bureau website. https://www.edb.gov.hk/attachment/en/teacher/prevention-of-student-suicides/Resource_Handbook_for_Schools_En.pdf.

Au, J. S., Yip, P. S., Chan, C. L., & Law, Y. W. (2004). Newspaper reporting of suicide cases in Hong Kong. *Crisis, 25*(4), 161–168. https://doi.org/10.1027/0227-5910.25.4.161.

Brenner, L. A., & Homaifar, B. Y. (2009). Deployment-acquired TBI and suicidality: Risk and assessment. In L. Sher & A. Vilens (Eds.), *War and suicide* (pp. 189-202). New York, NY: Nova Science Publishers, Inc.

Cheng, Q., Fu, K. W., Caine, E., & Yip, P. S. (2014). Why do we report suicides and how can we facilitate suicide prevention efforts? *Crisis, 35*, 74–81.

Chu, X., Zhang, X., Cheng, P., Schwebel, D., & Hu, G. (2018). Assessing the use of media reporting recommendations by the World Health Organization in suicide news published in the most influential media sources in China, 2003–2015. *International Journal of Environmental Research and Public Health, 15*(3), 451. https://doi.org/10.3390/ijerph15030451.

Department of Mental Health and Substance Abuse World Health Organization. (2008). *Preventing suicide a resource for media professionals.* WHO publications.

Discuss. (2018). *做人真係好辛苦, 生存在世都唔知為乜*. Retrieved from https://www.discuss.com.hk/viewthread.php?tid=27709059&page=2.

Dovel, M. D. (2016, December 4). Psychology today: Suicide prevent mobile device app being developed. *Suicide Solution.* Retrieved from http://suicidepreventionsolutions.blogspot.com/2016/12/g.html.

Education Bureau. (2018, March). A Resource Handbook for Schools: detecting, supporting and making referral for students with suicidal behaviours. Retrieved from https://www.edb.gov.hk/attachment/en/student-parents/crisis-management/about-crisis-management/Resource_Handbook_for_Schools_e.pdf.

Final report by Committee on Prevention of Student Suicides. (2016). Education bureau. Retrieved form https://www.edb.gov.hk/attachment/en/student-parents/crisis-management/about-crisis-management/CPSS_final_report_en.pdf.

Firestone, L. (2013, September 5). Suicide prevention: The treatment that works. *Psychology Today.* Retrieved from https://www.psychologytoday.com/us/blog/compassion-matters/201309/suicide-prevention-the-treatment-works.

Ghasemi, P., Shaghaghi, A., & Allahverdipour, H. (2015). Measurement scales of suicidal ideation and attitudes: A systematic review article. *Health Promotion Perspectives, 5*(3), 156–168. https://doi.org/10.15171/hpp.2015.019.

Gould, M. S., Shaffer, D., & Greenberg, T. (2003). The epidemiology of youth suicide. In R. A. King & A. Apter (Eds.), *Suicide in children and adolescents* (pp. 1–40). Cambridge University Press.

HKFP's comprehensive guide to mental health services in Hong Kong|Hong Kong Free Press HKFP. (2018, June 26). Retrieved from https://www.hongkongfp.com/2016/06/26/hkfps-comprehensive-guide-to-mental-health-services-in-hong-kong/.

Hawton, K. & van Heeringen, K. (2009). Suicide. *The Lancet, 373*, 1372-1381.

Hogan, M., & Kennedy, K. (2011). Suicide in Hong Kong: Epidemiology, changing patterns, associated phenomena and prevention. *In Irish psychiatrist, 12* (1). Retrieved from http://www.mindmap.hk/wordpress/wp-content/uploads/2011/05/2011-Irish-Psychiatrist-Suicide-in-Hong-Kong.pdf.

How internet affects young people at risk of self-harm or suicide. (2013, October 31). *University of Oxford.* Retrieved from http://www.ox.ac.uk/news/2013-10-31-how-internet-affects-young-people-risk-self-harm-or-suicide.

Klein, M. C., Ciotoli, C., & Chung, H. (2011). Primary care screening of depression and treatment engagement in a University Health Center: a retrospective analysis. *Journal of American College Health, 59*(4), 289-295. https://doi.org/10.1080/07448481.2010.503724.

Labouliere, C. D., Tarquini, S. J., Totura, C. M. W., Kutash, K., & Karver, M. S. (2015). How much is learned by students participating in suicide prevention gatekeeper training? *Crisis, 36*(4), 274–280. https://doi.org/10.1027/0227-5910/a000323.

Larsen, M. E., Nicholas, J., & Christensen, H. (2017, January 18). Apps for suicide prevention: What the research says. *Psychiatric Times.* Retrieved from http://www.psychiatrictimes.com/telepsychiatry/apps-suicide-prevention-what-research-says.

Lau, C. W. (2016, March 16). 分析: 香港為何學生自殺事件不斷. Retrieved from https://www.bbc.com/zhongwen/simp/china/2016/03/160318_ana_hong_kong_youth_suicide.

Law, C. K., Yip, P. S. F., Chan, W. S. C., Fu, K. W., Wong, P. W. C., & Law, Y. W. (2009). Evaluating the effectiveness of barrier installation for preventing railway suicides in Hong Kong. *Journal of Affective Disorders, 114*, 254–262.

Law, Y., Wong, P. W., & Yip, P. S. (2010). Suicide with psychiatric diagnosis and without utilization of psychiatric service. *BMC Public Health, 10* (1). https://doi.org/10.1186/1471-2458-10-431.

Li, J. (2016, October 14). 'I don't want to add any more burden on you, Mum and Dad', says Chinese boy, 15, in suicide note. South China Morning Post. Retrieved from https://www.scmp.com/news/china/society/article/2028075/i-dont-want-add-any-more-burden-you-mum-and-dad-says-chinese-boy.

Linehan, M. M., Korslund, K. E., Harned, M. S., Gallop, R. J., Lungu, A., Neacsiu, A. D., McDavid, J., Comtois, K. A., & Murray-Gregory, A. M. (2015). Dialectical behaviour therapy for high suicide risk in individuals with borderline personality disorder. *JAMA Psychiatry, 72* (5), 475. https://doi.org/10.1001/jamapsychiatry.2014.3039.

Mann, J. J., & Currier, D. (2007). A review of prospective studies of biologic predictors of suicidal behavior in mood disorders. *Archives of Suicide Research, 11*(1), 3-16. https://doi.org/10.1080/13811110600993124.

Nock, M. K., Park, J. M., Finn, C. T., Deliberto, T. L., Dour, H. J., & Banaji, M. R. (2010). Measuring the suicidal mind: implicit cognition predicts suicidal behavior. *Psychological Science, 21*(4), 511-517. https://doi.org/10.1177/0956797610364762.

Oriental daily. (2016, February 19). *Suicide at Ting Kau Bridge: Total height of 62 metres, becoming a hotspot.* Retrieved from http://hk.on.cc/hk/bkn/cnt/news/20160219/bkn-20160219081606020-0219_00822_001.html.

Osman, A., Bagge, C. L., Gutierrez, P. M., Konick, L. C., Kopper, B. A., & Barrios, F. X. (2001). The suicidal behaviours questionnaire-revised (SBQ-R): Validation with clinical and non-clinical samples. *Assessment, 8*, 443–454.

O'Connell, K. (2013). Suicide prevention app aims to reach wider population. *WRVO Public Media.* Retrieved from http://www.wrvo.org/post/suicide-prevention-app-aims-reach-wider-population.

on.cc. (2016). 本學年20宗學生自殺 大學生佔8宗. Retrieved from http://202.125.90.231/hk/bkn/cnt/news/20160309/bkn-20160309205839126-0309_00822_001.html?eventsection=hk_news&eventid=402882b0533bcabd01535b747d3d6cb1.

Pao, S. (2018, July 29). 推手機App「Chat竇」供青少年傾吐. *Sing Pao Daily News.* Retrieved from http://www.singpao.com.hk/index.php?fi=news1&id=77702.

Pedersen, E. R., & Paves, A. P. (2014). Comparing perceived public stigma and personal stigma of mental health treatment seeking in a young adult sample. *Psychiatry Research, 219*(1), 143–150. https://doi.org/10.1016/j.psychres.2014.05.017.

Pompeo, A. (2014). College students' perceived and personal mental health stigma: The influence on help-seeking attitudes and intentions (Ph.D.). Montclair State University, United States - New

Jersey. Retrieved from: http://search.proquest.com/psycinfo/docview/1525999386/abstract/C284EBEFBCCF4BBFPQ/14?accountid=13265.
Preventing suicide: A Global imperative. (2014). *World Health Organization*. Retrieved from http://apps.who.int/iris/bitstream/handle/10665/131056/9789241564779_eng.pdf;jsessionid=969F67939D60B3E3E0C962C06CEF30E2?sequence=1.
Reynolds, W. M. (1991). *Adult Suicide Ideation Questionnaire: Professional manual*. Odessa, FL: Psychological Assessment Resources.
Rudd, M., Bryan, C., Wertenberger, E., Peterson, A., Young-McCaughan, S., Mintz, J., et al. (2015). Brief cognitive-behavioural therapy effects on post-treatment suicide attempts in a military sample: results of a randomized clinical trial with 2-year follow-up. *American Journal of Psychiatry, 172*(5), 441–449. https://doi.org/10.1176/appi.ajp.2014.14070843.
Samaritans Hong Kong (2018). Youth Programme. Retrieved 18th February 2018 Retrieved from: https://samaritans.org.hk/services/youth-programme/.
Seligman, M. E. P. & Csikszentmihalyi, M. (2000). Positive psychology: An introduction. *American Psychologist, 55*, 5-14.
Seligman, M. E. P., Steen, T. A., Park, N., & Peterson, C. (2005). Positive psychology progress: Empirical validation of interventions. *American Psychologist*, 60, 410-421.
Shum, A. (2016, April 22). *Suicide prevention and mental health*. The Hong Kong Jockey Club, Centre for Suicide Research and prevention, The University of Hong Kong. Retrieved from https://www.edb.gov.hk/attachment/tc/teacher/student-guidance-discipline-services/lecture-notes/lecture-notes-201516/20160422_seminar_2.pdf.
Smith, A. (2015, April 1). *U.S. Smartphone Use in 2015*. Pew research Center. Internet & technology. Retrieved from http://www.pewinternet.org/2015/04/01/us-smartphone-use-in-2015/.
Stay Alive Suicide Prevention App|Grassroots Suicide Prevention|Suicide Prevention Charity. (2019). Retrieved from https://www.prevent-suicide.org.uk/stay_alive_suicide_prevention_mobile_phone_application.html.
Substance Abuse and Mental Health Services Administration. (2012). *Preventing suicide: A toolkit for high schools*. Center for Mental Health Services, Substance Abuse and Mental Health Services Administration.
The Samaritans. (2017). *Service delivery and reporting*. Retrieved from http://www.wisegiving.org.hk/en/donation/search/ngodetails.aspx?id=122&page=report.
Torous, J., Friedman, R., & Keshavan, M. (2014). Smartphone ownership and interest in mobile applications to monitor symptoms of mental health conditions. *JMIR mHealth and uHealth, 2* (1), e2. https://doi.org/10.2196/mhealth.2994. PMID: 25098314; PubMed Central PMCID: PMC4114412.
Who cares wins. (2017, August). *Centre for suicide research and prevention, The Hong Kong Jockey Club, The University of Hong Kong*. Retrieved from http://csrp.hku.hk/file/newsletter/201708/files/assets/common/downloads/CSRP%20Newsletter%20(Issue%202017%20Aug).pdf.
Wilson, T. D. (2009). Know thyself. *Perspectives on Psychological Science, 4*, 384–389.
World suicide prevention day—life-saving crisis app is available to download now. (2014, September 9). *DCP strategic communication ltd*. Retrieved from http://www.dcppr.co.uk.
Yip, P. S. F., Caine, E., Yousuf, S., Chang, S. S., Wu, K. C., & Chen, Y. Y. (2012). Means restriction for suicide prevention. *Lancet, 379*(9834), 2393–2399.
Yip, P. S., Law, C. K., Fu, K. W., Law, Y. W., Wong, P. W., & Xu, Y. (2010). Restricting the means of suicide by charcoal burning. *The British Journal of Psychiatry, 196*(3), 241–242. https://doi.org/10.1192/bjp.bp.109.065185.

Chapter 4
Potentials for Using Cognitive and Neurological Measures for Characterizing Suicide Risk

Solutions to the current problems in assessing suicide risk

As mentioned, prediction and prevention of suicide are difficult because many individuals who experience suicidal behaviour may avoid discussing this with others (Nock et al., 2010). Sharing feelings and thoughts can often trigger feelings of stigmatization and this can also lead to difficulties in predicting suicidality because assessments are largely based on clinical interviews and self-report measures (Wilson, 2009). Molero et al. (2014) reported that very often patients who have attempted suicide explicitly denied having suicidal ideation in their last clinical reports before the attempt. Another study conducted by Qin and Nordentoft (2005) also demonstrated that suicide risk increased immediately after patients were released from hospital care following their self-report that they were no longer experiencing suicidal tendencies. It was noted that some patients deliberately reported lower intention of suicide to avoid prolonged hospitalization. This highlights the importance of developing alternative measures for identifying individuals with suicide risk. One potential option would be to use measures of cognitive and neurological processing. Support for this suggestion is based on past research that used cognitive tasks to show how deficits in executive functions were associated with suicidality (Cha et al., 2010; Jollant et al., 2008, 2010; Keilp et al., 2008, 2013; Mann et al., 2006; Westheide et al., 2008).

Based on the ample findings which have pinpointed suicidality to be related to depression, difficulties in attentional control, and executive functions, the use of cognitive tasks has been suggested to be one objective indicator for individuals suffering from emotional and cognitive difficulties. The performance in various cognitive tasks can help to determine whether high and low suicide risk individuals differ in these cognitive performances in general, or whether the difference is more apparent under emotional interference (positive, negative, or neutral). Based on prior findings that have established the link between cognitive deficits and suicidality in Chap. 2 (Johnston et al., 2017; Jollant et al., 2011; Wagner et al., 2012; Willeumier et al., 2011), it is also postulated that differences in cortical activity are related to suicidality and this could serve as a potential marker for characterizing suicide risk.

E. Ong, *Early Identification and Intervention of Suicide Risk in Chinese Young Adults*,
https://doi.org/10.1007/978-981-16-7641-3_4

4.1 Impairment of Attentional Control for Characterizing Suicide Risk

Researchers have suggested that behavioural tests may better help to understand and predict future suicidal thoughts or attempts (Nock et al., 2010). Cognitive assessments were developed based on the assumption that individuals at potential suicide risk respond in a different way when they are presented with suicide-related cues as opposed to neutral cues (Nock & Banaji, 2007, Nock et al., 2010). Although the limited ability of attentional control among suicide attempters was discussed in the past, some researchers such as Wenzel and Beck (2008) suggested that there is a vicious cycle in cognitive processing that makes a person more prone to engage in suicidal thoughts (Chung, 2015). According to this cognitive model, individuals with dispositional factors may lead them to be more prone to suicide risk. These include having a neurotic or perfectionistic personality, impulsivity, or problem-solving deficits, exacerbate psychiatric disturbance, and hopeless feelings when a person attempts to deal with life stress. Thus, suicidal individuals are likely to experience hopelessness, perceive that there is no solution but suicide to relieve their stress or pain (attributing to suicide schema). Once the suicide schema is activated, they become preoccupied with suicidal thoughts that there is no other option to solve their problems (state of defeat and entrapment as mentioned in Chap. 2). They, in turn, show selective attention toward suicide-related cues that could feed their suicidal thoughts. This fixation on suicide consequently worsens the current state of hopelessness and creates a vicious cycle that exacerbates suicidal ideation. According to the cognitive model (Wenzel & Beck, 2008), attentional bias toward suicide-related cues could be a behavioural marker to discriminate those who engage in suicidal ideation if accurately measured. Indeed, one of the commonly used behavioural measures has been modified to detect one's potential suicide risk, namely, the computerized emotional Stroop Task.

Past studies such as those of Cha et al. (2010) and Jung and Jeglic (2016) who have explored attentional bias with suicidality reported specific Stroop interference effect (attentional bias towards disorder-related cues) in the suicidal population. In Cha et al. (2010)'s study, participants' suicidal behaviour, depression, and hopelessness were first assessed by self-report questionnaires before the experiment, at 3-month and 6-month intervals following the experiment. These include the BHS, BSS, SBQ-R, BDI-II (see Table 5 for details). The participant's primary clinician in the emergency department was also asked to provide an initial assessment of the patient's suicidal behaviour within the next six months (see Fig. 4.1 for the experimental paradigm). Following their initial interview, patients were contacted by telephone and asked about their self-report rating of suicidal behaviours during the previous six months. The experiment involved an emotional Stroop task whereby each participant was presented with four types of words (positive, negative, neutral, and suicide-related words). As expected. Cha et al. (2010) found that those patients with a history of suicidal behaviours had an attentional bias to suicide-related words (as opposed to neutral words) compared to those who had never made suicide attempts. This

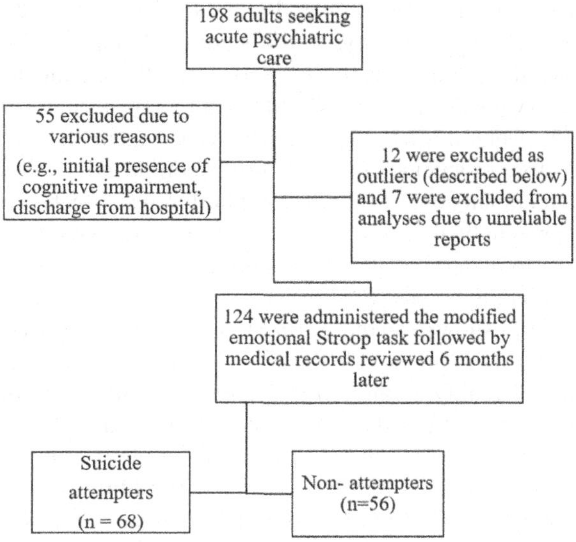

Fig. 4.1 Cha experimental paradigm

attentional bias was strongest for those who had made suicide attempts within the preceding 6 months (Chung, 2015). Further, they found that this suicide-specific attentional bias added significantly to the prediction of who would make a subsequent suicide attempt in the 6-month follow-up period when used with other self-report measures of suicidal behaviours.

The findings imply that measures of attentional bias may be particularly useful for clinicians to predict, above and beyond other clinical predictors (e.g., depression, past history of attempt), those individuals who go on to make a suicide attempt. While these results were very promising, it is unknown if these research findings can be generalized to a non-clinical population in which most individuals have never made a suicide attempt (Chung, 2015). In addition, it is unknown from the previous research findings if the EST, as a predictor of current and future suicidal behaviour among college students, outperforms commonly used self-report measures to assess suicidal ideation and behaviours (e.g., BHS, BSS, SBQ-R, BDI-II).

Considering that individuals with high suicidality exhibited a specific bias towards the word *suicide*, this could be particularly useful in situations where individuals with suicidal behaviours deny their suicide tendency through self-report questionnaires. As mentioned earlier, those who experience suicidal behaviour may avoid discussing this with others, and sharing feelings and thoughts can often trigger feelings of stigmatization. This can also lead to difficulties in predicting suicidality because assessments are largely based on clinical interviews and self-report measures (Wilson, 2009). However, this highlighted the usefulness of using the emotional Stroop task as an alternative for predicting suicide, a method that does not require self-disclosure of an individual.

Building on the evidence which has reported an attentional bias towards negative information in depressed patients (Keilp et al., 2001), Keilp et al. (2008) went on to specifically compared attentional deficits in depressed patients with varying degrees of suicidality. In the study, individuals with or without a past history of suicide attempts were assessed using Beck's medical damage rating of physical injury resulting from a suicide attempt (Beck et al., 1975). A total of 53 participants who were 'low lethality', 42 who were 'high lethality', 83 with depression but no past history of suicide, and 66 controls completed a colour Stroop task as a measure of attentional control (the Stroop interference effect). The Stroop interference effect is apparent by the additional response time required to name the colour of incongruent versus congruent words. This is due to difficulties inhibiting an automatic process of reading the word (Beall & Herbert, 2008; MacLeod, 1991; Ovaysikia et al., 2010). Results showed an increased Stroop interference effect in all depressed patients relative to non-patients, but the effect was most apparent in patients reporting one or more high lethality attempt(s) in the past. In addition to the lethality of the attempt, the frequency of lethal attempts and the proximity of the most recent lethal attempt was also associated with slower response time (Chung, 2015). Authors concluded that such interference may increase the susceptibility to engage in suicidal behaviours, and the deficit of attentional control combined with dysfunctions of emotion regulation could predict suicide risk (Keilp et al., 2008).

The findings suggest that deficits in attentional control (indexed by lower accuracy and slower response times in the Stroop tasks) may predict suicide risk in clinical populations. Importantly, this replicated their earlier findings (Keilp et al., 2001) and shows that the extent of the attentional bias, as measured using the Stroop paradigm may be a useful indicator of suicide risk. Some researchers named the attentional bias towards negative stimuli as a *negativity bias*. Though the emotional Stroop effect is consistently reported in prior studies, this effect has been shown to be more robust in depressed patients than in the non-clinical population. In particular, there are more instances of negativity bias with a larger emotional Stroop effect for negative information (e.g., words such as sad, down, hopeless) than for positive information. A meta-analysis conducted by Epp et al. (2012) from Chung, 2015 showed that the severity of depressive symptoms correlated positively with the response time in the Stroop tasks, again illustrating that negative bias is one significant feature in individuals with depression. Similarly, Reinholdt-Dunne et al. (2009) explored the cognitive basis of individuals with anxiety and also found that high anxiety and poor attention control predicted high cognitive interference by emotional facial expressions. If fixation on suicide-relevant information is evident among suicidal individuals as Wenzel and Beck (2008) proposed, those who engage in suicidal ideation are more likely to have difficulties inhibiting task-irrelevant information if the information is suicide-related. However, there remain sparse studies that have examined the attentional bias of individuals with suicidal behaviours.

One explanation for this is that depressive individuals may have attentional bias and enhanced sensitivity to information congruent to their emotional state (Epp et al., 2012; Gotlib et al., 1996). This is based on the supposition of the mood-congruency hypothesis (Bower, 1981; 1991) which explains the influence of emotion on information processing. The model posits that individuals would prioritize the processing of emotional information consistent with their current mood states. Therefore, a positive mood state will facilitate the processing of positive information whilst negative moods will facilitate the processing of negative information (Bower, 1981). From this perspective, when depressed individuals feel negative they will also pay more attention to negative information, and subsequently, it is more difficult to inhibit the meaning of the word and focus on the colour-naming task.

The attentional bias for emotional information (sometimes also called a processing advantage) is explained from the evolutionary perspective where it is beneficial to prioritize such information that may signal environmental danger (Ohman et al., 2001). However, there are instances in which this bias can lead to processing costs, therefore attentional control would be crucial to maintain focus on task-relevant information in the presence of distraction (Riddle, 2007). Gotlib et al. (2004) explored the extent of attentional bias in depressive patients and healthy controls using images of emotional faces. Facial stimuli depicting sad, angry, and happy expressions were used in an emotional Stroop task. In line with the mood congruency hypothesis, it was predicted that depressed patients would exhibit a bias consistent with their emotional state and would preferentially focus on sad faces. Results showed that depressed participants exhibited attention to depression-relevant (sad) faces but not to other faces such as angry and happy faces. Gotlib and Joormann (2004, 2010) argued that the attentional bias in the depressed group may manifest depressed individuals to become more vulnerable to negative information, and have more difficulties in inhibiting irrelevant negative information. Concurrently, these are also the common factors contributing to the increasing intensity of depressive symptoms (Gotlib et al., 2004).

In previously mentioned studies, inhibition supports the orientation of attention, behaviour, thoughts, and emotions through the ability to actively ignore irrelevant information (Blasi et al., 2006; Boehler et al., 2010; Diamond, 2013). The ability to exert inhibitory control is essential to enable individuals to behave in socially appropriate ways. It can also help to suppress unwanted thoughts or distractions that occur or are presented together with important, relevant information. Excessive worrying and rumination are characteristics of anxiety and depression (Joormann & Gotlib, 2010) and it has been suggested that these are a result of an inability to inhibit negative thoughts.

Followed from the findings of Gotlib et al. (2004), Gotlib et al. (2010) suggested that depression is characterized by ruminative responses to negative emotional states and distressing life events, the inability to regulate one's own negative emotion, increased elaboration of negative information, and difficulties disengaging from negative material. Evidently, these emotional disturbances correspond to the deficits in inhibition, attention, and working memory. This is because when depressed individuals have an attentional bias for negative information, their cognitive abilities to deal with overriding prepotent responses, to inhibit the processing of irrelevant material, the ability to respond flexibly and to adjust adaptively to changing situations are all thought to be disrupted. Gotlib et al. (2010) concluded that among all cognitive aspects, deficits in inhibitory control play a central role in the exacerbation of depression.

Complementing the proposal of Keilp et al. (2008) which is to use the Stroop interference effect to predict suicide risk, Jollant et al. (2011) extended this idea and found that the emotional Stroop task could similarly be used to differentiate suicide attempters from those without suicide risk. Jollant et al. (2011) used the severity of cognitive deficits as indexed by performance in the Stroop task to distinguish depressed patients with a past suicide act from patients without a past suicide act and healthy controls. Results showed that individuals with suicidal behaviour experienced more difficulties with the task as they were more distracted by negative or suicide-related stimuli. This shows that the Stroop task can be a useful method for predicting suicide.

A recent study (Dockrill, 2017) conducted by the research team at Carnegie Mellon University investigated how brain imaging techniques can identify individuals with suicidal thoughts. The study (Just, 2017) involved 34 young adults (17 controls, and 17 with a history of suicidal thinking or past attempts). All participants were presented with keywords (see Table 4.1) whilst placed in an fMRI machine that measures brain activity by monitoring blood flow. During the scan, individuals were presented with 10 words related to suicide along with 10 positive words and 10 negative words, and they were asked to reflect on their meaning (Ruiz, 2017).

. It was proposed that how suicidal individuals think about suicide and emotion-related concepts can be revealed using machine learning to analyze that brain activity. From the brain activity recorded and the emotional responses they indicated, the researchers isolated six terms—'death', 'cruelty', 'trouble', 'carefree', 'good', and 'praise'—and five brain areas that most clearly distinguished the suicidal ideators from the control group.

Just and his team used computational models to map how the brain processes complex thoughts, whether that's things like scientific concepts or the tangled combinations of ideas that represent human action. They discovered that 91% of the time, it correctly determined which participant had a history of suicidal thoughts, and which didn't. That is the subset of these data were able to recognize that 15 of 17 patients

Table 4.1 Showing word list used in the experiment

Suicide	Positive	Negative
Apathy	Bliss	Boredom
Death	Carefree	Criticism
Desperate	Comfort	Cruelty
Distressed	Excellent	Evil
Fatal	Good	Gloom
Funeral	Innocent	Guilty
Hopeless	Kindness	Inferior
Lifeless	Praise	Terrible
Overdose	Superior	Trouble
Suicide	Vitality	Worried

belonging to the suicide group, and 16 of 17 healthy individuals as belonging to the control group. Additionally, the software analyzing these algorithms also successfully identified (94% accuracy) which individuals had previously attempted suicide. The team noticed that in particular, the brain responses to the terms 'death', 'lifeless', and 'carefree' were the most accurate.

Currently, researchers have used the same techniques to try and isolate what suicidal tendencies might look like in terms of our brain's electrical activity, by searching for neural signatures that give away emotional responses such as sadness, shame, anger, and pride. It is suggested that the processing of different emotions is associated with differential brain activation, and therefore neural imaging data could be an objective measure to reflect emotional processing. The neurological findings concluded that suicidal feelings and thoughts are deeply intertwined with the way the brain processes information, this challenges the common stereotype that suicidal individuals could change their perspective if they just tried hard enough (Fig. 4.2).

A clear limitation is that this study was based on small sample size (N = 34) and follows on from some very specific assumptions regarding maps of brain activity and emotions (Just, 2017). It is yet unclear how broadly these results could apply to any practical outcome, but the initial findings shed a positive light that more data could help develop a method that has clinical applications in the near future. It is reasoned that with a larger sample the data could be more generalizable, more confidence in predicting future suicidal behaviour, and could give clinicians a way to identify, monitor, and even intervene with distorted thinking that so often characterizes seriously suicidal individuals (Dockrill, 2017; Ruiz, 2017). While the technique

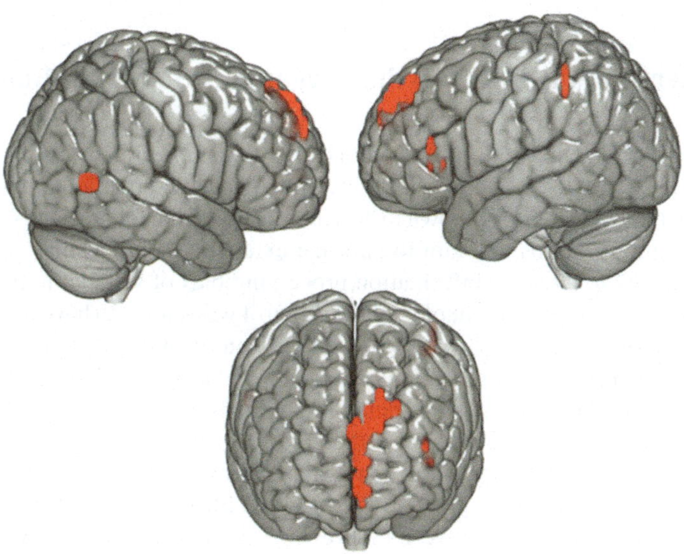

Fig. 4.2 Discriminating brain regions for distinguishing between suicidal ideator and control group membership from (Just, 2017)

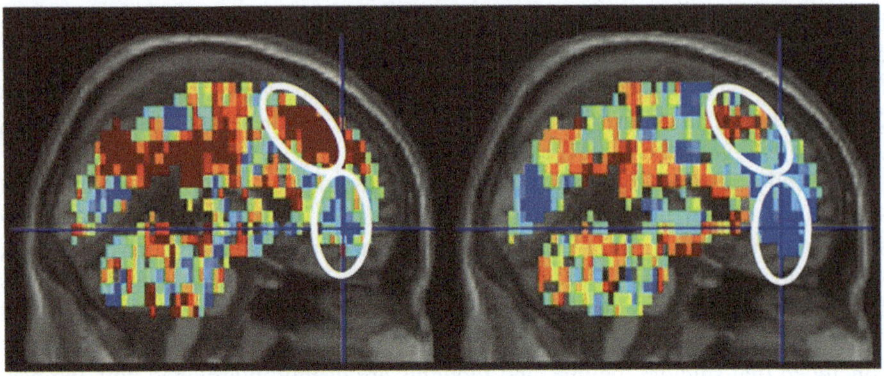

Fig. 4.3 Suicide attempter (left) versus the control group (right)

is promising, fMRI is not easily accessible or cheap (Dockrill, 2017). This creates another limitation for Just's study since fMRI is only available in advanced research institutions and requires cooperative patients, it will never be widely available to a large population such as mental health patients under the NHS in England or the Hospital Authority in HK. This is why Just and his colleagues aimed to see if EEG can serve as an alternative tool that is more easily and economically accessible which detects functionality of the brain similar to the fMRI. Indeed this relatively affordable tool can similarly decode how the brain responds to key concepts related to suicide and positive and negative feelings (Fig. 4.3).

4.2 Interventions by Reverting Negative Attentional Bias

As outlined earlier, clinicians and educators struggle to find effective ways to reduce the prevalence of suicide. Nonetheless, given that specific attentional bias towards suicide-related information is shown to be a promising marker characterizing suicidal behaviours, interventions that aim to alter the extent of such bias may prove to be a useful strategy to alter the information processing bias of suicidal individuals. In addition, since the improvement of attention control was shown to have a pivotal role in the regulation of emotions, it is suggested that interventions that aim to improve specific bias such as suicide-related information may be an effective way to alleviate the recurrence of the symptoms in suicidal individuals.

Together with some of the adjunctive therapies (e.g. meditation, cognitive therapy, and neurofeedback training) that aim to help patients by strengthening the attentional control processes and reducing negativity bias, the Stroop effect has recently been implemented to provide objective measures for monitoring the therapeutic effectiveness of interventions (Malinowski et al., 2017). For example, the effectiveness of mindfulness meditation intervention on cognitive processing was assessed using performance in a Stroop task. During mindfulness practice, individuals will try to

Fig. 4.4 Relaxation achieved by practicing Mindfulness meditation

maintain a moment-by-moment awareness of thoughts, feelings, bodily sensations, and surrounding environment, through a gentle, nurturing lens. The trainers will pay attention to one's thoughts and feelings without judging them as a right or wrong way to think in a particular way. When practicing mindfulness it is essential to let your own thoughts tune into sensing fully of the surrounding environment, the present moment rather than rehashing the past or imagining the future. This means that there will be increase body sense awareness, more relaxation, reduction of pain, and enhancing well-being through practicing Mindfulness meditation (Fogel, 2011). Regular practices have been shown to be effective in treating sleep disorders, obsessive–compulsive disorder, cancer, headache, depression, and stress reduction. It is also useful in helping individuals prepare for and recover from medical interventions. These effects are supported by parasympathetic nervous system (relaxation) activation, reduced muscle tension, and a lowering of stress hormones (Fig. 4.4).

In the study by Malinowski et al. (2017), participants were randomly allocated to the mindfulness training group or an active control group. In the mindfulness group participants were instructed to conduct 10 min of mindfulness practice five times per week. To match the mindfulness training condition as closely as possible, participants in the active control group took part in brain training that involved active, effortful cognitive processes. This included doing an arithmetic calculation that required effortful cognitive processing and activated a wide range of frontal and parietal brain regions implicated in attention. Improvement in attentional control was shown by better performance in a counting Stroop task (lower response times across all trials). This task differs from the classical Stroop task as it was a combination of a counting Stroop task and an emotional Stroop task. In each trial, a word stimulus (a word of either ONE, TWO, THREE, or FOUR) was presented in either in the congruent or incongruent condition. Participants are instructed to indicate how many words are presented on the screen by button press (between one and four words). In an incongruent condition, for example, the word "TWO" would be presented three times. Participants have to inhibit the word and respond to the number of words. This means that to complete this task, executive control is essential in the response conflict condition (i.e. when the meaning of a presented number word conflicts with the number of words that are presented and need to be responded to). Results showed greater improvement in attentional control can help to give objective indicators in terms of the therapeutic effectiveness of meditation training compared to the active control group.

While the benefits of mediation have been frequently documented in scientific journals, some of the negative side effects may have not been openly discussed (Ireland, n.d.). For example, some people although rarely may report the experience of meditating to be a frustrating or even agonizing process that will bring close contact with one's own inner conflicts (live strong website). Rather than a metamorphosis, some individuals find that the very act of sitting very still for up to 20 min is difficult to achieve. In addition, without prior education on meditation people can make the most rudimentary mistakes in sitting that will cause negative side effects. Livestrong posits that if individual inner thighs are not flexible, sitting in a cross-legged pose on a hard floor will result in over-focus on the source of muscular discomfort rather than finding a union with the breathing exercise during meditation. While it is well known that meditation can have numerous benefits, its role in improving some aspects may have been overstated. For instance, a recent review from ("Even Meditation Has Limitations," 2018) on a variety of meditation studies has been conducted by scientists at Coventry University (UK), Massey University (New Zealand), and Radboud University (Netherlands). It was found that most of the initial positive results reported by individuals practicing meditation disappeared when the meditation groups were compared to other groups that engaged in tasks unrelated to meditation.

Another setback of meditation was raised from a book titled: "Meditation: the dark side" (Douglas Todd). It was suggested that practicing too much meditation may exacerbate inappropriate detachment from others and manifest insensitivity to others. In support of this, David Treleavan, a specialist in spirituality and health, has suggested that "sustained attention to the body can lead to a dissociative, or freeze, response" that he has named "contemplative dissociation." (Fogel, 2011). This typically occurs when the present moment of body sense awareness touches old physical or psychological wounds that have never been resolved. The result is that one gets stuck in the pain and can't get out. Using more psychological language, this is a form of rumination or somatization focused on pain and dysphoric feelings. He added that using meditation may not only lead to escape from their own shadows but to escape from others.

4.2.1 *Attention Bias Modification that Reverts Negative Attentional Bias*

With the argument that attentional control is important, recent research shows that attention biases to emotional information can be trained and untrained in individuals with affective disorders using attention bias modification (ABM; Boffo et al., 2017; Ferrari et al., 2016). As with training to divert attention away from negative stimuli, Ferrari et al. (2016) have introduced the use of ABM training as a cost-effective intervention for depressed patients alongside their usual care including taking medication and CBT interventions. Acknowledging that the extent of negativity bias noted in depressed individuals contributes to the development and maintenance of depression, the ABM intervention was reported to help reduce the negativity bias in depressed patients and therefore have a therapeutic value (Fig. 4.5).

Although the research in ABM is quite recent and existing evidence of its effectiveness on suicidal individuals is lacking, its effectiveness in clinical samples has shown some promising results. For example, depressed individuals are characterized by increased avoidance behaviour, and enhanced sensitivity (bias) to negative cues and punishment, and reduced attention to positive and rewarding stimuli (see also Pizzagalli et al., 2011), and ABM training has been implemented to help these patients. Wells and Beevers (2010) conducted a study involving 126 patients diagnosed with depression, they were randomly allocated to a positive training (towards positive and away from negative stimuli), a placebo (i.e. sham ABM) training, or a control condition (continuous attentional bias assessment). The effectiveness of ABM intervention was evaluated at 1, 6, and 12 months. The results consistently showed the ABM to be successful in reducing symptoms of depression after as little as four weeks of training.

More recently Ferrari et al. (2016) assessed the outcome of training through the measures of mood response to stress, depressive symptoms, and cognitive abilities (i.e., measures of attentional bias for verbal stimuli, cognitive control, and positive mental imagery). Similar to the use of the Stroop performance as outcome

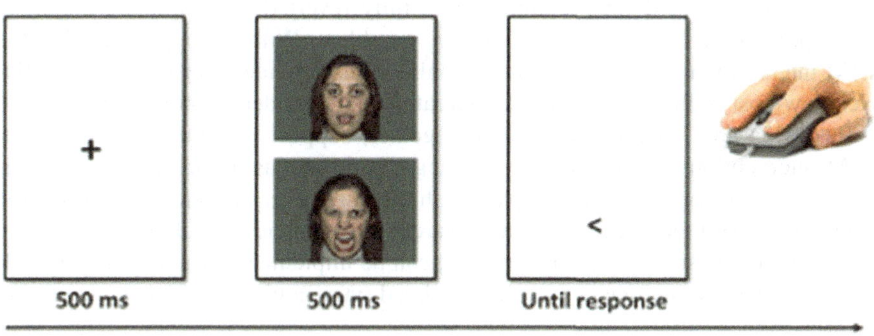

Fig. 4.5 Attention bias modification adopted from (Altheimer, 2014)

Table 4.2 Neuroimaging studies of groups with suicide attempters from (Cox et al., 2018)

Authors and year	Group with history of suicide attempts	Group(s) without attempts	Methods	Findings
Functional magnetic resonance imaging studies				
Jollant et al. (2008)	13 males with MDD, Mean age = 40 yrs	14 Diagnostic controls 16 Healthy control	Response to intense or mild, angry or happy face stimuli, compared to responses to neutral face stimuli	↑ Response in lateral and ↓ in superior frontal cortex to angry versus neutral, ↑ anterior cingulate gyrus to mild happy versus neutral, ↑ cerebellum to mild angry versus neutral, relative to Diagnostic controls
Jollant et al. 2010)	13 males with MDD, Mean age = 38 yrs	12 Diagnostic controls 15 Healthy control	Iowa gambling task, regions of interest	↓ Lateral OFC and occipital cortex activation during risky relative to safe choices, relative to Diagnostic controls Poorer gambling task performance, relative to Diagnostic controls
Marchand et al. (2012)	6 males with MDD with self-harm, 5 with attempts, Mean age = 28 yrs (overall MDD sample)	16 Diagnostic controls	Motor activation task	↓ Putamen activation and altered functional connectivity in a network involving bilateral motor/sensory cortices and striatum, left temporal and inferior parietal lobule regions, and right posterior cortical midline structures

(continued)

Table 4.2 (continued)

Authors and year	Group with history of suicide attempts	Group(s) without attempts	Methods	Findings
Reisch et al. (2010)	8 females with attempts, Mean age = 39 yrs	None	Activation during recall of mental pain and suicide action during recent suicide attempts	Recall of mental pain was associated with ↓ activation in DLPFC, rostral PFC, and premotor regions. Recall of suicidal action was associated with ↑ activation in the medial PFC, Anterior cingulate cortex and hippocampus

MDD Major depressive disorder

depression (Allen & Reznik, 2015), anger (Allen, 1998), stress, and post-traumatic stress disorder (Meyer et al., 2015). The FCA measure can be defined in various ways. It is a comparison between power in the alpha band (8–13 Hz) on the left side compared with the corresponding power on the right side. Note that alpha power is inversely related to cortical activity, which means that greater alpha power on the left would indicate lower cortical activity on that side (Coan & Allen, 2004), the logarithm of average alpha power on the left side minus the right, which is equivalent to the log of the ratio of the powers:

$$\log(\text{right alpha power}) - \log(\text{left alpha power}) = \log\left(\frac{\text{right alpha power}}{\text{left alpha power}}\right)$$

Due to individual differences in the thickness of the scalp, there are differences in the degree of cortical activity detected between different individuals making the study of individual differences in brain lateralization difficult. The asymmetric index (uV^2) avoids this issue because it allows the comparison of relative activity in the left and the right cortical regions (Davidson et al., 2000). Alpha asymmetry is calculated by subtracting overall activity in the alpha frequency band at left electrodes from alpha activity at right electrodes. With this measure, any unwanted individual variance such as skull thickness or scalp-related impedence can be removed (Coan & Allen, 2004). Given the inverse relationship between alpha power and cortical activity (Oakes et al., 2005), positive alpha asymmetry scores are interpreted as left-frontal activity relative to right, while negative scores are interpreted as right-frontal activity.

Taken together, frontal asymmetries of alpha, beta, or gamma frequency bands can be interpreted with respect to the Approach-Withdrawal model mentioned earlier, that is the extent of motivation towards (approach) or away from (avoidance) a stimulus. Frontal asymmetry can be extracted from EEG headsets with electrodes located at frontal scalp regions (ideally, F3 and F4) (Frontal Asymmetry 101, 2017). The excellent time resolution of the EEG allows the analysis of short-term changes in motivation over the course of a stimulus presentation (e.g., picture- or video-based advertisements, trailers, videos, shows), also in mobile applications beyond stationary lab setups (field and in-store studies).

4.3.3 Medical Grade Versus Consumer EEG Systems

Bringing brain research tools like EEG devices out of the lab into the pockets of practitioners and researchers may fundamentally change the current way of measuring brain activities. While most of the current techniques are limited to research clinics and require excessive set-up, new consumer EEG devices connected to standard, off-the-shelf mobile devices may offer new ways without these constraints (Link et al. n.d.). This allows neuropsychological assessment and research in mobile settings, possibly even in remote areas with limited accessibility and infrastructure, thus bringing the equipment to the patient instead of bringing the patient to the equipment. Due to the constraints and high costs of conventional EEG machines, there are increasing studies of lateralized brain activity using commercial EEG headsets instead of the conventional EEG machines found in laboratory settings. Numerous studies have compared quantitative EEG signal and test–retest reliability of medical and consumer EEG systems in order to evaluate their potential application in clinical research and clinical trials (Ratti et al., 2017). Newly popularized consumer EEG systems were evaluated due to their low cost, wide accessibility, and potential for home-based studies in challenging populations (see Table 4.3 for EEG systems comparison). Among the popular applications of consumer EEG systems are meditation and relaxation training as well as coping with anxiety or pain. Recent investigations have been exploring their utility beyond gaming: NeuroSky was shown to be able to detect the onset of stage 1 sleep (Van Hal et al., 2014) and there has also been interest in assessing consumer EEG within brain-computer interfaces (Bialas &

Table 4.3 EEG systems comparison

	Muse	Mindwave	B-Alert X24	Enobio 20
Company	**Interaxon**	**NeuroSky**	**Advanced brain monitoring**	**Neuroelectrics**
Channels	2	1	20	20
Sampling rate	220 Hz	512 Hz	256 Hz	500 Hz
Wet/dry electrodes	Dry	Dry	Wet	Wet
Signal quality check	Yes	Yes	Yes	Yes
Impedance check	N/a	N/a	Yes	Yes
Setup time (minutes)	5	3	20–25	20–25

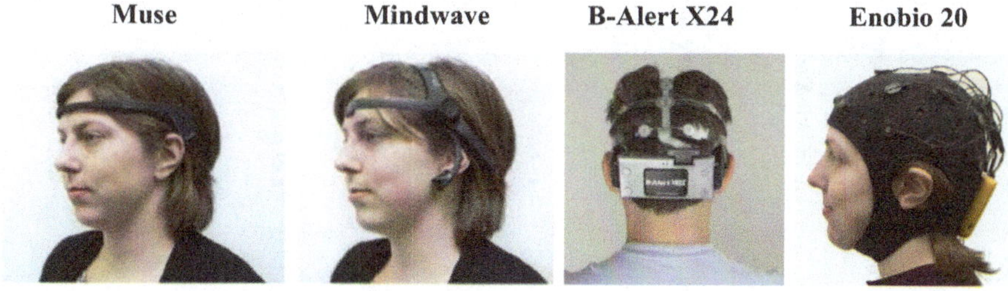

Fig. 4.6 This study provided evidence that fairly good quality EEG data can be successfully collected from consumer EEGs (Ratti et al., 2017)

Milanowski, 2014; Kim et al., 2015; Taherian et al., 2017). The application of simpler EEG systems which consists of 6-channels is also being explored for emergency settings (Jakab et al., 2014). Although utilizing a more complex headset, a prior evaluation showed that commercially available multi-lead consumer EEG systems, such as the Emotiv EPOC 16-electrode cap, may also have value in evaluating clinical conditions (Schiff et al., 2016) (Fig. 4.6).

Muse Mindwave B-Alert X24 Enobio 20

Compared to medical-grade EEG devices, consumer EEG systems have the benefits of being more convenient and easy to set up. The downside is that the data quality is compensated by artifact susceptibility especially those which use dry electrodes. The data are also particularly prone to noise such as eye blinks and muscle movement with eye-opening also likely contributed to this relative artifact (Ratti et al., 2017). Additionally, the assessment performed by consumer EEG systems is, by their nature, limited and confined to the only anatomical brain region covered by the few channels, precluding multi-networks evaluations. Overall, a consumer EEG system can be a useful way to collect EEG data especially as a self-help application, but the varying limitations on usability, data quality, and reliability should be accounted for.

4.3.4 Comparison of Commercial EEG Headset

Considering that the use of a relatively low-cost commercial EEG device is a viable option for measuring brain activity, this part will now focus on the comparison of a range of device available EEG devices. Aside from the biggest advantage of commercial EEG devices for their low cost, these systems are also flexible in terms of their advances in EED electrode design and configuration (Burnet & Turner, 2017). For example, the use of dry or saline electrodes means that there is significantly reduced preparation time for the setup and is more comfortable than the traditional EEG systems used in laboratory research. In addition, these systems can interface with commodity PCs, Macs, and mobile phones directly through standard interfaces

Table 4.4 Showing a summary of consumer-grade EEF system adopted from (Burnet & Turner, 2017)

Manufacturer	Emotiv a	OpenBCI	OpenBCI b	OpenBCI	Wearable Sensing c	Brain rhythm Inc.	Brain rhythm Inc	Brain products e
System name	EPOC (+)	Mark IV	Nova	Supernova	DSI-24	BR32S	BR8 Plus	actiCAP Xpress
Number of electrodes	14	8/16	8	16	24	32	8	32
Electrode type	Saline electrodes	Wet, dry, or active	Wet, dry, or active	Wet, dry, or active	Foam or Spring-loaded	Foam or Spring-loaded	Dry	Passive, active
Flexible locations	No	Yes	Yes	Yes	No	No	No	Yes
Flexible reference	No (Mastoid/P3)	Yes	Yes	Yes	No	Yes	No	Yes
Price	$799	$2000	$1000	$1700	$20,000	$12,000	$4500	$6990
Sampling rate internal	2500	250	250SPS	125SPS	300 Hz	250 Hz	1000 Hz	100 kHz
Access to raw data	No	Yes	Yes	Yes	Yes	Yes	Yes	Yes
Output file type	EDF	CSV	CSV	CSV	CSV and EDF	EDF	CSV and EDF	EEG

A https://www.emotiv.com/
B http://openbci.com/
C http://www.wearablesensing.com/
D http://www.bri.com.tw/about.html
E http://www.brainproducts.com/

and work in rooms that are not specially shielded for EEG. The wireless connections between the EEG collection headsets and the host computer recording the data providing excellent ease of use in complex environments.

With these advantages listed, it implies that the commercial EEG device the opportunities for moving EEG out of specialized, purpose-built laboratories and into more naturalistic settings are many. Within reasonable limits, some amount of EEG can now be collected almost anywhere. The major drawback of these systems is that they are low-density, ranging from one or two electrodes up to 16 or 32 for some of the more expensive mid-tier systems. The research uses one of the most renowned systems which has been reviewed by some researchers. They commented that these EEG systems are highly sophisticated in the use of both clinical research applications and in educational settings, with relatively low cost. Likewise, there are new systems in the 10,000 USD range that claim to offer performance equivalent to systems costing 2 to 10 times as much. The table summarizes some of the EEG systems that are multi-electrode (with a minimum of 8 sensors) and that either have previously been used in some form of research or show a strong potential for such use. Based on the comparison of EEG devices above, it was concluded that while the earlier systems like the Emotiv may have challenges for use in research, these consumer-grade EEG systems represent a useful addition to certain types of EEG research (Burnet & Turner, 2017) (Table 4.4).

4.3.5 The Use of EEG Emotiv

EEG Emotiv, a relatively low-cost EEG device that is more easily accessible than the traditional EEG or MRI. The EEG Emotiv EPOC/EPOC+ offers a headset with 14 electrodes. The electrodes provided are at international 10–20 locations: AF3, F7, F3, FC5, T7, P7, O1, O2, P8, T8, FC6, F4, F8, AF4 (see Fig. 4.7). Another advantage is

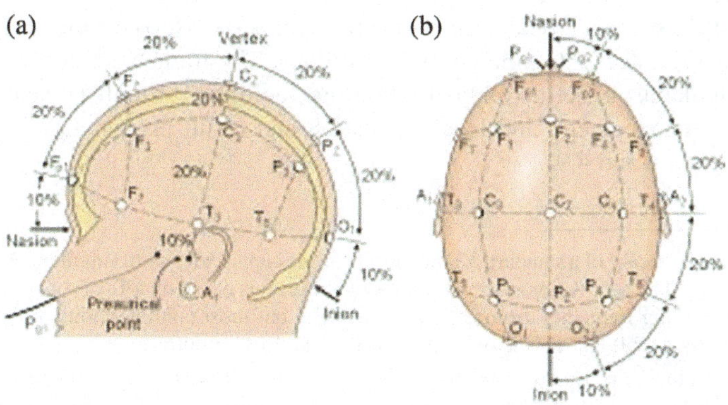

Fig. 4.7 International 10–20 system

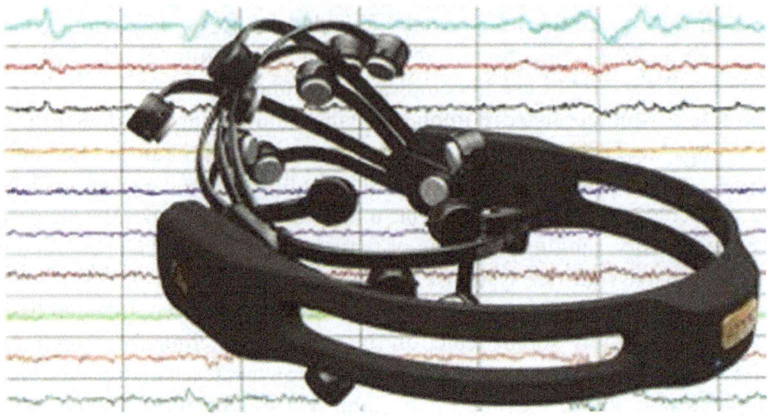

Fig. 4.8 A sample picture of a portable EEG tool used outside the laboratory setting

that the Emotiv EPOC/EPOC + uses saline felt electrodes to provide a good electrical connection (Burnet & Turner, 2017). As noted above the system provides data to the user at an effective sampling rate of 128 Hz, although per the technical specifications it works at a rate of 1024 Hz internally. The downsampling is for various technical reasons including wireless transmission to the receiver. Resolution is approximately 0.5 microvolts (14 bits).

Turner et al. (2017) gave merits to the use of this commercially low-cost EEG device due to its portability, which opens doors to collecting data in many places other than laboratories such as schools, child-care centers, hospitals, and private clinical practices. This offers a meaningful application for a diverse range of research aims that are not attainable with conventional methods such as fMRI and traditional EEG. Turner et al. (2017) also remarked that the frontal cortical asymmetry can be reliably collected by the use of low-cost EEG hardware. With a series of experiments comparing EEG Emotiv with other consumer EEG systems such as the OpenBCI,[1] and the Brain Rhythm Inc,[2] it is argued that the EEG Emotiv favors robust measurements the best such as alpha or other spectral comparisons, or for the study of slow changes over longer EEG time-course recordings. The framework consists of three main components: EEG driver and recording facilities, Stimuli presentation and experiment management, and local evaluation and result presentation from Sjölie (2011) (Figs. 4.8 and 4.9).

[1] The OpenBCI consists of a standard 32 channel electrode cap, it can record simultaneously from up to 16 electrodes. The acquisition system for the EEG headset is based on a Texas Instruments ADC, which has sampling frequency from 250 Hz to 16 kHz, but most configurations of the OpenBCI equipment work at 250 Hz. This is twice the speed of the EEG Emotiv.

[2] Compared to the EEG Emotiv, the Brain Rhythm Inc is a relatively new company supporting EEG, offering 8 and 32 channel wireless EEG systems. Similar to the OpenBCI, the system can use spring-loaded dry electrodes or an innovative foam-block type dry electrode. Their 32-channel system (the BR32S) uses an electrode cap similar to traditional research EEG systems.

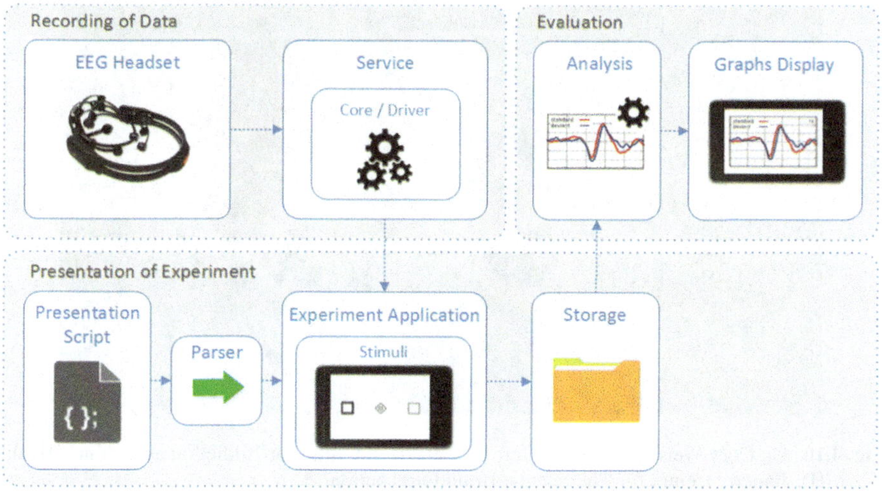

Fig. 4.9 Showing an overview of the framework's system architecture from (Link et al., n.d.)

4.4 Interventions by Altering Neural Activation

4.4.1 Repetitive Transcranial Magnetic Stimulation (rTMS)

As mentioned earlier, suicidal thinking comorbids with many other disorders including post-traumatic stress disorder, bipolar disorder, schizophrenia, and borderline personality disorder. Approximately 90 percent of individuals who have made suicide attempts were also diagnosed with at least one of these disorders (Centre for Addiction and Mental Health, 2018). Currently, the most common current treatments available for disorders such as depression are antidepressant medications and evidence-based psychotherapy. Although many patients respond to these treatments, only a third enter complete and sustained remission. Among those who received treatment, many have failed to improve. This leads to a condition called *Treatment-resistant depression* which defines individuals who do not experience a noticeable improvement in their symptoms after trying at least two different antidepressant medications. Indeed, almost 40% of individuals with depression are treatment-resistant, raising an urge to explore other forms of treatments for them (Centre for Addiction and Mental Health, 2018) (Fig. 4.10).

The rTMS is a non-invasive brain stimulation technique that directs magnetic pulses at a targeted area of the brain (Weissman et al., 2018). It consists of rapidly alternating magnetic fields applied to the scalp to induce small, focal electrical currents in the cortex. During rTMS, a small, insulated electromagnetic coil is placed on the scalp. A bank of capacitors is then rapidly discharged into the coil, which converts the electrical activity into a pulsed magnetic field of low or high frequency. The current then passes through the cranium with minimal impedance.

Fig. 4.10 Dr. Cory Weissman and Dr. Jeff Daskalakis in Centre for Addiction and Mental Health (CAMH), Temerty Centre for Therapeutic Brain Intervention

These magnetic fields in turn generate electric currents in the brain. Upon delivery of sufficiently intense TMS to the targeted area, the cortical neurons depolarize, and action potentials are generated. Currently employed technology generates a powerful magnetic field of approximately 1.5 T (comparable to that of a standard MRI) for a brief period, which penetrates up to approximately 3 cm beneath the coil surface (Yip & Carpenter, 2010).

According to a recent study conducted by Weissman (2018), the rTMS has been demonstrated to be an effective way for reducing suicidal thoughts (N = 156) who have failed to recover well from other treatments on depression. In these studies, rTMS was applied to the dlPFC five times a week for either three or six weeks. Participants were randomized to receive rTMS in one of three ways: to both the right and left frontal lobes (bilateral rTMS), the left frontal lobe only (unilateral rTMS), or, as a comparison group, sham rTMS, which is similar to a placebo. Results showed that 40% of individuals who received bilateral rTMS reported in the study reported that they no longer experienced suicidal thoughts after receiving bilateral rTMS (Weissman et al., 2018). In contrast, 27% of those who received unilateral rTMS, and 19% of those who received sham rTMS no longer experienced suicidal thoughts. The promising findings suggest that rTMS may offer a new way to prevent suicide in individuals with hard-to-treat depression, as well as other mental illnesses. Interestingly, the decreases in suicidal ideation were not strongly linked to reductions in the severity of depression symptoms (Centre for Addiction and Mental Health, 2018). Weissman further added that suicidality is not necessarily just a symptom of depression—it may be a related, but separate entity. Given that suicidal ideation occurs across multiple mental illnesses, identifying an effective treatment may prevent suicide for a broad spectrum of individuals with affective disorders.

While left unilateral rTMS is the most common type, the findings suggest that targeting the right frontal lobe may be key to treating suicidal thinking (Centre for

Addiction and Mental Health, 2018). Earlier research in individuals with depression and suicidal ideation has shown that this brain region may be linked with impulsivity and difficulties with regulating emotions. In future studies, the researchers plan to zero in on the right frontal lobe. It is now well established that the rTMS is safe, well-tolerated, and causes no known side effects beyond an occasional headache, and very rarely, seizure or tinnitus. With the moderately efficacious for medication-resistant depression, questions remain about patient selection, how best to deliver the treatment (i.e., parameter optimization), and its place in the treatment algorithm relative to existing treatments for resistant depression (Yip & Carpenter, 2010).

4.4.2 Transcranial Direct Current Stimulation (tDCS)

Johnston et al. (2017) agree with the speculation that neurological data may help clinicians to develop new strategies to minimize risk factors and therapies designed to strengthen vulnerable brain circuits. Therefore, the data may serve as a method to assist suicide prevention. For example, recent research has implemented the use of another non-invasive tool that fits well in the criteria, namely transcranial direct current stimulation (tDCS; Boggio Rocha et al., 2008). This is a method whereby a weak electrical current (1–4 mA) is passed over the scalp using electrodes. The current can stimulate the cortical activity of the corresponding region (Silva et al., 2017). This intervention does not merely elicit action potentials, but it is thought to manipulate neuronal activity and enhance neuroplasticity.

The use of tDCS has shown some promising results for the treatment of depression (Knotkova et al., 2012; Rigonatti et al., 2008). Following just two weeks of tDCS treatment, depressives showed a significant decrease in the severity of symptoms reported. In addition, tDCS stimulation has obtained some positive results showing improvement in cognitive performance after repeated usage. These include enhanced performance in impulse control, working memory, attention, and inhibitory control in healthy participants (Boggio et al., 2008). This shows that tDCS may be used as a form of intervention that could improve cognitive and emotional aspects at the same time (Fig. 4.11).

4.4.3 Transcranial Direct Current Stimulation

As it was unclear from previous studies what specifically mediates the effects of tDCS on learning and performance of these tasks, Coffman et al. (2012) included an Attentional Network Test[3] (ANT) in their study to identify the extent to which

[3] The Attentional Network Task (ANT) was developed to assess the operation of three attentional networks in participants: alerting, orienting, and executive control (Petersen & Posner, 2012). The

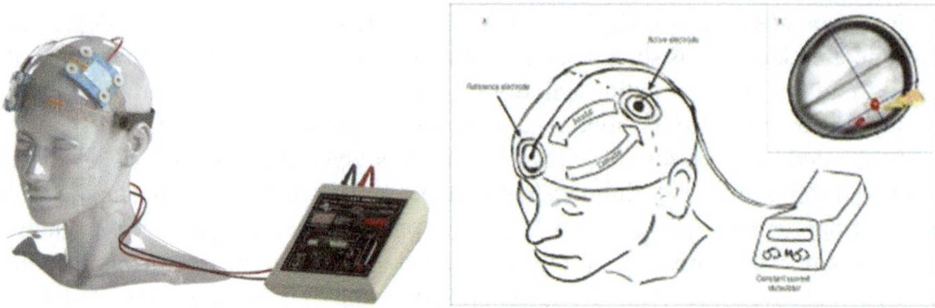

Fig. 4.11 Transcranial direct current stimulation headset

attention is modified by tDCS applied to the inferior frontal cortex. They examined how tDCS stimulation improves learning and performance in the task by comparing the response times for three forms of attention: alerting, orienting, and executive network. These executive function aspects were assessed by task performance in the Attentional Network Task (ANT) which consists of a cued reaction time task (Posner, 1980) and a flanker task (Eriksen & Eriksen, 1974). Nineteen participants received tDCS (either a low (0.1 mA) or high (2.0 mA) stimulation) and completed the ANT before and after training (baseline-test). Results indicated that tDCS was effective in improving attention measures following just 30 min of receiving tDCS. The improvement was most significant on measures of all attentional measures, particularly measures for the alerting and executive network. This is important since that difficulty in attentional control was one key factor identified for the manifestation of suicidal behaviour. Having an intervention that targets frontal cortical activity as well as attention control may seem ideal, however, it is noteworthy that improved responses to the alerting cues in the Coffman et al. (2012) study was only found following stimulation over the location of F10, which is an area in front of the temporal lobe but below the F4 (the PFC). Although the use of tDCS has shown some promising results for treating depression (Knotkova et al., 2012; Rigonatti et al., 2008), its effectiveness for treating individuals with high levels of suicidality remains speculative and warrants further investigation. In acknowledging that the difficulty in recruiting left frontal activities might have been an underlying cause for impaired inhibitory control found in suicidal individuals, this has led to the idea that interventions that target the correction of such brain lateralization may shed light on treating suicidal individuals (Fig. 4.12).

task requires participants to indicate with a speeded button press response whether a centrally presented arrow points to the left or to the right.

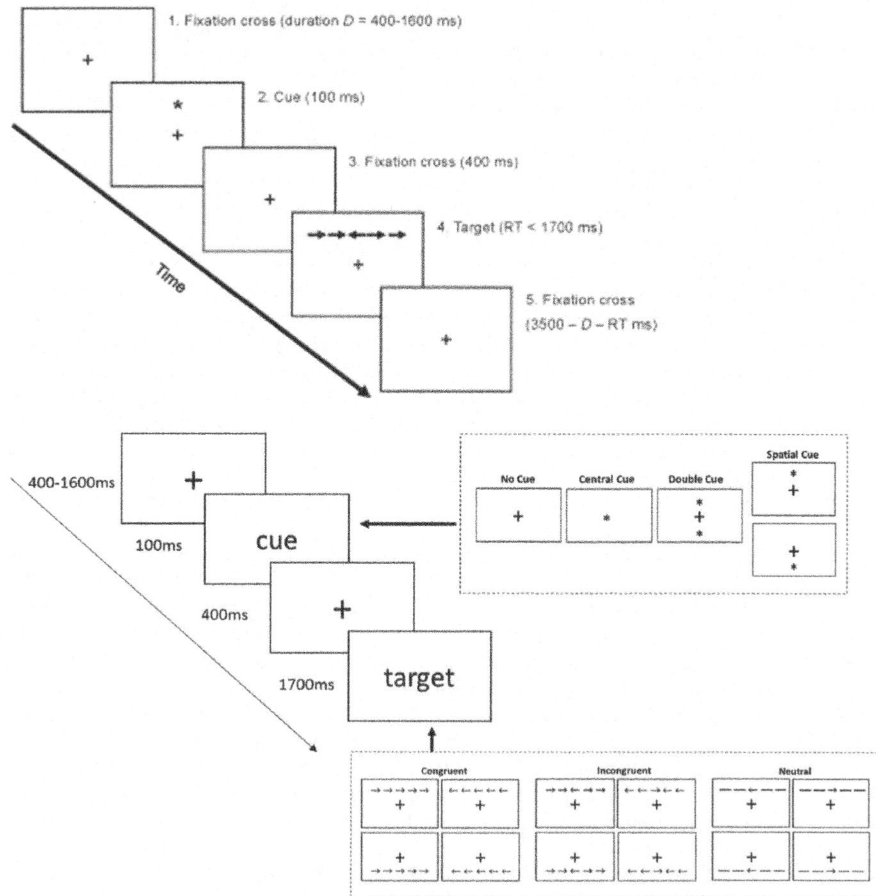

Fig. 4.12 Attentional network test

References

Allen, J. J., & Reznik, S. J. (2015). Frontal EEG asymmetry as a promising marker of depression vulnerability: Summary and methodological considerations. *Current Opinion in Psychology, 4*, 93–97.

Babiloni, C., Lizio, R., Marzano, N., Capotosto, P., Soricelli, A., Triggiani, A. I., Cordone, S., Gesualdo, L., & Del Percio, C. (2015). Brain neural synchronization and functional coupling in Alzheimer's disease as revealed by resting state EEG rhythms. *International Journal of Psychophysiology, 103*, 88–102. https://doi.org/10.1016/j.ijpsycho.2015.02.008.

Beall, P., & Herbert, A. (2008). The face wins: Stronger automatic processing of affect in facial expressions than words in a modified Stroop task. *Cognition & Emotion, 22*(8), 1613-1642. https://doi.org/10.1080/02699930801940370.

Beck, A. T., Beck, R., & Kovacs, M. (1975). Classification of suicidal behaviors: I. Quantifying intent and medical lethality. *American Journal of Psychiatry, 132*(3), 285-287. https://doi.org/10.1176/ajp.132.3.285.

Blasi, G., Goldberg, T. E., Weickert, T., Das, S., Kohn, P., Zoltick, B., et al. (2006). Brain regions underlying response inhibition and interference monitoring and suppression. *The European Journal of Neuroscience, 23*(6), 1658–1664.

Boehler, C. N., Appelbaum, L. G., Krebs, R. M., Hopf, J. M., & Woldorff, M. G. (2010). Pinning down response inhibition in the brain-conjunction analyses of the stopsignal task. *NeuroImage, 52*(4), 1621–1632.

Boffo, M., Willemen, R., Pronk, T., Wiers, R., & Dom, G. (2017). Effectiveness of two web-based cognitive bias modification interventions targeting approach and attentional bias in gambling problems: Study protocol for a pilot randomised controlled trial. *Trials, 18* (1). https://doi.org/10.1186/s13063-017-2190-2.

Boffo, M., Pronk, T., Wiers, R., & Mannarini, S. (2015). Combining cognitive bias modification training with motivational support in alcohol dependent outpatients: study protocol for a randomised controlled trial. *Trials, 16* (1). https://doi.org/10.1186/s13063-015-0576-6.

Boggio, P., Rocha, R., da Silva, M., & Fregni, F. (2008). Differential modulatory effects of transcranial direct current stimulation on a facial expression go-no-go task in males and females. *Neuroscience Letters, 447*(2–3), 101–105. https://doi.org/10.1016/j.neulet.2008.10.009.

Bower, G. H. (1981). Mood and memory. *American Psychology, 36*, 129–148. https://doi.org/10.1037/0003-066X.36.2.129.

Bower, G. H. (1991). Mood congruity of social judgements, in emotion and social judgements (pp.31–53). New York, NY: Pergamon.

Burnet, D. H., & Turner, M. D. (2017). Expanding EEG research into the clinic and classroom with consumer EEG Systems.

Centre for Addiction and Mental Health. (2018, May 3). Brain stimulation reduces suicidal thinking in people with hard-to-treat depression, new CAMH study shows. Retrieved from https://www.camh.ca/en/camh-news-and-stories/brain-stimulation-reduces-suicidal-thinking-in-people-with-hard-to-treat-depression.

Cha, C., Najmi, S., Park, J., Finn, C., & Nock, M. (2010). Attentional bias toward suicide-related stimuli predicts suicidal behaviour: Correction. *Journal of Abnormal Psychology, 119*(4), 874–874. https://doi.org/10.1037/a0021512.

Chung, Y. (2015). *Use of the modified emotional stroop task to detect suicide risk in college students.* Doctoral dissertation. Retrieved from https://academicworks.cuny.edu/cgi/viewcontent.cgi?article=1541&context=gc_etds.

Coan, J., & Allen, J. (2004). Frontal EEG asymmetry as a moderator and mediator of emotion. *Biological Psychology, 67*(1–2), 7–50.

Coffman, B. A., Trumbo, M. C., & Clark, V. P. (2012). Enhancement of object detection with transcranial direct current stimulation is associated with increased attention. *BMC Neuroscience, 13*(1), 108–115. https://doi.org/10.1186/1471-2202-13-108.

Davidson, R. J., Jackson, D. C., & Kalin, N. H. (2000). Emotion, plasticity, context, and regulation: Perspectives from affective neuroscience. *Psychological Bulletin, 126*(6), 890–909. https://doi.org/10.1037//0033-2909.126.6.890.

Diamond, A. (2013). Executive functions. *Annual Review of Psychology, 64*(1), 135–168.

Dockrill, P. (2017, October 31). New AI could help us avert tragedy by identifying people with suicidal thoughts. *Science Alert*. Retrieved from https://www.sciencealert.com/new-algorithm-identifies-people-suicidal-thoughts-analysing-brain-scans-ideation-emotion.

Epp, A., Dobson, K., Dozois, D., & Frewen, P. (2012). A systematic meta-analysis of the Stroop task in depression. *Clinical Psychology Review, 32*(4), 316-328.

Ferrari, G. R., Becker, E. S., Smit, F., Rinck, M., & Spijker, J. (2016). Investigating the (cost-) effectiveness of attention bias modification (ABM) for outpatients with major depressive disorder (MDD): A randomized controlled trial protocol. *BMC Psychiatry, 16*(1), 370–384. https://doi.org/10.1186/s12888-016-1085-1.

Fogel, A., (2011, May 4). The limits of mindfulness. *Psychology Today*. Retrieved from https://www.psychologytoday.com/us/blog/body-sense/201105/the-limits-mindfulness.

Gotlib, I. H., & Joormann, J. (2010). Cognition and depression: Current status and future directions. *Annual Review of Clinical Psychology, 6*(1), 285–312. https://doi.org/10.1146/annurev.clinpsy.121208.131305.

Gotlib, I., Krasnoperova, E., Yue, D., & Joormann, J. (2004). Attentional biases for negative interpersonal stimuli in clinical depression. *Journal of Abnormal Psychology, 113*(1), 127–135. https://doi.org/10.1037/0021-843x.113.1.121.

Gotlib, I. H., Roberts, J. E., & Gilboa, E. (1996). Cognitive interference in depression. In I. G. Sarason, G. R. Pierce, & B. R. Sarason (Eds.), *Cognitive interference: Theories, methods, and findings* (pp. 347–377). Lawrence Erlbaum Associates Inc.

Gotlib, I. H., & Joormann, J. (2010). Cognition and depression: current status and future directions. *Annual Review of Clinical Psychology*, 6(1), 285-312.

Gotlib, I. H., Hamilton, J. P., Cooney, R. E., Singh, M. K., Henry, M. L., & Joormann, J. (2010). Neural processing of reward and loss in girls at risk for major depression. *Archives of General Psychiatry, 67*(4), 380-387. https://doi.org/10.1001/archgenpsychiatry.2010.13.

Johnston, J. A., Wang, F., Liu, J., Blond, B. N., Wallace, A., Liu, J., Landeros- Weisenberger, A. (2017). Multimodal neuroimaging of frontolimbic structure and function associated with suicide attempts in adolescents and young adults with Bipolar disorder. *American Journal of Psychiatry, 174*(7), 667-675. https://doi.org/10.1176/appi.ajp.2016.15050652.

Jollant, F., Lawrence, N. S., Olie, E., O'Daly, O., Malafosse, A., Courtet, P., & Phillips, M. L. (2010). Decreased activation of lateral orbitofrontal cortex during risky choices under uncertainty is associated with disadvantageous decision-making and suicidal behaviour. *NeuroImage, 51*(3), 1275–1281. https://doi.org/10.1016/j.neuroimage.2010.03.027.

Jollant, F., Lawrence, N., Olié, E., Guillaume, S., & Courtet, P. (2011). The suicidal mind and brain: A review of neuropsychological and neuroimaging studies. *The World Journal of Biological Psychiatry, 12*(5), 319–339.

Jollant, F., Lawrence, N. S., Giampietro, V., Brammer, M. J., Fullana, M. A., Drapier, D., Phillips, M. L. (2008). Orbitofrontal cortex response to angry faces in men with histories of suicide attempts. *American Journal of Psychiatry, 165*(6), 740-748. https://doi.org/10.1176/appi.ajp.2008.07081239.

Jollant, F., Lawrence, N. S., Giampietro, V., Brammer, M. J., Fullana, M. A., Drapier, D., Courte, P., & Phillips, M. L. (2008). Orbitofrontal cortex response to angry faces in men with histories of suicide attempts. *American Journal of Psychiatry, 165*(6), 740–748. https://doi.org/10.1176/appi.ajp.2008.07081239.

Joormann, J., & Gotlib, I. H. (2010). Emotion regulation in depression: Relation to cognitive inhibition. *Cognition & Emotion, 24*(2), 281–298. https://doi.org/10.1080/02699930903407948.

Just, M. A., Pan, L., Cherkassky, V. L., McMakin, D., Cha, C., Nock, M. K., & Brent, D. (2017). Machine learning of neural representations of suicide and emotion concepts identifies suicidal youth. *Nature Human Behaviour, 1*, 911–919. https://doi.org/10.1038/s41562-017-0234-y.

Keilp, J., Gorlyn, M., Oquendo, M., Burke, A., & Mann, J. (2008). Attention deficit in depressed suicide attempters. *Psychiatry Research, 159*(1–2), 7–17.

Keilp, J. G., Gorlyn, M., Russell, M., Oquendo, M. A., Burke, A. K., Harkavy-Friedman, J., & Mann, J. J. (2013). Neuropsychological function and suicidal behaviour: Attention control, memory and executive dysfunction in suicide attempt. *Psychological Medicine, 43*(3), 539–551. https://doi.org/10.1017/S0033291712001419.

Keilp, J., Sackeim, H., Brodsky, B., Oquendo, M., Malone, K., & Mann, J. (2001). Neuropsychological dysfunction in depressed suicide attempters. *American Journal of Psychiatry, 158*(5), 735–741.

Knotkova, H., Rosedale, M., Strauss, S. M., Horne, J., Soto, E., Cruciani, R. A., Malaspina, D., & Malamud, D. (2012). Using transcranial direct current stimulation to treat depression in HIV-infected persons: The outcomes of a feasibility study. *Frontiers in Psychiatry,3*, 59–66. https://doi.org/10.3389/fpsyt.2012.00059.

MacLeod, C. (1991). Half a century of research on the Stroop effect: An integrative review. *Psychological Bulletin, 109*(2), 163–203. https://doi.org/10.1037/0033-2909.109.2.163.

Mann, J. J., Currier, D., Stanley, B., Oquendo, M. A., Amsel, L. V., & Ellis, S. P. (2006). Can biological tests assist prediction of suicide in mood disorders? *International Journal of Neuropsychopharmacology*, *9*, 465–474.

Molero, P., Grunebaum, M., Galfalvy, H., Bongiovi, M., Lowenthal, D., Almeida, M., Burke, A. K., Stevenson, E., John Mann, J., & Oquendo, M. A. (2014). Past suicide attempts in depressed inpatients: Clinical versus research assessment. *Archives of Suicide Research, 18*(1), 50–57. https://doi.org/10.1080/13811118.2013.803446.

Nock, M. K., Park, J. M., Finn, C. T., Deliberto, T. L., Dour, H. J., & Banaji, M. R. (2010). Measuring the suicidal mind: implicit cognition predicts suicidal behavior. *Psychological Science, 21*(4), 511-517. https://doi.org/10.1177/0956797610364762.

Oakes, T. R., Pizzagalli, D. A., Hendrick, A. M., Horras, K. A., Larson, C. L., Abercrombie, H. C., Gross, J. J. (2005). The cognitive control of emotion. *Trends in Cognitive Sciences*, *9*, 242-249.

Ohman, A., Flykt, A., & Esteves, F. (2001). Emotion drives attention: Detecting the snake in the grass. *Journal of Experimental Psychology: General*, 130, 466–478.

Posner, M. I. (1980). Orienting of attention. *Quarterly Journal of Experimental Psychology., 32*, 3–25.

Qin, P., & Nordentoft, M. (2005). Suicide risk in relation to psychiatric hospitalization: Evidence based on longitudinal registers. *Archives of General Psychiatry*, *62*, 427–432.

Ratti, E., Waninger, S., Berka, C., Ruffini, G., & Verma, A. (2017). Comparison of medical and consumer wireless EEG systems for use in clinical trials. *Frontiers in Human Neuroscience, 11*, 398. https://doi.org/10.3389/fnhum.2017.00398.

Riddle, D. (2007). Brain aging. Boca Raton: Taylor & Francis.

Rigonatti, S. P., Boggio, P. S., Myczkowski, M. L., Otta, E., Fiquer, J. T., Ribeiro, R. B., Nitsche, M.A., Pascual-Leone, A., & Fregni, F. (2008). Transcranial direct stimulation and fluoxetine for the treatment of depression. *European Psychiatry, 23*, 74–76. https://doi.org/10.1016/j.eurpsy.2007.09.006.

Ruiz, R. (2017, November 1). How your brain responds to certain words might predict your suicide risk? *MashableAsia.* Retrieved from https://mashable.com/2017/10/31/suicide-risk-words-neuroscience/#DGysk6qN8gqY.

Silva, A. F., Zortea, M., Carvalho, S., Leite, J., Torres, I. L., Fregni, F., & Caumo, W. (2017). Anodal transcranial direct current stimulation over the left dorsolateral prefrontal cortex modulates attention and pain in fibromyalgia: randomized clinical trial. *Scientific Reports, 7*(1). https://doi.org/10.1038/s41598-017-00185-w.

Turner, M. D., Burner, D. H., & Turner, J. A. (2017, March). Expanding EEG research into the clinic and classroom with consumer EEG systems. Paper presented at Undergraduate Research Conference, Georgia State University.

Wagner, G., Schultz, C. C., Koch, K., Schachtzabel, C., Sauer, H., & Schlösser, R. G. (2012). Prefrontal cortical thickness in depressed patients with high-risk for suicidal behavior. Journal of Psychiatric Research, 46(11), 1449-1455. https://doi.org/10.1016/j.jpsychires.2012.07.013.

Weissman, C. R., Blumberger, D. M., Brown, P. E., Isserles, M., Rajji, T. K., Downar, J., Mulsant, B. H., Fitzgeral, P. B., & Daskalakis, Z. J. (2018). Bilateral repetitive transcranial magnetic stimulation decreases suicidal ideation in depression. *Journal of Clinical Psychiatry, 79* (3). https://doi.org/10.4088/JCP.17m11692.

Wells, T., & Beevers, C. (2010). Biased attention and dysphoria: Manipulating selective attention reduces subsequent depressive symptoms. *Cognition & Emotion*, *24*(4), 719-728. https://doi.org/10.1080/02699930802652388.

Westheide, J., Quednow, B. B., Kuhn, K.-U., Hoppe, C., Cooper-Mahkorn, D., Hawellek, B., Wagner, M. (2008). Executive performance of depressed suicide attempters: the role of suicidal ideation. *European Archives of Psychiatry and Clinical Neuroscience*, *258*(7), 414-421.

Willeumier, K., Taylor, D. V., & Amen, D. G. (2011). Decreased cerebral blood flow in the limbic and prefrontal cortex using SPECT imaging in a cohort of completed suicides. *Translational Psychiatry*, *1*(8), e28-e28. https://doi.org/10.1038/tp.2011.28.

Wilson, T. D. (2009). Know thyself. *Perspectives on Psychological Science*, *4*, 384–389.

Wilson, T. D. (2009). Know thyself. *Perspectives on Psychological Science, 4*, 384–389.

Yip, A. G., & Carpenter, L. L. (2010). Transcranial magnetic stimulation for medication-resistant depression. *The Journal of Clinical Psychiatry, 71*(04), 502–503. https://doi.org/10.4088/jcp.10ac06054blu Yee Man Lui, Y. (2019). 【2017回顧】平均每9.3日一青年人自殺數據解構為何踏上不歸路.

Chapter 5
Conclusions and Future Directions

5.1 Implications and Summary

In the early chapters of this book, several issues regarding the existing approach in assessing suicide risks and issues within the current mental health services system have been highlighted. It is clear that something needs to be done to clarify the divergent definitions of suicide, to further develop suicide risk assessment, reduce current waiting times to interventions, and to fill in the evidence-practice gap. It is vital that evidence-based research has to seek new path and transcend professional boundaries. Scientists need work hands in hands with practitioners to successfully design, innovative, evidence-based treatment for the advanced IT world.

There is a considerable number of studies that have established the link between cognitive impairments and neurological deficits in relation to suicide. Yet, these findings are mainly based on clinical populations of patients who had a past history of one or more suicide attempts. As any attempt could be fatal, past research argues that suicide prevention by early identification of individuals at risk of suicide is essential before reaching a dangerous level of suicidality (Palmer, 2004; Klonsky & May, 2015). Therefore, the findings based on clinical populations may not be helpful in this perspective. The focus of the research in this thesis was non-clinical populations, which gives wider application to the preventive and identification measures in predicting suicidality. What had been unclear prior to the present research was a lack of empirical evidence on the neurological or cognitive basis of individuals with mild forms of suicidality. Therefore the current research sets out to investigate these factors underlying the development of suicidal behaviours. Another important issue highlighted in this book is that after reviewing the recent interviews and therapies available as assessment and prevention, it is noted that help offered to those in need has remained in the old and traditional ways adopted over three decades ago. Indeed, suicide assessment and intervention have not advanced appreciably at similar levels as the rapid development of I.T.

E. Ong, *Early Identification and Intervention of Suicide Risk in Chinese Young Adults*,
https://doi.org/10.1007/978-981-16-7641-3_5

Drawing from the issues highlighted in the relevant parts of this book, a series of theoretically-driven factors associated with suicide behaviour namely; executive function deficits, abnormal neural activities, information processing bias, affective disorders; and to examine proximal predictors for suicide progression. These factors were identified to confer early stages of suicidality, especially in the student population. All the empirical evidence raised was based on previous suicide models which specified that suicide behaviour arises when there is an attentional bias to particular life events reflecting signals of defeat, difficulty in inhibiting irrelevant emotional distractions, and insufficient strategies to solve problems. Summarizing the information in accordance with the Escape theory and the Cry of Pain model described earlier, it is suggested that they are generally consistent with the appraisal and information processing bias proposed by these models and provide empirical support towards the influence of these variables in impacting suicide behaviour. The SAMS, in particular, explains how information processing bias links to increased suicidality. It is postulated that in the long term, when negative information increases, is elaborated and becomes easily accessible, a suicide schema is formed. This is a semantic network comprising various stimuli, possible responses, and emotionally stored information related to suicide (Johnson et al., 2008; Panagioti et al., 2014). The suicide schema may influence individuals as it biases them to process more negative rather than positive information. This may enhance emotionally congruent information processing and retrieval of more mood-congruent memories related to suicide.

With a clear understanding of the arising of suicidal behaviour, a review of the literature was presented in the earlier Chapter to establish the direction that global research has taken and the associated trends regarding the prevalence of suicidal behaviour. Although suicidality is a well-explored field of study, a review of previous studies highlighted that limited data were available regarding the investigation of an early stage of suicide. This has caused an obstacle for exploring strategies for early prevention of suicide, especially in a student population in which the prevalence of suicide is increasing at an alarming rate. Therefore, the book investigated the cognitive and neurological underpinnings of suicide at an early stage in the suicide path. Moreover, it has identified a list of common factors associated with suicide. One of the noteworthy insights from the prior literature was that the approach of studying the interaction of risk and protective factors is more effective in predicting suicidality than merely exploring the risk factors alone (Johnson et al., 2008; Joormann & Gotlib, 2010; Rajappa et al., 2011). The etiological explanations of suicide have moved away from the conventional risk factors to address how executive functions and neural activities, as well as how individuals cope with situations, may interact with suicidality.

In terms of the neurological investigation of suicidality, the literature suggests that asymmetrical frontal brain activation is linked to different degrees of affective disorder and suicidality. Among these findings, the alpha (α) frequency band is often used to investigate frontal asymmetry because it reflects a relaxed state of wakefulness (Allen et al., 2004). An increase in the alpha frequency band signifies a resting state with relatively low levels of cortical activity. Conversely, when the cortex is active such as when an individual is engaged in a cognitive task, the alpha frequency band is significantly reduced (Davidson et al., 2000). To measure frontal alpha asymmetry, the EEG is ideal because it is relatively cheap and easily accessible, thus it is a standard tool used to measure the correlates of relative hemispheric dominance.

Specific recommendations as to what researchers and theorists can do in the future to advance our understanding of suicide and suicide interventions are offered. In the previous parts of this book which were substantiated with supporting and debating evidence of suicide research so far, present knowledge gained from established theoretical backgrounds, and highlight future directions for suicide research and prevention. In their opinion, one new dimension to innovative suicide assessment is the use of objective measures rather than the traditional measure such as self-report inventories and interviews. The launch of easily accessible neuroimaging tools and widely accepted use of mobile apps serve as potentials to make an important contribution to helping suicide individuals in the future.

5.2 Ethical Challenges and Limitations

Although several of the key cognitive functions were discussed in this book, it is noteworthy that it did not exhaustively cover all potentially cognitive variables that may be associated with suicidal behaviour. For example, autobiographical memory and cognitive flexibility (Miranda et al. 2011) were important cognitive predictors of suicidality that were not considered as potential measures or implemented as a form of suicide assessment. These could have been discussed in tandem with the attentional bias specified since the numerous suicide models also purport that maladaptive cognitive processes serve to increase the chance of activating a suicide schema, such as hopelessness, which may trigger cognitive processes associated with suicidal acts. For example, selective attention to suicide-relevant environmental cues and attentional fixation.

Regarding the use of neurological tools to better understand the underlying mechanisms of suicidal behaviour, although empirical evidence has been raised to show some promising results in its predictability, there remain unresolved issues. For example. Neurological tools as they stand seem to help objectively visualize a human brain ‘in action’, the complex assumption that jumps from a very subjective experience (e.g. feeling depressed or suicidal) to electromagnetic/neurological signals are hardly known. All these assumptions are only based on raw data drawing probabilistic covariances rather than scientific causal connections. Many neurologists make interpretations based on designs and theories. Still, it is unclear how complex phenomena such as when someone is in a state of suicidal crisis can be grasped by simply reading some neurological data. Moreover, the idea of applying video games, stimulating images on a computer screen instead of exploring how suicidal individuals interact with the real world and social issues may also raise questions on the ecological validity. After all, neuroimaging data are bound to momentary states, and inferences on personality are hardly warranted.

5.3 Conclusion

The work and evidence presented so far have provided some empirical evidence to continue neurological research in the suicidal population. It seems clear that in terms of behavioural and emotional responses to deal with stressful life events, we should not try to avoid the problems and should be encouraged to use different levels of strategies to cope better and have healthier psychological outcomes in reducing the risk of suicide. These might be easier to state than to carry out since the ability to utilize adaptive coping strategies and emotion regulations is somewhat limited to individuals with well-functioning brains only, as suggested by many neurologists. Those who are disadvantaged by having impairments with attentional control or difficulties with recruiting the essential brain regions to carry out work may be predisposed to an increased risk of suicide. Nevertheless, interventions are presently available that could alter these neurological and cognitive differences, and this may help the vulnerable group to be protected from emotional disturbance in advance. From the supporting evidence, it is evident that executive functions, brain activities, and may both be used to identify individuals at risk of suicide in non-clinical populations, and this should be accounted for in future treatment and prevention programs. Neuroimaging techniques for monitoring and manipulating brain functions are developing rapidly. Prudence and restraint in their application seem advisable. Nevertheless, scientists have still not fully answered questions as to how the different regions of the brain may interact, or how abnormal brain activities may predict suicidality or other affective disorders. The suggestion for promoting innovation in the future research and prevention of suicidal behaviour in order to stimulate research and theorizing so that our understanding of suicide will progress. The chapter ends with providing food for anyone interested in studying suicide or is in contact with someone encountering suicidal behaviour. This book highlights theoretical and methodological challenges that have plagued the field of suicide research. It is hoped that the knowledge gained can help to stimulate new ideas and interventions in the difficult fight against suicidal behaviours. It was concluded that as the neurological mechanism of resilience research is currently in the stage of an early investigation, the present research should be regarded as only a starting point for further work.

References

Allen, J. J., & Kline, J. P. (2004). Frontal EEG asymmetry, emotion, and psychopathology: The first, and the next 25 years. *Biological Psychology, 67*(1–2), 1–5. https://doi.org/10.1016/j.biopsycho.2004.03.001

Allen, J. J., Urry, H. L., Hitt, S. K., & Coan, J. A. (2004). The stability of resting frontal electroencephalographic asymmetry in depression. *Psychophysiology, 41*(2), 269–280. https://doi.org/10.1111/j.1469-8986.2003.00149.x

Davidson, R. J., Jackson, D. C., & Kalin, N. H. (2000a). Emotion, plasticity, context, and regulation: Perspectives from affective neuroscience. *Psychological Bulletin, 126*(6), 890–909. https://doi.org/10.1037//0033-2909.126.6.890

Davidson, R., Marshall, J., Tomarken, A., & Henriques, J. (2000b). While a phobic waits: Regional brain electrical and autonomic activity in social phobics during anticipation of public speaking. *Biological Psychiatry, 47* (2), 85–95.

Joormann, J., & Gotlib, I. H. (2010). Emotion regulation in depression: Relation to cognitive inhibition. *Cognition & Emotion, 24*(2), 281–298. https://doi.org/10.1080/02699930903407948

Klonsky, E. D., & May, A. M. (2015). The three-step theory (3ST): A new theory of suicide rooted in the "ideation-to-action" framework. *International Journal of Cognitive Therapy, 8*(2), 114–129. https://doi.org/10.1521/ijct.2015.8.2.114

Rajappa, K., Gallagher, M., & Miranda, R. (2011). Emotion dysregulation and vulnerability to suicidal ideation and attempts. *Cognitive Therapy and Research, 36*(6), 833–839. https://doi.org/10.1007/s10608-011-9419-2

Bibliography

Altheimer, G. (2014, December 8). Attention bias modification training for social anxiety. *Emotion on the Brian.* Retrieved from http://sites.tufts.edu/emotiononthebrain/2014/12/08/attention-modification-training-for-social-anxiety/

Assessment of suicide risk in people with depression. (n.d.). Retrieved from http://cebmh.warne.ox.ac.uk/csr/clinicalguide/docs/Assessment-of-suicide-risk--clinical-guide.pdf

Centre for Suicide Research. (n.d.). *Assessment of suicide risk in people with depression.* Department of Psychiatry, University of Oxford. Retrieved from http://cebmh.warne.ox.ac.uk/csr/clinicalguide/explaining.html

Cheng, A. T., Chen, T. H., Chen, C., & Jenkins, R. (2000). Psychosocial and psychiatric risk factors for suicide: Case-control psychological autopsy study. *British Journal of Psychiatry, 177*(04), 360–365. https://doi.org/10.1192/bjp.177.4.360

Cox Lippard, E. T., Johnston, J. A. Y., & Blumberg, H. P. (2014). Neurobiological risk factors for suicide insights from brain imaging. *American Journal of Preventive Medicine, 47* (3 0 2), S152–S162. https://doi.org/10.1016/j.amepre.2014.06.009

CSRP, The Hong Kong Jockey Club Centre for Suicide Research and Prevention. (2015b). *Method used in completed suicide in Hong Kong.* Retrieved from http://csrp.hku.hk/statistics/

Davidson, R. (2004). What does the prefrontal cortex "do" in affect: Perspectives on frontal EEG asymmetry research. *Biological Psychology, 67*(1–2), 219–234.

Davidson, R., & Fox, N. (1989). Frontal brain asymmetry predicts infants' response to maternal separation. *Journal of Abnormal Psychology, 98*(2), 127–131. https://doi.org/10.1037//0021-843x.98.2.127

Davidson, R. J., Ekman, P., Saron, C. D., Senulis, J. A., & Friesen, W. V. (1990). Approach-withdrawal and cerebral asymmetry: Emotional expression and brain physiology: I. *Journal of Personality and Social Psychology, 58*(2), 330–341. https://doi.org/10.1037/0022-3514.58.2.330

DoReMiFa 歷險記. (n.d.). Retrieved from https://doremifa.edu.hk/en/about-us

Even Meditation Has Limitations. (2018, August 8). Retrieved from https://psychcentral.com/news/2018/02/06/even-meditation-has-limitations/132184.html

General Anatomy. (2014, May 6). SlideShare. Retrieved from https://www.slideshare.net/seharasif1234/general-anatomy-19-b

Gotlib, I., & Cane, D. (1987). Construct accessibility and clinical depression: A longitudinal investigation. *Journal of Abnormal Psychology, 96*(3), 199–204. https://doi.org/10.1037//0021-843x.96.3.199

Gotlib, I., & McCann, C. (1984). Construct accessibility and depression: An examination of cognitive and affective factors. *Journal of Personality and Social Psychology, 47*(2), 427–439. https://doi.org/10.1037//0022-3514.47.2.427

Hawton, K., Saunders, K. E., & O'Connor, R. C. (2012). Self-harm and suicide in adolescents. *The Lancet, 379*(9834), 2373–2382. https://doi.org/10.1016/S0140-6736(12)60322-5

Headline Daily. (2021). 馬鞍山國際學校女生疑情困墮樓亡. [online]. Available at: https://hd.stheadline.com/news/realtime/hk/1922341/%E5%8D%B3%E6%99%82-%E6%B8%AF%E8%81%9E-%E9%A6%AC%E9%9E%8D%E5%B1%B1%E5%9C%8B%E9%9A%9B%E5%AD%B8%E6%A0%A1%E5%A5%B3%E7%94%9F%E7%96%91%E6%83%85%E5%9B%B0%E5%A2%AE%E6%A8%93%E4%BA%A1. [Accessed 27 July 2021].

Hong Kong Jockey Club for suicide research and prevention. (2005, July 31). *Research findings into suicide and its prevention.* Retrieved from https://csrp.hku.hk

Ireland, K. (n.d.). Meditation techniques for sports. *Leaf Group.* Retrieved from https://www.sportsrec.com/106002-meditation-techniques-sports.html

ISSUE SEP 2016. (2016, September 9). Connected for suicide prevention, 1–16. Retrieved from http://csrp.hku.hk/wp-content/uploads/2016/09/csrp_newsletter_2016_sept_en.pdf

Johnson, J., Gooding, P., & Tarrier, N. (2008). Suicide risk in schizophrenia: Explanatory models and clinical implications, The Schematic Appraisal Model of Suicide (SAMS). *Psychology and Psychotherapy: Theory, Research and Practice*, 81(1), 55-77.

Jollant, F., Guillaume, S., Jaussent, I., Bellivier, F., Leboyer, M., Castelnau, D., Malafosse, A., & Courtet, P. (2007). Psychiatric diagnoses and personality traits associated with disadvantageous decision-making. *European Psychiatry, 22* (7), 455–461.

Keilp, J. G., Grunebaum, M. F., Gorlyn, M., LeBlanc, S., Burke, A. K., Galfalvy, H., Oquendo, M. A., & Mann, J. J. (2012). Suicidal ideation and the subjective aspects of depression. *Journal of Affective Disorders, 140* (1), 75–81.

Law, C. K., Yip, P. S., & Caine, E. D. (2011). The contribution of charcoal burning to the rise and decline of suicides in Hong Kong from 1997–2007. *Social Psychiatry and Psychiatric Epidemiology, 46*(9), 797–803.

LCQ12: Prevention of child and youth suicide. (2015, October 14). Retrieved from https://www.info.gov.hk/gia/general/201510/14/P201510140538.htm

Miranda, R., Gallagher, M., Bauchner, B., Vaysman, R., & Marroquín, B. (2011). Cognitive inflexibility as a prospective predictor of suicidal ideation among young adults with a suicide attempt history. *Depression and Anxiety, 29*(3), 180-186

Ng, R. (2020). Mental health crisis in Hong Kong: Its current status and collective responses from mental health professionals in Hong Kong. *Psychiatric Times, 37* (1). Retrieved from https://www.psychiatrictimes.com/mental-health/mental-health-crisis-hong-kong

O'Connor, R. C., & Nock, M. K. (2014). The psychology of suicidal behaviour. *The Lancet Psychiatry, 1*(1), 73–85.

Office for National Statistics. (2015). Suicides in the United Kingdom, 2013 Registrations—ONS. Retrieved from https://www.ons.gov.uk/peoplepopulationandcommunity/birthsdeathsandmarriages/deaths/bulletins/suicidesintheunitedkingdom/2015-02-19

Office for National Statistics. (2016). Suicides in the United Kingdom, 2013 Registrations—ONS. Retrieved from https://www.ons.gov.uk/peoplepopulationandcommunity/birthsdeathsandmarriages/deaths/bulletins/suicidesintheunitedkingdom/2016registration

Ovaysikia, S., Tahir, K. A., Chan, J. L., & DeSouza, J. F. (2011). Word wins over face: Emotional Stroop effect activates the frontal cortical network. *Frontiers in Human Neuroscience, 4*, 234–242. https://doi.org/10.3389/fnhum.2010.00234

Palmer, C. J. (2004). Suicide attempt history, self-esteem, and suicide risk in a sample of 116 depressed voluntary inpatients. *Psychological Reports, 95*, 1092-1094

Panagioti, M., Gooding, P. A., Taylor, P. J., & Tarrier, N. (2014). Perceived social support buffers the impact of PTSD symptoms on suicidal behaviour: Implications into suicide resilience research. *Comprehensive Psychiatry, 55*, 104–112

Parry, S. (2005). Taking the easy way out? *South China Morning Post.* Retrieved from https://www.scmp.com/article/484827/taking-easy-way-out

Pereira, A., & Cardoso, F. (2015). Suicidal ideation in university students: Prevalence and association with school and gender. *Paidéia (ribeirão Preto), 25*(62), 299–306. https://doi.org/10.1590/1982-43272562201503

Pizzagalli, D. A. (2010). Frontocingulate dysfunction in depression: Toward biomarkers of treatment response. *Neuropsychopharmacology, 36*(1), 183–206. https://doi.org/10.1038/npp.2010.166

Ratti, E., Waninger, S., Berka, C., Ruffini, G., & Verma, A. (2017). Comparison of medical and consumer wireless EEG systems for use in clinical trials. *Frontiers in Human Neuroscience, 11*, 398. https://doi.org/10.3389/fnhum.2017.00398

Suicide prevention and intervention: Cross-cultural perspectives. (2017, January 23). Retrieved from http://www.psychiatryadvisor.com/suicide-and-self-harm/cultural-differences-have-an-impact-on-suicide-education-prevention/article/633257/

Suicide WHO. (2018, August 24). Retrieved from http://www.who.int/news-room/fact-sheets/detail/suicide

The Wellness Centre. (n.d.). *The new life psychiatric rehabilitation association.* Retrieved from https://www.nlpra.org.hk/EN/our_services/community%20support%20services

Topick. (2016). 廿歲港大生墮樓亡. Retrieved from https://topick.hket.com/article/1386468/廿歲港大生墮樓亡

Wang, Y. (2017, September 8). Suicide statistics show slight increase in number of suicides by young people in Hong Kong—But there's also good news. *South China Morning Post, Young Post.* Retrieved from https://yp.scmp.com/news/hong-kong/article/107260/suicide-statistics-show-slight-increase-number-suicides-young-people

Watson, S. (n.d.). What are the advantages and disadvantages of fMRI? How stuff works. Retrieved from https://science.howstuffworks.com/fmri4.htm

We need to talk: Getting the right therapy at the right time .(n.d.). *The Mind for better mental health.* Retrieved form https://www.mind.org.uk/media/280583/We-Need-to-Talk-getting-the-right-therapy-at-the-right-time.pdf

What is Dialectical Behaviour Therapy (DBT)? (n.d.). Retrieved October 17, 2018, from https://behavioraltech.org/resources/faqs/dialectical-behaviour-therapy-dbt/

Williams, J. M. G. (2006). Capture and rumination, functional avoidance, and executive control (CaRFAX): Three processes that underlie overgeneral memory. *Cognition and Emotion, 20*(3–4), 548–568. https://doi.org/10.1080/02699930500450465

Wong, P. W., Caine, E. D., Lee, C. K., Beautrais, A., & Yip, P. S. (2014). Suicides by jumping from a height in Hong Kong: A review of coroner court files. *Social Psychiatry and Psychiatric Epidemiology, 49*, 211–219.

Wong, P. W., Liu, P. M., Chan, W. S., Law, Y. W., Law, S. C., Fu, K. W., Li, H. S., Tso, M. K., Beautrais, A. L., & Yip, P. S. (2009). An integrative suicide prevention programme for visitor charcoal burning suicide and suicide pact. *Suicide and Life-Threatening Behaviour, 39* (1), 82–90. https://doi.org/10.1521/suli.2009.39.1.82

Yip, P. S., & Chen, F. (2014). A study on the effect of exclusion period on the suicidal risk among the insured. *Social Science & Medicine, 110*, 26–30.

Paul Y. I. P, Chan, W. L., Cheng, Q., Chow, S., Hsu, S., Law, Y., Lo, B., Ngai, K., Wong, K. Y., Xiong, C., & Yeung, T. K. (2020). A 24 h online youth emotional support: Opportunities and challenges. *The Lancet Regional Health—Western Pacific, 4*, 100047. https://doi.org/10.1016/j.lanwpc.2020.100047

Zhu, Y., Jiang, H., Su, H., Zhong, N., Li, R., Li, X., Chen, T., Tan, H., Du, J., Xu, D., Yan, H., Xu, D., & Zhao M. (2018). A newly designed mobile-based computerized cognitive addiction therapy app for the improvement of cognition impairments and risk decision making in methamphetamine use disorder: Randomized controlled trial. *JMIR Mhealth Uhealth, 6* (6). https://doi.org/10.2196/10292

The manufacturer's authorised representative in the EU is Springer Nature Customer Service Centre GmbH, Europaplatz 3, 69115 Heidelberg, Germany. If you have any concerns regarding our products, please contact ProductSafety@springernature.com

Printed and bound by CPI Group (UK) Ltd, Croydon, CR0 4YY
30/09/2026
02225307-0017